Disability in Wonderland

Disability in Wonderland
Health and Normativity in Speculative Utopias

AMANDA MARTIN SANDINO

McFarland & Company, Inc., Publishers
Jefferson, North Carolina

This book has undergone peer review.

LIBRARY OF CONGRESS CATALOGUING-IN-PUBLICATION DATA

Names: Sandino, Amanda Martin, 1987– author.
Title: Disability in wonderland : health and normativity in speculative utopias / Amanda Martin Sandino.
Description: Jefferson, North Carolina : McFarland & Company, Inc., Publishers, 2023 | Includes bibliographical references and index.
Identifiers: LCCN 2023008816 | ISBN 9781476683034 (paperback : acid free paper) ∞
ISBN 9781476650203 (ebook)
Subjects: LCSH: Disabilities in literature. | Disabilities in motion pictures. | Utopias in literature. | Utopias in motion pictures. | LCGFT: Literary criticism.
Classification: LCC PN56.D553 S36 2023 | DDC 809/.933561—dc23/eng/20230322
LC record available at https://lccn.loc.gov/2023008816

BRITISH LIBRARY CATALOGUING DATA ARE AVAILABLE

ISBN (print) 978-1-4766-8303-4
ISBN (ebook) 978-1-4766-5020-3

© 2023 Amanda Martin Sandino. All rights reserved

No part of this book may be reproduced or transmitted in any form or by any means, electronic or mechanical, including photocopying or recording, or by any information storage and retrieval system, without permission in writing from the publisher.

Front cover image © Sternfahrer/Shutterstock

Printed in the United States of America

*McFarland & Company, Inc., Publishers
Box 611, Jefferson, North Carolina 28640
www.mcfarlandpub.com*

"To Richard, who followed the White Rabbit."

Table of Contents

Preface 1

Introduction 11

CHAPTER 1
Crip Futurity and Literary Utopias   33

CHAPTER 2
Finding Criptopia in Baum's Oz Series   69

CHAPTER 3
Middle Era Wonderlands: A Turn to the Dark Side   94

CHAPTER 4
Alienation and *Charlie and the Chocolate Factory*   105

CHAPTER 5
Nostalgia, Fan Fiction,
and the Wayward Children Series   117

CHAPTER 6
The Underland and the Rejection
of the Medical Model of Disability   137

CHAPTER 7
Alice in the Underland   157

Conclusions   170

Chapter Notes   175

Works Cited   177

Index   191

Preface

This book will build upon various concepts of criptopia in providing a rereading of the speculative fiction canon that moves marginalized voices to the center. The term "criptopia" has been popular among various Tumblr communities and can refer to a world much like our own, but without compulsory ablebodiedness or the troubles of socially inscribed disability ("Criptopia"). I utilize this concept to refer to a more traditional utopic "no place," where persons with disabilities are both permitted and part of the definition of normate. I specifically consider literary utopic spaces intended for child audiences that are inhabited to some extent by persons with disabilities. I find that, unlike adult utopic fiction, the utopic wonderland of children's literature, as seen in Oz, Narnia, Wonderland, and Neverland, offers a space that is far more inclusive of disability and other marginalized groups. Rather than following the "woman as reward" trope so often depicted in early U.S. American utopic literature and speculative fiction—including Bellamy's *Looking Backward*, Butler's *Erewhon*, Morris's *News from Nowhere*, Perkins Gilman's *Herland*, Greg's *Across the Zodiac*, Serviss's *Edison's Conquest of Mars*, and numerous others—these narratives follow female protagonists. Thus, the criptopic spaces of children's wonderlands offer the possibility of a positive future that is more diverse in terms of dis/ability and gendered power relationships.

The open diversification of the speculative fiction genre during the twentieth and 21st centuries is unpacked by analyzing fan fiction, filmic representations, non-canonical coquels, sequels, and prequels of historic texts. New iterations and readings of older texts demonstrate that not only were marginalized persons present in historic speculative fiction texts, including those pre-dating the 1960s civil rights movements, but also show how these communities have actively responded to their

Preface

erasure from texts in this genre. I argue that these trends deconstruct the narrative of normality and alternative history supported by the Sad Puppies and Rabid Puppies, who purport that speculative fiction has been and should continue to be predominantly White, able bodied, neurotypical, male, heterosexual, and cisgender. Speculative fiction has not historically been homogenous nor its utopic visions gray, as this text will show. And newer, more diverse narratives actually and actively build upon historical texts often placed in the margins but still essential to the building of the speculative fiction genre.

In Chapter 1, "Crip Futurity and Literary Utopias," I present some of the ways that current scientific efforts and speculative fiction texts have attempted to remove disability from existence in their idealized worlds. Innovations that seek to rectify disabling conditions are considered in depth, including prenatal testing and resulting abortions and eugenics through genetic engineering. In this chapter, I argue that such scientific and literary endeavors complement one another to create an anti-disability ideology, a popular perspective whereby disabled bodies and minds are seen as a failure of contemporary science capable of being rectified with future generations. In this manner, persons with disabilities are perceived as needing cures to inhabit an idealized or utopic world.

This chapter also builds upon my understanding of criptopia. Criptopia, in this study, exists as a utopic space in which persons with disabilities are not only permitted to exist, but also treated as equally viable to the normate or part of a broadly defined understanding of the normate. Historically, utopic spaces in literature have largely erased or eliminated both physical and mental disabilities, often through eugenic practices or the assumption that, in a more perfect society, these perceived imperfections would simply cease to exist. I particularly discuss the wonderland utopia of Oz by L. Frank Baum, specifically the well-known *Wizard of Oz*, in relation to earlier and arguably grayer utopic texts, including Samuel Butler's *Erewhon*, Edward Bellamy's *Looking Backward*, and William Morris's *News from Nowhere*.

Finally, I define what characteristics are indicative of the wonderland, including: (1) a heroine's journey, (2) monsters, fairy folk, or talking animals, (3) rules that differ largely from those of the real world in terms of morality, science, and economics/government, (4) physicality and

Preface

literal existence otherwise known as geographic realism, (5) visitations by children or child-like figures from our own world, usually female, (6), and monarchs and tyrants interrupted by the visit of the human protagonist (7).

In Chapter 2, "Finding Criptopia in Baum's Oz Series," I argue that the fantasy world of Oz offers a quintessential criptopic wonderland space unlike those created by earlier twentieth-century authors. Drawing upon the characteristics introduced in the previous chapter, I demonstrate the manner in which the wonderland framework exists within Baum's Oz, particularly his first text in the series, *The Wizard of Oz*. Baum's Oz embodies a criptopia in an overt and narratively significant manner. This chapter introduces readers to the techniques of deep reading, fan culture awareness, and intertextual understandings of this influential text.

By offering an in-depth reading of *The Wizard of Oz* in relation to its subsequent texts by Baum, I demonstrate how bodies in wonderlands constantly undergo metamorphoses. Differences, rather than being hierarchical, are shown to be equally valuable within unique contexts. While the protagonist, Dorothy Gale, acts as a quintessential normate figure outside of Oz, her normalcy in and of itself is questioned and, at times, shown to be disabling within the context of this wonderland.

While the early wonderland is particularly marked by optimism and a lack of consequences, the middle period is wholly marked by far more traumatic events occurring both in the real world and the wonderlands themselves, including war, torture, descriptions of death, displacement, and unresolved conflict. This period, which is the subject of Chapter 3, "Middle Era Wonderlands: A Turn to the Dark Side," is furthermore characterized by change, such that texts written early during this period, for example *The Lion, the Witch, and the Wardrobe* (written in approximately 1949), are still significantly more cheerful and utopic than those written closer to the start of the underland period, such as *The NeverEnding Story* film (1984). By the time the contemporary wonderland period begins, the wonderland has in some ways transformed into a dystopic space, or at least a space that often reads as less than pleasant to anyone but the stories' heroes themselves. Happy endings are no longer guaranteed and permanent death becomes a clear possibility.

Preface

In this chapter, I define the underland/dark wonderland drawing upon Seanan McGuire's Wayward Children series and the wonderland guidelines from Chapter 1. In doing so, I offer a more in-depth overview of the yet underdiscussed middle period of the wonderland. Essentially, this chapter looks at the time of rapid narrative change between the wonderland and underland/dark wonderland texts, and the early and current wonderland periods. Particular texts highlighted in this chapter include *Glinda of Oz* (1920), *Charlie and the Chocolate Factory* (1964), *Bridge to Terabithia* (1977), *A Wrinkle in Time* (1962), and *The Little Prince* (1943).

Essentially, these "in-between" texts start to offer darker elements to the wonderland while still offering a happy ending and fewer negative consequences. Furthermore, these earlier narratives largely avoid permanent states of disability, offering impossible cures within their wonderland contexts that are shunned by the latter period. Yet, these texts nonetheless do not ignore the reality of suffering; instead, they merely focus on pain and other negative sensations as temporary or curable.

In Chapter 4, "Alienation and *Charlie and the Chocolate Factory*," I offer a deeper dive into the middle wonderland period between World War I and the fall of the Berlin Wall. In particular, I demonstrate that the lives of the authors, often directly impacted by World War II, deeply affected the manner in which childhood itself became depicted in their works. Many of the easy joys of childhood were lost for these writers, and this hardship is reflected in the lives of their characters through a lack of access to such things as toys, sugar, and play time; the permanent loss of a loved one, often a parent, friend, or sibling; and severe physical suffering, including depictions of characters dying of thirst and starvation. The child protagonists of the middle wonderland period, epitomized by Charlie Bucket of *Charlie and the Chocolate Factory*, remain good and kind, yet they experience true loss and suffering despite their goodness.

While Charlie Bucket's father is notably alive in the 1964 novel, Charlie nonetheless lives through horrific conditions. I discuss not only Charlie's scarceness of resources but also, how they alienate him from the other children who receive the Golden Tickets to Willy Wonka's Chocolate Factory. While Augustus Gloop, one of the many antagonists in *Charlie*, is characterized by gluttony, Charlie himself nearly dies

Preface

of starvation prior to winning his Golden Ticket. Violet Beauregarde chews gum almost religiously and in a highly competitive manner, bragging about beating her best friend's record for number of days chewing the same piece of gum. Yet her competition leads to severe individualism, something that marks her severely at odds with the more community-oriented Bucket family. Similarly, while Charlie's father loses his job as a "toothpaste cap-screwer" and becomes a snow shoveler, Veruca Salt's father is able to pay workers at his peanut factory to search for a Golden Ticket for Veruca. The women who work at his factory are said to shell peanuts all day long, sitting bored on an assembly line as they complete a monotonous task. Mr. Salt has such an excess of money that he can provide for Veruca's every want, including shutting down the production side of his business for nearly four days in order to procure Veruca's Golden Ticket. Even a mind-numbing job on such an assembly line would be a blessing for Mr. Bucket, in contrast.

Mike Teavee, however, offers clear insights into the shift of medium at play in this generation of wonderlands. For the young man is obsessed with television, while Charlie and his family rely heavily upon newspapers for their news. In this chapter, I explain the shift of focus in this study from largely print-based mediums to a larger library of media types, and how Dahl and his contemporaries deal with such a shift in their works. Many of the authors of the middle and contemporary periods simply wrote across a multitude of mediums, often driven more by the need for a paycheck than genuine interest. For example, Roald Dahl worked not only on novels but also radio programs, television series, and films, including the 1971 *Willy Wonka & the Chocolate Factory*. This multimodal writing, in which not just text but images and sounds are considered, has much in common with the early wonderlands in that they look toward adaptation; *Peter Pan* notably began as a play while *The Wizard of Oz* and *Alice in Wonderland* were adapted into stage plays almost immediately upon finding success. From the beginning, then wonderlands have looked beyond the page; I argue that this is an element indicative of this genre in and of itself, and something which perhaps make these texts more appealing due to the detailed worldbuilding.

Titled "Nostalgia, Fan Fiction, and the Wayward Children Series," Chapter 5 works as a fitting companion to Chapter 7 in considering

Preface

the ways in which power has come to affect the wonderland narrative. Building on Seanan McGuire's Wayward Children series and its surrounding commentary, I contend that fan culture has become a key component of the wonderland subgenre. In particular, fan culture has made it such that many contemporary wonderlands comment upon their predecessors, often while actively adapting them. For example, Gregory Macguire's *Wicked* tellingly considers *The Wizard of Oz* from The Wicked Witch of the West's perspective, asking readers to consider if they too wouldn't be angry with someone who had just murdered their sister and stolen magic shoes from her corpse.

While the earliest wonderland tales have entered the public domain, I also contend, in this chapter, with the strangeness of which wonderlands may be legally built upon in traditional publication venues and which have been relegated to fan culture. Theoretically, fan publications, such as fan fiction, should be considered to have equal merit to their traditionally published counterparts. Yet, this has been far from the case, meaning that those who, say, are not privileged enough to gain legal access to the Roald Dahl estate may create *Charlie and the Chocolate Factory* fanvids, while the notably wealthy Tim Burton can simply make his own for-profit production. This distinction, I contend, actually works in direct opposition to many of the current underland narratives, in that persons from the hegemonic classes continue to be those most likely to gain access to traditional publication and production resources.

In Chapter 6, "The Underland and the Rejection of the Medical Model of Disability," I use Jordan Peele's *Us* as a case study for the underland and as an example for regression in terms of disability representation. Offering a framework or the dark wonderland or underland, I focus on key examples in the contemporary wonderland era, including Peele's *Us*, *And Then Emily Was Gone* (Lees, et al.), *Pan's Labyrinth* (del Toro), American McGee's *Alice* videogames, and *Stranger Things* (The Duffer Brothers). This chapter will clarify the transformation of the wonderland into a negativized space as the utopic is increasingly seen as contextual (i.e., "one person's utopia is another's dystopia"). I then offer an overview of disability in new horror media with a particular emphasis on the dark wonderland as a space of negativized bodily difference using these examples. I contend that this shift marks a notable critique

Preface

of earlier wonderlands, in line with the current literary shift away from the utopic and toward this dystopic.

Chapter 7, "Alice in the Underland," offers a deeper analysis of Jordan Peele's *Us* in conversation with Grant Morrison and Dave McKean's *Arkham Asylum* (1989) and Jan Švankmajer's (1988) *Alice*. The terror elements of these three adaptations, especially *Us* as discussed with the earlier two works, acts to undermine fundamental binaries in utopic literatures, including good vs. evil, healthy vs. unhealthy, and sane vs. insane. In particular, these works demonstrate that those who are disenfranchised by such distinctions are often from marginalized groups; it is power, rather than objective realities, that determines where a person is located in such dichotomies.

In *Us*, this power differential is literalized by the original Red knocking out the original Adelaide and taking her place; she literally disempowers her upper-world counterpart. When we first delve into this film, the Tethered seem to be clearly situated as the villains. After all, we see them quickly attack the Wilsons and the Tylers are all slaughtered by their Tethered counterparts in a matter of seconds; the script describing the scene as a "seven second massacre" (62). Yet, once it is revealed that the woman we have known as Adelaide for the entire film began as a Tethered and took the original Adelaide's place, our perspective begins to shift. We are asked to wonder who began the project of placing human beings underground, what makes them different from their Untethered counterparts, and, most importantly, whether the Tethered may be the actual victims of the story, or at least co-victims with the above grounders. Interestingly, more persons who can be confirmed as Tethered are actually killed than their above-ground counterparts; this distinction is notably difficult to make for many characters, as the human chain at the end of the film depicts a fair number of Tethered *not* wearing the signature red jumpsuit. In terms of above-ground persons killed by Tethered, there are the four Tylers, a newscaster, and a man holding an "11:11" sign. We can presume that many of the other bodies seen in the background are Untethered but cannot be sure; as Adelaide and Red's switch demonstrates, it is very easy to confuse the twins. In contrast, eight Tethered are clearly killed by the Wilsons, all of them named characters in the script: the four Tethered Tylers and the four Tethered Wilsons. While the number of Tethered characters

Preface

holding hands at the end of the film seem to represent a large number, the possibility that literally every U.S. American may have a Tethered counterpart suggests that the Untethered are actually winning the fight; especially given that U.S. military helicopters are clearly being weaponized against the scissor-wielding army. If we are to sympathize with the Tethereds' suffering and rage, it becomes difficult to see them as the "bad guys" of the film, especially non-violent characters such as Pluto. The line between good and bad is meaningfully blurred, in terms of good vs. evil characters, the good vs. the bad life, and the utopic and dystopic.

Arkham Asylum (1989) and *Alice* (1988) further this blurring of the binary in wonderland spaces. *Alice* depicts the White Rabbit, on the command of the Red Queen, executing two playing cards by decapitating them with scissors. The folk of Wonderland seem to be largely vilified until the end of the film, when it becomes clear that the inhabitants of wonderland are in some way imbued with life by Alice herself. If the playing cards are represented by her actual cards, the caterpillars by socks, human-like creatures by dolls, and so on, then we are left to question who the Red Queen's counterpart is. Rather than being based on a playing card, it seems that Alice may herself be the regular world counterpart to the Red Queen; the last line in the film is given by Alice, who comments about the White Rabbit: "He's late, as usual. I think I'll cut his head off" in a manner much like the Red Queen.

Arkham Asylum moves creatures from wonderland into the titular Elizabeth Arkham Asylum for the Criminally Insane. Figures such as the Caterpillar and Mad Hatter are portrayed not only as mentally disabled but as villainous, in contrast to Batman, who is meant to be sane and good. Yet, by the end of the comic, Batman himself is unsure of his sanity as well as his goodness. After all, in the service of "the good," he has hurt and killed many people, whether marked as villains or not. Tellingly, one of the last major actions in the graphic novel is the death of the hospital's administrator, Dr. Charles Cavendish, at the hands of his subordinate, therapist Dr. Ruth Adams. Cavendish is choking Batman to death at the time, meaning that Adams is theoretically slitting her superior's throat to save the story's hero. Yet, as soon as Cavendish is killed, Adams is horrified and filled with remorse. She repeats to herself that she "didn't mean to" and shows signs of being traumatized by the experience. Batman, however, seems completely unperturbed by the violent death he has just witnessed, merely stating that Cavendish "got what he deserved" and moving on to the next step in his plans; Morrison's script tellingly notes that "Batman doesn't give a damn for [Adams's] feelings." It is very clear that Batman is just as, if not more, violent and mentally ill than the inmates of Arkham Asylum.

In these narratives, light, open space, and above-groundness became equated with privilege. They are locations inhabited by those of the hegemonic classes, the minority of the characters in the works who live an exquisite life at the expense of those who rarely, if ever, see those privileged spaces. These stories come from authors who have seen the earlier wonderlands and recognized themselves those in the other who dwells beneath; the underland narrative acts as a postmodern critique of the early wonderland, in particular, and its focus on middle-to-upper class Whiteness, cisheterosexuality, and colonizer positionalities. Thus, these narratives tend to come from those erased or disenfranchised by earlier narratives. The wonderland has been reclaimed in being critiqued; the underland thus becomes a tool for empowerment.

Finally, the book concludes with an overview of the three periods of wonderlands in relation to disability and what they mean in terms of broader U.S. culture. For, as disability rights movements seemingly gain more ground and credibility, these narratives simultaneously turn away from particular parts of the crip community and the concept of criptopia. The disabled hero denies the possibility of cure but, in doing so, appears to become increasingly violent while turning any space she inhabits into a dystopia. While the wonderland becomes a space of critical utopia studies characterized by the pessimism of the post–Cold War era, so too does it reflect pessimism regarding cripfuturity in the face of gene editing technologies and the revival of eugenics.

Introduction

Loss of home is perhaps one of the themes best translated from L. Frank Baum's 1900 *The Wizard of Oz* to its popular 1939 film adaptation. Throughout the MGM classic, Dorothy consistently expresses her desire to return home and the phrase "there's no place like home" becomes at once a magic spell able to transport Dorothy back to Kansas and a tagline for the film as a whole. While Dorothy's house in Kansas notably facilitates Dorothy's emergence as a heroine in Oz when the house falls upon the Wicked Witch of the East, killing her, the literal destruction of home is negated in the film due to use of an "it was all a dream" trope. While, in the film, Dorothy does ultimately return to a home and a house that is still intact, in the original book, Dorothy's family must still recover from their farm's destruction following Dorothy's return to Kansas. Eventually, due to the financial hardship attached to the loss of their house, Aunt Em and Uncle Henry must seek money-making opportunities elsewhere, including San Francisco and Australia, before eventually relocating to Oz for good.

In the non–Ozian parts of Earth, ships inevitably sink, lands inevitably break open, and homes inevitably are destroyed. In the wake of disasters outside of Oz, Dorothy finds refuge in the magical world, while she generally returns home after defeating or otherwise killing persons in Oz. While literary critic Charity Gibson has already considered *The Wizard of Oz* as a modernist work, drawing upon arguments such as its subversion of the master narrative, early feminist tendencies, and fixation on the technological, I argue that it is rather these many losses, particularly that of home both conceptually and literally, that mark both mark the Oz series thematically as a modernist work of children's literature *and* the early wonderland narratives as texts steeped in modernism's vision for narrative change.

Introduction

Published between the years of 1865 and approximately 1914, most early wonderland texts fits chronologically in the time typically associated with modernism yet have rarely been considered as works, and I would argue key texts, of modernist literature. Both successful and well read by parents, caretakers, and children alike, the wonderland contributes significantly to modernist children's literature, especially the youth-oriented avant-garde movement termed the "kindergarde" by Dana Teen Lomax (viii). Lomax defines the kindergarde via the experimental, particularly highlighting the following aspects:

> [1] The writers ... try to be themselves and write in ways that make sense to them—even if they have to make up words or rearrange sentences or scramble up the page or forget punctuation on purpose or change the way a story can go.
> [2] These writers spend their time closely looking at and thinking about things. Like many of you, they wonder about the world and what could be, what might be, what's real.
> [3] They take creative risks. They commit to their strange ideas.
> [4] They don't always do as they are told or follow the instructions about how to act on paper or in society. They remind us that there are lots of way to be.

The three quintessential early wonderland series—the Land of Oz books, the *Peter Pan* books, and the *Alice in Wonderland* books—clearly meet all four of these criteria. For (1), one might easily look at Baum's respelling of the word "gnomes" in his work, choosing instead to write "nomes" as silent g's or Lewis Carroll's propensity for nonsense words and neologisms (i.e., "chortle" and "galumphing" from *Through the Looking-Glass*). Even J.M. Barrie reworked the meaning of the word "kiss" to mean a token of affection, in *Peter Pan* either an acorn button or thimble. Secondly (2), inanimate objects in wonderland works literally come to life—including playing cards, once-dead fairies, scarecrows, and men made of tin. Ordinary substances such as water and clocks become the (unintentional) downfall of villains. Thirdly (3), these fantastic worlds are nothing if it not strange. In the first book of the Oz series, *The Wizard of Oz*, the word "strange" occurs 36 times, notably in the following instances:

> Then a strange thing happened. [...] The house whirled around two or three times and rose slowly through the air. Dorothy felt as if she were going up in a balloon...

Introduction

> She stood looking eagerly at the strange and beautiful sights...
> She felt lonely among all these strange people...
> "How strange it all is!"...

The word "strange" in and of itself also appears 28 times in *Peter Pan*. While only 5 times in *Alice in Wonderland*, the word is famously substituted for "curious," which appears 21 times in the first book. Furthermore, the rules of these worlds are estranged from those of ours. Magical creatures exist, people are able to fly, bodies shrink to the size of mice before growing to the size of houses, animals talk, and so many other impossible things occur.

Finally (4), the rules of law, if not the entire power systems within these worlds are notably disparate from those of the real world. While interrupted by the coming of a usually female protagonist, we are given lands ruled over by magicians and animals, pirates and mermaids, and playing cards come to life. In Wonderland, Alice finds that the sentencing of a defendant comes *before* a trial (Carroll, *Alice in Wonderland*), while Ojo is thrown into prison for picking a six-leaved clover (Baum, "The Patchwork Girl of Oz"), and many of the lost boys are sentenced to walk the plank seemingly for the crime of procuring a surrogate mother (Barrie, *Peter Pan*).

Yet it is furthermore the loss of home that most attaches these early wonderlands series to modernism. For though these early child protagonists demonstrate sorrow for their loss of home, they are, with few exceptions, always returned to the "real" world. U.S. American and British modernism is largely signified through mourning, as clarified in literary scholar Seth Moglen's *Mourning Modernity*:

> American modernism is famously a literature of loss ... the writers we have come to call modernist ... remind us of something important: that many writers in this period have experienced losses so fundamental as to have become constitutive of identity; that these men and woman had lost so much that they felt themselves to *be* lost—disoriented, unmoored, cut off from the continuities of a social order that seemed itself to be shattering [44].

This loss of self, identity, and placement in the social order, while largely present in these early works, become increasingly present in the middle period of the wonderland (approximately 1918–1988) and uprooted

Introduction

altogether with an overhaul of normalcy in the late wonderland period (approximately 1988–present). As Dorothy weeps at the thought of never seeing Kansas, Aunt Em, and Uncle Henry again, so too do other early adventurers to wonderlands mourn their inabilities to return to the so-called "real" world. However, being in the early wonderland period, they don't need to worry *too much*, as they are in a narrative period marked by happy endings in children's literature.

Disability in the Wonderland

In the U.K. and U.S., the end of what disability studies historian Kim E. Nielsen terms the "institutionalization era" of disability, the period during which most persons with disabilities were either jailed within traditional prisons or placed within often prison-like psychiatric facilities, intersected with the rise of high modernism and the wonderland narrative in the late 19th and early 20th century. The increased representation of persons with disabilities in Anglophone literatures occurred simultaneously to these cultural and artistic movements. These intersecting aesthetic and ideological periods were marked by a purposeful break from tradition and an increased confidence in the ability of science and technology to master and cure the natural world. The context of this time period ensured that the concept of disability would be developed and increasingly scrutinized. Interweaving literary modernism and disability was so prevalent during this period that it led to the development of Lennard Davis's notion of "dismodernism," a theory which "argues for commonality of bodies within the notion of difference," essentially the idea that "we are all nonstandard" ("The End of Identity Politics," 268). Michael Davidson builds upon this idea in his *Concerto for the Left Hand,* explaining that "the aesthetic values that art historians and literary scholars use to explain these changes are seen differently through a disability optic" (xii–xiii). For example, a poem written by a deaf poet, a painting by an artist who has low vision, and a dance performed by an artist with one leg offer insightful and unique aesthetic values and ideas. The positionality of these creators as persons with disabilities inscribe new meanings, leading us to question what it means to be beautiful and create art (Davidson xii–xiii).

Introduction

The concept of the normate, or "the corporeal incarnation of culture's collective, unmarked, normative characteristics" (Garland-Thomson 10), itself began to be more thoroughly questioned during the institutionalization era. Thus, wonderlands must be interpreted with this contextual understanding in order to see the cultural shift that was occurring at the time. As disability theorists Mitchell and Snyder explain, reconsiderations of classic texts through a disability studies lens shows that, contrary to popular belief, "people with disabilities have been the object of representational treatments, but [also] that their function in literary discourse is primarily twofold: disability pervades literary narrative, first, as a stock feature of characterization and, second, as an opportunistic metaphorical device" (47).

Alongside the increased presence of persons with disabilities in conventional spaces, such as living on main street rather than secluded within hospitals, prisons, and asylums (Davis, "Introduction," 5), came the increased presence of such persons in literature. This representation was furthered by a deeper understanding of disability in the broader population as well as a growth in the number of persons surviving injuries and illnesses to live with disabilities outside of an institutional context. This shift modified the concept of humanness itself, such that a human's essential personhood, which had previously been conceptually moved from the soul to the brain with the rise of humanism, shifted again to exist within a person's DNA or genetic material (Vidal). This change occurred as increasing numbers of individuals who worked in factories and other high-risk occupations and World War I veterans became a larger part of the general population while having visible neurological and physical disabilities that normate persons could encounter in everyday life (Mcleod ii). These particular categories of disabilities were non-genetic and due to injury or trauma, ensuring a differentiation that normalized returning veterans, particularly within patriotic postwar U.K. and U.S. cultures.

While previous studies have considered the historical significance and presence of persons with disabilities in literatures of the U.S. and U.K., this book specifically considers unique representations of disability in children's speculative literature, popular adaptations of classic speculative fiction, and fan fiction writings responding to such texts. This study is driven by intertextuality and the intermingling of

Introduction

experiences expressed in literatures with those on main street. For example, the 1939 film interpretation of L. Frank Baum's wonderland, *The Wizard of Oz*, is so influential from a cultural studies perspective that it is in many ways more significant than the original text. As explained by film theorist Robert Stam's pivotal text on novel to film adaptation, the use of medium rather than content can be the key indicator of success and proliferation. The differentiation and elevation of the film makes even more practical sense when one realizes that many of *The Wizard of Oz*'s intended audience members are not yet able to read. Throughout most of the film's history, it has held a G rating,[1] marking it as proper viewing material for everyone by the MPAA; however, Common Sense Media, a leading educational review organization, suggests that the original book only be read by children over 8 years of age. In short, the film is simply more accessible to a child viewership than the book.

This study also considers a particular subgenre, that of the child-oriented utopic wonderland, within the modernist timeframe by asking, "What contributions do wonderlands make to understanding the intersections of the utopic and disabled bodies in U.S. and U.K. literature?" In this book, the wonderland is understood as a version of the utopic "no place" or idyllic community, a definition which will be built upon in subsequent chapters. Numerous terms will need to be defined through a cultural studies lens because terminology works toward "binding words in certain activities and their interpretation" and framing "words in certain forms of thought" (Williams 15). As words depend upon their contexts and cultures, clarifying my own usage is particularly essential as a prelude to this study.

Terms

Because words often have unique meanings within specific contexts, the societal impact of word choices must be examined beyond their academic understandings. As explains cultural studies critic Raymond Williams in *Keywords*:

> ...we use the same words for most everyday things and activities, though with obvious variations of rhythm and accent and tone. Some of the variable

Introduction

> words, say lunch and supper and dinner, may be highlighted but the differences are not particularly important. When we come to say "we just don't speak the same language" we mean something more general: that we have different immediate values or different kinds of valuation, or that we are aware, often intangibly, of different formations and distributions of energy and interest. In such a case, each group is speaking its native language, but its uses are significantly different, and especially when strong feelings or important ideas are in question. No single group is "wrong" by any linguistic criterion, though a temporarily dominant group may try to enforce its own uses as "correct" [10].

Williams's groundbreaking text took as its premise the importance of the cultural understanding of words over etymological conceptions. For example, the literal and etymological meaning of the word "decimate" refers to the reduction of something by 1/10th ("deci" from the Greek for "ten"); but, because the average person often uses this term to refer to complete destruction, under Williams's understanding, the second definition is more useful from a cultural studies and public humanities perspective. Furthermore, one should not take one's usage of a term for granted, as knowledge, per cultural studies, is:

> ...not a product of research that can be validated only in established disciplines and by credentializing institutions, but as a process that is responsive to the diverse constituencies that use and revise the meanings of the keywords that govern our understandings of the present, the future, and the past [Burgett and Hendler 3].

Our definitions for terms can shift based on numerous contextual factors, necessitating that, when a term such as "wonderland" is used as a study keyword, it should be explained according to the author's particular conception of it, as included below.

Criptopia. The concept of a utopia as a vision of the world that adheres to certain ideals and needs is not a new concept, but the term "criptopia" has largely emerged as a portmanteau following the appropriation of the term "cripple" through the use of the word "crip" in disability activism.[2] As explained at the 2017 Sex Disability Conference:

> Crip is considered to be an inclusive term, representing all disabilities: people with vastly divergent physical and psychological differences. Crip represents the contemporary disability rights wave and is an "insider" term for disability culture. Not to be confused with a gang name, the term Crip within the disability community reflects the political reclaiming of the

Introduction

historically derogatory term "cripple," which not only diminished the person to an image of ugliness but also excluded those with non-physical disabilities from the disability community ["Crip Theory"].

Combining this word for disabled identity with the concept of utopia, an imagined but desired place characterized by perfection, suggests the imagining of a perfect world in which persons with disability are not just permitted to exist, but to thrive. As explained in the popular article "Criptopia" by Josie Byzek, managing editor of *New Mobility*, "the magazine for active wheelchair users," this concept imagines a space in which everything is "perfectly accessible, affordable and accommodating."

Crip Futurity. Related to the concept of criptopia, the idea of crip futurity considers the temporal existence of persons with disabilities. In his review of Alison Kafer's *Feminist, Queer, Crip*, fellow intersectional disability theorist Robert McRuer offers a genealogy for her politics of crip futurity:

> While attuned to Lee Edelman's critique of a narrow reproductive futurism invested in an idealized childhood, Kafer writes more in a Muñozian vein and (as Feminist, Queer, Crip was published in the year of his death) carries on or crips a Muñozian legacy. "Queer kids, street kids, kids of color—all of the kids cast out of reproductive futurism, have been and continue to be framed as sick, as pathological, as contagious," Kafer writes (32). Although her book is not a direct response to [Muñoz's magnum opus] *Cruising Utopia*, she explicitly calls on readers to "do the work" Muñoz imagined, "and to do it with attention to how [these] different populations are demarcated differently" in relation to idealized notions of the future (34) [532].

Similar to queer or queer persons in Edelman's *No Future*, Kafer reads the depiction and understanding of persons with disability in Anglo-American culture as consistently *future-less*, with disability acting as a condition upon which one's future is effectively ended or precluded (33). In his review, McRuer notes that most futurists "can only conceive of a future from which disability has been purged" (532). Thus, the purpose of crip futurity is to imagine a future, often a utopian one, in which disability and the communities surrounding its various conditions have not been eliminated. My understanding of crip futurity in this monograph builds on such a model of criptopia based in queer, disability, feminist theory.

The reproduction-based futurism of queer theorist Lee Edelman is

Introduction

examined via the concept of biofuturity in poet and disability theorist Michael Davidson's "Pregnant Men: Modernism, Disability, and Biofuturity in Djuna Barnes." Davidson interrogates Edelman's concept of the queer "death drive," the call for a conception of queer time that is based in the present, accepting one's futurity as ending with one's individual death rather than continuing via one's blood lineage. In his deconstruction of the term, Davidson analyzes the rhetoric utilized by euthanasia proponents, essentially critiquing the normate-based decision that certain crip lives are "not worth living" (209), a narrative that negates certain crip futures *and* presents. In his examination of the popular 2004 film *Million Dollar Baby*, in which a boxer is rendered paraplegic after an accident, he notes that there is an assumption of a "body that, could it speak, would want not to be born" (209). A more recent example of such a conception is Jojo Moyes's 2012 novel *Me Before You* and the boycotting of the 2016 adaptation by many disabled communities. The storyline in both texts follows a wealthy upper-class British man, Will, as he seeks to end his life following an accident that leaves him quadriplegic. When his new caretaker and love interest, Louisa, learns that his mother has agreed to support his physician-assisted suicide in six months, should he still wish to terminate his life, she attempts to convince him that his life is still worth living. Despite Will and Louisa falling in love, Will chooses to end his life after the six-month period. Regardless of having access to the highest quality healthcare, a supportive and wealthy family, and a loving partner, this character still feels that death is preferable to life as a quadriplegic. As disability and queer rights activist Jax Jacki Brown explains:

> Let's be clear here: Will ends his life solely on the basis of having disability... As a wheelchair user, I am deeply concerned that this film perpetuates these messages: that the lives of people with disabilities are not worth living, and that people with disabilities cannot be worthy partners... When able-bodied people feel as though they want to die, we get them help and talk about suicide prevention, but when people with disabilities are depressed, there's a large subset of society sending the message that it's understandable and wanting to legislate to help them do it.

With this movement toward a now and future based in self rather than coupling and reproduction, the concept of biofuturity for the disabled body extends to biological reproduction *of* and *by* persons with

Introduction

disabilities. In Chapter 1 of this study, I therefore consider the implications of genetic modification, prenatal testing, and disability-based abortions in relation to crip futurity, asking if the future, as depicted in utopian fiction, must preclude the continued existence of certain disabilities and their related crip communities.

Speculative Fiction. Sometimes used interchangeably with sf or science fiction, this term has been broadly used to include adventure fiction, mysteries, weird fiction, detective novels, fantasy, and even horror literature. Many contemporary authors whose works might otherwise be categorized as science fiction, such as Nalo Hopkinson, explain that the history of science fiction has mostly negated the presence of women and persons of color (Rutledge and Hopkinson 591). Some groups, such as the alt-right ideological Hugo voting blocs the Rabid Puppies and the Sad Puppies, implicitly consider science fiction to be intended for White, male, straight, normate, and cisgender audiences. As such, the term "speculative fiction" is often applied when referring to a more diversified vision of the genre as it has existed from the late 20th century, from the civil rights movements of the 1960s to the present. This definition can also be extended to address fiction that considers our world(s) from a broader, societal lens:

> ...as a set of literatures that examine the effects on humans and human societies of the fact that we are toolmakers. We are always trying to control or improve our environments. Those tools may be tangible (such as machines) or intangible (such as laws, mores, belief systems). Spec-fic [short for speculative fiction] tells us stories about our lives with our creations [Nelson and Hopkinson].

In terms of the present work, the term "speculative fiction" is differentiated from "science fiction" and "fantasy" because I use it to refer to various aforementioned genre fiction in a broad, all-encompassing lens that historically includes compositions by persons belonging to marginalized groups.

Wonderland. While numerous definitions for this term exist, these understandings build upon the Oxford English Dictionary's generalized depiction of a wonderland as "a. An imaginary realm of wonder and faery ... b. A country, realm, or domain which is full of wonders or marvels" ("wonderland, n."). Thus, in approaching this book from a cultural studies perspective, it is imperative to understand the societal uses of

Introduction

the term "wonderland" or "wonder" as an emotion. In fact, in his current project, professor of speculative fiction Glenn Willmott argues that it is the emotion of wonder rather than the existence of science or magic that builds the foundations of this genre (2). In his thought piece on this topic for the 2016 Modernist Studies Association conference, Willmott notes the common use of words such as "marvelous," "wonderful," "thrilling," "astounding," and "startling" in titles among the Golden Age of speculative fiction from the late-1930s to mid–1940s. Consider some of the more prominent texts indisputably linked to the concept of the wonderland: Lewis Carroll's *Alice in Wonderland*, J.M. Barrie's *Peter Pan, or The Boy Who Wouldn't Grow Up*, and L. Frank Baum's *The Wonderful Wizard of Oz*. While notably absent from the title of Barrie's key work, the term "wonderful" is quite common in the text itself, appearing six times and linked to the ability to fly through Peter's explanation: "You just think lovely, wonderful thoughts ... and they lift you up in the air." The broader term "wonder" appears 22 times. The other two key texts include the word in their very titles, suggesting that these terms were actually popular within the genre prior to the Golden Age.

Particularly significant additions to this definition include the wonderland as a literary utopic space intended for a predominantly child audience and a broader audience of persons concerned for their welfare. It is both this intended audience and the intended evoked emotion that mark the wonderland as distinct from the larger genre of utopic literature.

Periodization

The wonderland as a space of disability was largely defined by the average reader's lack of experience around persons with disabilities up until the start of World War II. When Alice in Wonderland first came out in 1865, persons with disabilities were largely sequestered in institutions and prisons, so that the normate had little personal interaction with persons with disabilities. As the Progressive Era spanned from *Alice*'s publication year to roughly 1890, so too did the U.S. see a rise in the popularity of eugenics and the forced sterilization of an estimated 65,000 Americans (Nielsen 100). It was only after the First World War

Introduction

that persons with disabilities, especially disabled war veterans, became a more common presence on main streets across the country, setting up the foundations for what would become the disability rights movement from the late 1960s to present.

The increasing presence of persons with disabilities in towns and cities across the United States affected and in turn was affected by wonderland texts. The eventual rise and success of the disability rights movements in these spaces had a particularly significant effect on these narratives, especially following the passage of the groundbreaking Americans with Disabilities Act introduced in 1988 and signed into law in 1990. I contend that the early wonderland period from 1865 to 1914, predominantly offered the wonderland as a positive alternative to spaces accessible to persons with disabilities. By the end of the two world wars, the middle wonderland period had begun, in which death and illness exist far more often in the wonderland space. During this time period, roughly 1914–late 1980s/early 1990s or from the start of World War I to approximately the end of the Cold War, disabilities, while still often temporary conditions, came to be associated with horrors such as war, disease, and death. Finally, in the late wonderland period, approximately late 1980s–present, we find not only an increased presence of disability but a shift from the utopic to dystopic wonderland as well. These more contemporary narratives offer visions of the wonderland that seem to both celebrate disability, particularly mental illness, while eschewing the medicalization of mind-body difference. Disability activist, scholar, and poet Eli Clare refers to the complicated relationship between persons with disabilities and the medical industrial complex as "grappling with cure." Yet, these narratives of contemporary dystopic wonderlands seem instead to deny cure altogether in ways that I contend are actually harmful to persons with disabilities, particularly those of us who do seek medical treatments.

Early Wonderlands

Early wonderland spaces often act in contrast to their real-world counterparts when it comes to disability; essentially, when persons with disabilities faced particularly harsh practices in the U.K. and U.S. historically, they were normalized within the wonderland. A key quote

Introduction

from *Alice's Adventures in Wonderland* highlights the commonality of such difference within Wonderland. As Alice worries to the Cheshire Cat about travelling amongst "mad people" such as the Mad Hatter and March Hare, the feline explains, "Oh, you can't help that ... we're all mad here. I'm mad. You're mad... You must be ... or you wouldn't have come here" (Carroll 33). English scholar Mark M. Hennelly, Jr., notes that the Wonderland as developed by Lewis offers an example of utopian carnivalesque, with bodies, laws, and power structures in constant states of change. Rather than being constrained by the rules of science or society, Alice's "identity might potentially be anything and everything" simultaneously (121).

Within such a world, both the social and medical definitions of disability also become suspect. Because reality itself is constantly shifting, particularly with regard to these larger categories of being, the body inhabited may remain the same yet cross the problematic binary of disabled/non-disabled. Yet, even further, the body itself may easily change, often in ways limited to fantasy worlds. Change in itself appears to be the only constant within the early wonderland, another feature of the carnivalesque. Russian linguist Mikhail Bakhtin particularly utilizes the term "carnivalesque" to describe the destabilization of such structures of power and control. He offers four categories to describe the carnivalesque, including (1) unity and interaction between peoples who do not usually inhabit the same spaces, (2) behavior that breaks from the ordinary and generally accepted, (3) the meeting of disparate, oppositional, or polarized persons or categories of being, and (4) an absence of the rules of respect and elevation of the profane. While these qualities may be applied to wonderlands across all of the time periods, the focus on the utopic or "wonderful" marks the early era as particularly dense with largely pleasant wonderland journeys. Exemplars in this period, such as *Peter Pan*, the *Alice* books, and the early Oz books offer wonder in the carnivalesque sense, of venturing to a new world of dis/order without any fear and openly discovering new knowledges (Hennelly, Jr., 104).

And arguably there is nothing to fear in these early wonderlands, unlike the worlds of the middle and late periods. As a book acts almost directly as a passage from the early to middle wonderland, C.S. Lewis's *The Lion, The Witch, and the Wardrobe* demonstrates qualities of

Introduction

both phases. Written predominantly during and in the aftermath of World War II, *The Lion* offers one of the more upsetting images of death included in a wonderland novel while also including far less affective images of death and suffering that better mark the early period. In short, it is essential to compare the deaths of Aslan and Tumnus the faun. While Tumnus's petrification takes place off page, his frozen expression, marked by Edmund, is one of profound grief. Upon finding the statue garden, Lucy responds too with sadness; however, within pages Aslan has begun unfreezing his fallen kin such that they are "none the worse for having been a statue."

In contrast, the death of Aslan is notably described in detail on the page, as watched by Lucy and Susan, as he is bound, shaved, muzzled, and eventually stabbed to death. Notably the actual moment of the stabbing is missed, as both girls look away, though Aslan's expression of grief rather than terror is offered instead. Like Tumnus, his reaction to death, however temporary, seems not to be fear but sorrow for his friends, his killers, or both. Also similar to Tumnus, Aslan is able to quickly return from death, in this case by way of the Deep Magic governing Narnia. Because he allowed himself, as an innocent, to be sacrificed in Edmund's stead, Aslan is able to be resurrected. For mere paragraphs, Lucy and Susan mourn over Aslan's corpse before it is taken back into the ground by magic and he reemerges alive, mane and all.

Yet, as temporary as these deaths in Narnia are, that of Aslan in particular is meant to trouble the reader; the narrator notes, "I hope no one who reads this book has been quite as miserable as Susan and Lucy were that night." Such sorrow offers a departure from the earlier wonderlands and attitudes toward death, which is largely absent or even more temporary in the Wonderland, Oz, and Neverland.

Peter Pan, notably showing fear for the first time in the narrative upon facing his potential death, only allows the emotion to fill him for the briefest of moments:

> Peter was not quite like other boys; but he was afraid at last. A tremour ran through him, like a shudder passing over the sea; but on the sea one shudder follows another till there are hundreds of them, and Peter felt just the one. Next moment he was standing erect on the rock again, with that smile on his face and a drum beating within him. It was saying, "To die will be an awfully big adventure."

Introduction

He is triumphant as he becomes trapped on a small rock with the waters rising to drown him. If he is to die, he will do so as he has lived, cockily and bravely. As such, he does not even take his rescue by the Never bird seriously, growing annoyed with her poor efforts at saving him as though he would just as soon drown after all.

Wendy, arguably the hero of the tale, also shows little fear in the face of death. When she and the lost boys are captured by Captain Hook and his crew, Wendy is told that her life may be spared if she promises to be the pirates' mother. Wendy, described as showing "disdain" and "contempt," refuses. Even when asked by Smee, Hook's first mate and arguably the kindest of the pirates, Wendy replies, "I would almost rather have no children at all." She remains proud, brave, and angry until Peter shows up to save her and the lost boys.

Similarly, Alice grows unafraid of death. At the end of her first novel, she encounters the Queen of Hearts, who famously shouts "off with their head," referring to about nearly everyone who surrounds her. Eventually, Alice grows irritated by the queen's behavior, as well as the justice system in her kingdom which allows for the sentencing of a defendant prior to a trial. "Stuff and nonsense," Alice finally shouts, interrupting the proceedings, "You're nothing but a pack of cards!" While she does scream "half of fright" when the entire card deck descends upon her, the book notes that she is also reacting "half of anger." Despite knowing that she may be sentenced to decapitation like so many around her, Alice speaks out at the trial of the Knave of Hearts for stealing the Queen's tarts each time the proceedings become particularly nonsensical or unjust.

Similarly, Dorothy's anger at the Wicked Witch in *The Wizard* overpowers her fear. When one of her silver slippers falls off and is taken by the witch, "the little girl, seeing she had lost one of her pretty shoes, gr[ows] angry, and s[ays] to the Witch, 'Give me back my shoe!'" When the witch refuses, Dorothy becomes increasingly enraged until she eventually picks up a bucket of water and throws it on the Wicked Witch. It is only when she sees the witch begin to melt that Dorothy becomes afraid, as she had merely intended to splash the shoe thief with water, not kill her. The scene mirrors an earlier one in which the Scarecrow, Tin Man, Toto, and Dorothy are scared by the Cowardly Lion when he attempts to bite Toto. "Heedless of danger," Dorothy gets between Toto and the Lion, slapping the latter in the face. She then scolds the lion for his cowardice, more angry than afraid.

The permanence of death and disability are erased in these early wonderlands, such that fear itself is largely removed as well. Permanent death is reserved for wicked characters, such as the Wicked Witch, while the presence of magic acts as a deus ex machina in seemingly irreparable situations. Disability appears to be almost omnipresent and ever-changing. Wicked characters, such as Captain Hook and the Wicked Witch, demonstrate the clear presence of disability through their prosthesis and weakness to water respectively. Yet so too do our heroes demonstrate disabilities, including the common literary trope of children who never age; the lost boys and all citizens of Oz are notably free of aging, rendering them almost inhuman in that "the common process of change and growth over the course of a human life" is removed (Michals and McTiernan). The binary between disabled/nondisabled becomes especially fraught, fluid, and changeable, such that many characters, such as Alice, go through significant physical and mental changes throughout their narratives.

Middle Wonderlands

While the binary between the disabled/nondisabled continues to be antagonized in the middle wonderland period, there comes with these works a tendency toward hierarchy. Essentially, it is generally understood within such wonderlands that it is better to be non-disabled or normative than disabled. So, should someone cross the barrier into a disabled existence, chances are that they will return to their normative selves by the end of the story; and most of these stories continue to offer traditionally "happy" endings.

In this section, I will particularly draw upon the examples of *Charlie and the Chocolate Factory* (1964) and its 1971 film adaptation; *The NeverEnding Story* (English translation released in 1983) and its 1984 film adaptation; and the final Narnia book, *The Last Battle* (1956). Each of the film adaptations and the ultimate Narnia book offer a particularly unique relationship to death, time, and change that demonstrates how the wonderland began to become a space in which horror could occur more abundantly and safety was far from guaranteed. *The Neverending*

Introduction

Story and *The Last Battle*, in particular, include depictions of apocalypses, images which were likely very present in the consciousness of the books' first readers during the Cold War.

The Last Battle offers perhaps the clearest departure from the early wonderland period; while the whole Narnia series is in many ways characteristic of the middle wonderland period, its final book provides a clear departure from the utopic. While the novel arguably offers a happy ending, in that nearly all major protagonists from the previous books in the series end up in the "true Narnia," also known as "Aslan's Country," this heaven-equivalent location is only reached by the death of said protagonists in a train crash. Death and destruction are key factors in this book, which mirrors the Book of Revelation in the Christian bible, and the Narnia of all the previous books is destroyed. While the majority of the protagonists, as well as the Pevensies' parents, both die and are brought to Aslan's Country, Susan Pevensie likely survives and cannot return to Narnia, a fact which strangely seems not to bother her siblings. Though the manner of their deaths also sounds horrific, the children, in the afterlife, note that they suffered no pain or fear. Edmund explains, "I felt not so much scared as—well, excited. Oh—and this is one queer thing. I'd had a rather sore knee, from a hack at rugger. I noticed it had suddenly gone. And I felt very light. And then—here we were." Similarly, Digory and Polly, who are described as being elderly, note that they were "unstiffened" in coming to Aslan's Country, as well as suddenly no longer feeling old. In the utopic vision of heaven to which the Narnian protagonists are admitted, there thus is emphasized a lack of disability and old age as key components of perfection.

A similar horror element within the context of a happy ending occurs in the 1971 film adaptation of *Charlie and the Chocolate Factory*, titled *Willy Wonka & the Chocolate Factory*. While both versions end with Charlie becoming the heir to Wonka's factory as the chocolatier approaches retirement, the film version offers very little in terms of what has befallen the other golden ticket holders. In the original novel, the children are physically altered by their experiences but are clearly seen from the glass elevator to be otherwise unharmed. Yet, when Charlie asks Wonka what has befallen his fellow children in the film, he is simply told, "I promise you they'll be quite all right. When they leave here, they'll be completely restored to their normal, terrible old selves.

Introduction

But maybe they'll be a little bit wiser for the wear." Wonka's use of the future tense suggests that the other children, even as Charlie sees all of his dreams come true, may still be suffering; Violet may still be getting the blueberry juiced squeezed out of her, Veruca and her parents may be burning in an incinerator, Mike may still be getting pulled "like chewing gum" in the stretching machine, while Augustus may still be getting mixed in a giant chocolate-mixing barrel (Dahl 136).

Additionally, Charlie appears to face actual danger in the filmic version of the factory rather than the book. While both contain a scene in which the Great Glass Elevator bursts through the ceiling of the chocolate factory, only Grandpa Joe seems afraid that he, Charlie, and Wonka will die from the crash in the book. In the film, we are also given a close up shot of Charlie with a clear expression of dread as the elevator continues upward. Similarly, both media include Fizzy Lifting Drinks, sodas which cause the consumer to float upward, but they are never drunk by Grandpa Joe or Charlie in the book. Instead, Wonka speaks of an Oompa-Loompa having drunk one and floated away into the sky, forgetting that he might burp to come back down. In the film version, both Grandpa Joe and Charlie drink the soda and enjoy its effects until they are nearly torn to shreds by a ceiling fan. It is only after screaming for help and finding nothing to hold onto that Grandpa Joe accidentally burps and the two float back down to safety.

Thus, while both versions of the story offer dark elements and actual fear of death, at least for some minor characters, the film adaptation demonstrates the further progression of the wonderland toward the underland. Willy Wonka's factory remains a place of magic but one in which may and likely will get one killed. The children deemed bad are potentially left in their altered states, suggesting disability as a punishment for bad behavior. And all the while Charlie, the good child, faces very little danger at all.

The Neverending Story is similarly transformed into a narrative more befitting the underland than wonderland in its filmic adaptation, *The NeverEnding Story*, which covers the first half of the novel. In both media, a once-wonderland world, Fantastica in the book and Fantasia in the films, has become consumed by a strange entity known as the Nothing as a result of the world's leader, the Childlike Empress, becoming ill. Two heroes offer the only chance of saving the land: Atreyu, a

Introduction

young boy from inside the book, and Bastian, a young boy reading the book. Notably, Bastian steals *The Neverending Story* in hopes of escaping figuratively into the fantasy world rather than process the emotions of having recently lost his mother and his father's subsequent difficulty adjusting to being a single parent. Yet, the film offers even more trouble for young Bastian in the forms of difficulties at school, a deep fear of horses despite his desire to learn riding, constant bullying, refusal to participate in school activities, and repeated dreams about his mother. While Bastian in the book also complains of bullying and difficulty with schoolwork, in addition to admitting to being a bit of a scaredy cat, the plot quite quickly moves into the novel within a novel of *The Neverending Story*. Furthermore, most of this information is provided quickly through a matter-of-fact discussion with the bookseller Carl Coreander in the book, while it is more emotionally told through a discussion between Bastian and his father in the film.

This difference merely sets the tone for the additional themes of loss, trauma, despair, and illness that pervade the film, even more strongly than in the book. While the Childlike Empress is said to be ailing from a mysterious illness, allowing the Nothing to take hold in Fantastica, few details are offered in the novel; she simply needs a new name in order to regain her powers and thus continue living on along with Fantastica. While readers of the book eventually learn that not only is the Childlike Empress sick, but dying, nearly 100 pages pass before such information is shared with the reader. Instead, the film offers the nearly hopeless reality that the Childlike Empress is dying and that her death will mean the end of Fantasia early in the film's narrative. Almost immediately, Bastian is given a world that parallels his own; his and his father's world has been seemingly destroyed by his mother's death, while the world of Fantasia similarly faces extinction should its matriarch perish. This trauma is mirrored again when Bastian bestows upon the Childlike Empress his mother's name, Moonchild, allowing her to survive and for Fantasia to be reformed.

Yet death remains a constant occurrence throughout the film despite the Childlike Empress' survival. A defining moment in the film sees Artax, Atreyu's horse, drowning in the Swamp of Sadness. While this event also occurs in the book and could have been heightened by Artax's ability to talk, Artax is arguably rendered less likeable in the

Introduction

book due to his arrogance and petulance. Additionally, Artax is rendered so depressed by the Swamp of Sadness that he actually begs Atreyu to leave him so that he might die. It is also clear that Atreyu might easily save Artax in the book by putting the protective amulet, AURYN, over both himself and the horse; Artax, however, refuses to allow this action on the grounds that the Childlike Empress may find it disrespectful. While Artax and Atreyu's final conversation in the book is rather logical, the film version is extremely emotional. As Artax sinks beneath the mud, Atreyu begins sobbing and begs Artax to keep fighting the sadness, wailing that he loves the horse and holding Artax until he sinks completely to his death. There is no hope for Atreyu to save Artax and the scene has become well-known for its negative impact on young viewers. In a 2019 interview with the cast and director, Atreyu's actor, Noah Hathaway, notes that "I feel like I sent people to therapy over that scene with Artax" (Cordero). Director Wolfgang Petersen talks about an urban legend surrounding the scene, which says that the horse playing Artax died during filming. While Artax was actually played by two different horses who both survived, the rumor adds an extra edge of terror to the scene of Artax's death. That the scene is followed by Atreyu nearly dying of thirst, hunger, and exhaustion, as well as the seeming suicide of the Rockbiter upon losing his friends, makes the film work even more toward becoming an underland narrative.

Furthermore, while the book offers resolution between Bastian and his father, no such healing occurs between the two characters in the film. While the book ends with Bastian's father coming to find him at the bookstore at which Bastian receives *The Neverending Story*, and the two embracing, no such reconciliation occurs in the first of *The Never-Ending Story* films. While Bastian has likely overcome his fear of riding horses after riding the luckdragon, Falkor, and has successfully scared off his bullies by chasing them with Falkor, it seems unlikely that little else will be resolved in Bastian's life. His escapism through fantasy, rather than being curtailed into acceptance of the "real" world, has instead been further indulged by Fantasia. As his father wants him to "keep [his] feet on the ground," it seems likely that Bastian and he will remain alienated from one another, which bears out in the second film. *The NeverEnding Story: The Next Chapter* begins with Bastian again fearful, this time displaying acrophobia which keeps him from being

Introduction

able to join the swim team. Rather than receiving support from his father, Bastian is left alone at night while his father goes out with "Ms. Station Wagon," allegedly to work late but likely actually for a romantic evening. The two remain at odds with one another until the very end of the second film.

Without the resurrection of Fantasia and its inhabitants at the end of the film, *The NeverEnding Story* would clearly act as an underland narrative. Yet the recovery of this wonderland, along with the clear rebirth of deceased characters such as Artax, shows the continued predilection for a more or less happy ending that marks middle wonderland narrative. Furthermore, the fact that the Childlike Empress must recover from her illness in order for Fantasia to be recreated continues to mark disability as something that must be removed from the wonderland by the end of a narrative. The Empress cannot have a chronic illness but, rather, a recurring but wholly curable difference that never manifests on a quotidian level.

Contemporary Wonderlands and the Underland

Finally, the contemporary wonderland period offers a more complex understanding of the disabled/nondisabled binary that more overtly questions normativity in and of itself. While these texts at times offer some of the same tropes and ableist conceptions of cure found in earlier wonderlands, they generally present underland narratives that instead present difference as something perhaps essential to the heroine's experience travelling through such spaces. Yet simultaneously these tales focus on the horrific rather than wonderful characteristics of their fantasy worlds.

In this study, I will look more in depth at the middle wonderland period in order to demonstrate how the shift between the early and middle period led to the dystopic focus of the contemporary underland period. While these stories grow darker in tone as they bring in themes of death, trauma, and loss that may become permanent, in doing so they also regularize human responses to tragedy, particularly in terms of mental disabilities. Thus, while still associated with negative experiences and suffering, the underland moves away from the model of cure and medicalization.

CHAPTER 1

Crip Futurity and Literary Utopias

The unlimited possibilities inherent in the futuristic, fictional worlds of speculative fiction make the genre ripe for the study of societal norms, the social identity of persons with disabilities, and the future of disability studies. Tales of utopias, specifically, offer a unique opportunity to see how authors envision idealized futures and the place of persons with disabilities in supposedly perfect worlds. However, such an understanding of disability, particularly crip futurities, cannot be deconstructed without first looking at the context of disability as a status within U.S. and U.K. cultures and across time. Thus, I begin this chapter with an overview of disability studies with particular emphasis on readings of disability history with its theoretical lens.

Following this overview, and in consideration of the future of the disabled body, I turn to visions of the utopic and the manner that persons with disabilities are included or entirely removed from such stories; such a narrative model in utopias outside of the realm of the wonderland, I argue, demonstrates broader Anglophone attitudes toward the lack of futurity for crip communities. By then turning to the subcategory of the utopic wonderland, I demonstrate how this idealized location is framed and the way it creates a space ripe for a celebration of difference, particularly in terms of the body and mind.

Understanding Disability in Context

Disability can be understood in multiple contexts, both social and medical. Under the social definition, disability exists primarily in a relational and political manner (Kafer 9). Essentially, it is not so much physical or mental conditions that render one disabled as it is society's inability to support or otherwise normalize disabled bodies in public spaces. The classic example, per disability studies theorist Tom Shakespeare, is that a wheelchair user is only rendered disabled by a lack of ramps, curb cuts, accessible routes, or other accommodations in certain places ("Social Model" 212). When spaces and ideas are made accessible to persons who may otherwise receive limited entry, they are no longer disabled in the social sense. Recognizing that disability in many cases also exists in a physical sense, disability studies scholar and medievalist Joshua R. Eyler notes: "When we speak of disability using the social model, we do so with an acknowledgment that impairment precedes disability, but it is the disability that is actually the debilitating force" (320). This understanding of disability as biologically, or at least physically, designated by physicians is known as the medical model of disability. Both social and medical definitions tend to exist simultaneously, complementing one another in our greater understanding of disability as a complex and intersectional issue.

In her discussion of disability and futurity, activist and theorist Alison Kafer refers to the disabled body as a "potential site for collective reimagining" (9). Given the possibilities of imagined worlds based in the future or an alternative present, it seems that speculative fiction is an area ripe for the negation of the factors contributing to disability in the social sense. However, these futurist visions instead tend to focus on the aspects constituting the medical model of disability, striving to negate the existence of disabilities entirely by imagining worlds replete with what bioethicist Glenn McGee terms "perfect babies." As McGee explains, "when an obstetrician refers to the 'healthy baby,' she is making a kind of 'reverse diagnosis'—if the infant presents no symptoms of illness, it is healthy" (116); thus, the citizens of utopic literary spaces are generally depicted as absent of any conditions differing them from the normate. Recently, disability rights advocates, particularly parents with disabilities or those with children with disabilities, have noted the troubling flip side of the phrase "as long as it's healthy." Often used as an alternative to offering a gender preference, the suggestion still provides a clear preference for a child of a certain type. In actuality, the philosophy that accompanies this notion is that one should celebrate the birth of a *healthy* child, but that the birth of an *unhealthy* child or an infant

1. Crip Futurity and Literary Utopias

with disabilities is not worth celebrating but, rather, mourning (Free; Roberts; Taylor).

Adding to such a critique, feminist theorist Sara Ahmed considers a second characteristic often used as a gauge for the worthiness of a child, and thus, a successful parent: happiness. Ahmed argues that in Anglophone cultures, "the obligation of the child to be happy is a repaying of what the child owes, of what is due to the parents given what they have given up. The duty of the child is to make the parents happy and to perform this duty happily by being happy or by showing signs of being happy in the right way" (*The Promise of Happiness*, 59). This norm, which Ahmed refers to as "the happiness turn," focuses on the way that happiness has been both normalized and marketed. She notes the high number of books available from 2005 onward that attempt to sell the concept of happiness as something achievable by all (*The Promise of Happiness*, 2). In combining these two concepts regarding the essentialness of happiness and healthiness, one also sees the rise of an industry for books directly related to raising an idealized baby who is both happy and healthy. Some of these texts include the following bestselling titles: *The Happiest Baby on the Block*; *Healthy Sleep Habits, Happy Child*; and *Peaceful Parent, Happy Kids*.[1] While there is nothing inherently wrong with being happy or wishing general health for one's child, Ahmed states that the trouble arises with societal conceptions of what happiness should look like. Largely, she argues, happiness is used to reify normative lifestyle choices, categories, and ways of being, such that parents hope that their children will not be queer or disabled in order to guarantee them "happier" lives (*The Promise of Happiness* 19). The ultimate outcome of such a desire for one's child, however well intentioned, does not work to combat prejudice against marginalized groups but instead eliminates the marginalized group rather than the prejudice itself. For example, while there are clear societal advantages to being born as one who is at least medically defined as male, most countries ban sex-based abortion and limit scientific techniques for gender selection. While being sexed as female means that one will face sex-based discrimination, whether or not one identifies with one's assigned sex, larger society has not sought to end the birth of girls. Instead, efforts such as the various feminist movements have focused on combatting sex-based discrimination and the patriarchy as a whole.

Disability in Wonderland

Yet, such a futuristic conception of unity through extreme, and often forced, homogeneity, as would be created through the elimination of disability, has long been considered in speculative fiction. In a particularly useful example, the protagonist of Ursula K. Le Guin's 1971 novel *The Lathe of Heaven*, George Orr, seeks to subvert racism by reimagining all humans with a gray complexion; in this novel, George is able to change the current state of the world through his dreams, which he learns to control. However, instead of ending prejudice on Earth, George's alteration simply moves the prejudice to focus on alternative characteristics to race. Simultaneously, his attempt to create a utopic future becomes notably *dystopic* through the alterations that occur to persons on a deeper level than skin color. George realizes that his attorney friend, a mixed-race woman named Heather, simply cannot exist sans her racialized identity, internally noting that "she could not have been born gray. Her color, her color of brown, was an essential part of her, not an accident. Her anger, timidity, brashness, gentleness, all were elements of her mixed being" (130). Similarly, individuals whose senses of self are inexorably linked to identities such as queer, crip, female, Latino/x, and other positionalities, may be rendered entirely other to themselves when removed from such markers.

In short, to be in a position of marginalization and to recognize oneself as rendered inferior is a joyless experience. Most social movements, Ahmed explains, have thus "struggled against rather than for happiness" (*The Promise of Happiness*, 2). As a result, the "killjoy" comes to represent the feminist figure because, in coming to understand the existence of the patriarchy, one simply cannot accept it and be happy with one's subordination. By desiring happiness for our children, we must therefore question what that this happiness should look like and whether it would not be better to wish for a cause-driven or self-validated child. Happiness, according to Ahmed, is often utilized as a mechanism for silencing persons who have legitimate reasons for being unhappy through the recognition of the cisheteropatriarchy, sustained racial injustice, neuronormativity and other forms of ableism, as well as other instances of regularized and system discrimination. In relation to the figure of the feminist killjoy, Ahmed discusses the counter concept of the feminist snap, which results from persons trying not to be the "killjoy" that addresses and gives voice to such injustices; the feminist

1. Crip Futurity and Literary Utopias

snap occurs as a result of maintaining the pressure of silence. This tension continues to accumulate until, against the imperative to be happy or at least maximize the potential for the happiness of others, this rage snaps free:

> When you are estranged from happiness—and happiness can be what you shatter just by turning up or speaking up—so much else is revealed. And so we might be there, listening to the happy hum of family life; you might be having conversations where only certain things are brought up. Someone says something problematic. If you find something problematic, you have a problem. If you find something problematic, you become a problem. So, you respond quietly, perhaps. You might be speaking quietly, or you might be getting wound up, recognizing with frustration that you are being wound up by someone who is winding you up. Being wound up: you become tighter, and tighter, the more you are provoked. Tighter, tighter, tighter still, gasp, there is no air left: until, snap [Ahmed, "Snap!"].

The desire that one's child be happy is not problematic in itself. Rather, it is the manner in which this desire manifests and becomes a tool for normalizing and controlling others that becomes the problem. Certain characteristics are universally assumed to make all persons happy, such as marriage, caring for children, and other regularized social institutions and relationship types. However, Ahmed notes that "different people are made happy by different things; we have a diversity of likes and dislikes" (*The Promise of Happiness* 118–119). There is no standard model for what happiness looks like; instead, there is simply a normalized model for behavior that one is pressured to follow under the justification that it will "make one happy."

Furthermore, the promise of happiness is simply not accessible to all persons at all times, while some persons will be chronically *unhappy*. In his essential 1917 essay "Mourning and Melancholia," Freud notes that people can rarely control their responses to loss. Mourning deals explicitly with sorrow that results from the loss of a love object, an experience over which the mourner usually has little or no control. Melancholia is also experienced as a result of loss, but without the actual absence of a love object. This latter experience, now characterized as melancholic depression and a subset of major depressive disorder ("MDD," APA, *DSM IV*), is even less navigable by an individual than mourning. When the moment of loss that causes mourning passes, over time the separation between the mourner and the love object becomes normalized. To put it simply, one generally copes with the loss and "moves on." But, in melancholic depression, the individual continually experiences the moment of loss, even when an actual loss has not actually occurred outside of the person's mind. Furthermore, beyond depressive conditions, additional health factors can continuously limit the ability of certain people to be happy, such as structures of ableism, racism, and the cisheteropatriarchy. Additionally, as noted by psychologist Todd B. Kashdan, conditions such as loneliness and insomnia can severely limit one's ability to be happy while even "the pressure to be happy makes people less happy." Addressing issues similar to those discussed by Sara Ahmed but from the perspective of psychology, Kashdan comes to a similar conclusion:

> Think about what you want written on your tombstone.
> Here lies Todd Kashdan, a man who put every ounce of effort into being a happy person.
> Here lies Todd Kashdan, a man who strived to be a good friend, a good husband, a good father, while trying to make the world a slightly better place.

While the concept of "goodness" is as fraught and multifaceted as that of happiness, the second epitaph demonstrates how focusing on an outward approach to life may be preferable to a general goal of being happy. Essentially, Kashdan asks, when we think of revolutionary figures known as leaders of movements for positive social change, we rarely focus on their personal fulfillment; few people think of someone such as Martin Luther King, Jr.'s, legacy and say, "Yes, his movement did a lot for civil rights in the U.S. *But was he happy?*" Kashdan's understanding mirrors Ahmed's argument that a cause-driven life may be a better desire for one's child than happiness or happiness alone.

Similarly, the conception of health varies widely from person to person. Although the desire for a healthy child may build upon common fears and anxieties surrounding perinatal death (Brockington, Macdonald, and Wainscott), popular online parenting resources also demonstrate a fixation on fears surrounding birth defects (Dreisbach). And such a fear regarding defect largely focuses on potential mental illnesses, such as autism spectrum disorder (ASD) and Down syndrome. Such a finding agrees with the arguments of historian and science

1. Crip Futurity and Literary Utopias

philosopher Fernando Vidal. Vidal purports that one's personhood in Anglophone cultures has largely shifted from being based in the soul to the mind, with the brain as the model for selfhood in the contemporary era. Yet Vidal's studies into the nature of personhood and identity go even further, suggesting that we are currently undergoing a shift beginning in the 21st century whereby "genetics have been linked to fundamental selfhood issues" (6). An identity determined by one's unique DNA now poses the greatest challenge to personhood as defined by one's brain. An example of this shift may be seen in the rising popularity of genetic testing companies, such as 23andMe and Ancestry.com's AncestryDNA. Thus, it has become essential to understand the question of health in terms of recent technologies that categorize congenital disabilities, which largely render a child "unhealthy" at birth, as conditions to be corrected. After all, the logic goes, one may be comfortable having a child with a disability, but one may question the morality of bearing a child who will continue a line of disabled persons indefinitely. For example, the popular *What to Expect When You're Expecting* web complement to the bestselling pregnancy guide by Heidi Murkoff includes the article "The Benefits of Prenatal Testing."[2] While the article itself neither prescribes nor proscribes prenatal testing, the title misleadingly suggests that prenatal testing is a wholly positive or "beneficial" decision.

This and other articles that seek to appeal to persons across various belief systems often fail to address the real-life implications of such potentialities, namely disability-based abortions and prenatal gene editing. As of 2017, CRISPR-Cas9 has become an effective tool for prenatal gene editing. Gene editing is now able to prevent the conditions that lead to congenital heart disease prior to birth, leading to the need to analyze bioethical concepts surrounding prenatal testing, abortions based upon diagnoses, and possibilities for contemporary eugenic practices. Responding to the proliferation of access to and support for disability-based abortions, lawmaker Kevin Shinkwin of the United Kingdom (U.K.) described such practices as a form of eugenics, the practice of attempting to "improve" the genetic quality of humanity by promoting reproduction between individuals that possess perceived positive traits while discouraging it from those who possess perceived negative traits. Such a practice has largely been used to threaten the continued

Disability in Wonderland

existence of certain racial groups, persons who identify as queer or genderqueer, the poor, and those with hereditary disabilities (Hansen and King; Snyder and Mitchell, "Compulsory Feralization"). Citing statistics from the U.K. Department of Health, Shinkwin notes that the "overall number of abortions on the grounds of disability, regardless of the point of gestation at which they occurred, has grown by 68 percent over the last 10 years" (qtd. in Tennant). While the exact numbers for disability-based abortions are difficult to find in the United States, largely due to the impact of Roe v. Wade prior to the decision being overturned in 2022, and the privacy surrounding abortion offered to parents in the U.S. per the Fourteenth Amendment, an estimated 85–90 percent of positive prenatal tests for Down syndrome result in abortions (Ouellette 212). Shinkwin states that some of the conditions that resulted in abortions following prenatal testing in the U.K. in 2015 were largely curable, non-life-threatening conditions or constituted conditions that were disabling solely in the social sense. Consider, for instance, the staggering statistic that these tests resulted in the abortion of 11 embryos with cleft lips and/or palettes, conditions that are almost always curable, non-life threatening, and largely aesthetic. As explained by the U.S. Centers for Disease Control: "With treatment, most children with orofacial clefts [cleft lips or cleft palates] do well and lead a healthy life. Some children with orofacial clefts may have issues with self-esteem if they are concerned with visible differences between themselves and other children" ("Facts about Cleft Lip and Cleft Palate"). As the biotechnology surrounding prenatal screening has advanced, a wider array of conditions and identities have been identified in embryos, including traits such as "sex, neural tube defects, deafness, trisomy 13, anencephaly, adult-onset genetic disorders (e.g., Huntington's), Down syndrome, and an increased likelihood to develop certain cancers" (Ouellette 212). Bioethics instructor and legal scholar Alicia Ouellette explains that the number of traits detectable prior to birth will only increase with future technical innovation:

> Advances in genetic and other prenatal testing appear likely to reveal even more information about developing fetuses, such as hair and eye color, skin pigmentation, and autism spectrum disorder...
>
> As genetic testing becomes more available, less invasive, and more robust, questions arise about "which conditions can and should be tested for [before implantation and] prenatally... And as science evolves, we need to

1. Crip Futurity and Literary Utopias

ask: should prenatal testing include autism, breast cancer risk genes, or even one's sexual orientation?"

The question for many stakeholders, particularly those who identify as members of disability communities, is whether eliminating the existence of certain or all congenital disabilities constitutes a eugenic practice that threatens current persons with disabilities and their communities. From this perspective, I question if such efforts strive to eliminate a disability-based or crip identity. With the increase of active genetics and prenatal testing, the practical implications of the drive to have a happy and healthy baby may at least strive to remove disability as a category of being.

As science fiction develops into scientific fact through genetic modification and other biomedical innovations, persons with disabilities and their advocates have come to question whether such technologies constitute eugenic policies or at least progress towards eugenics ideals. As professor of special education Solveig Magnus Reindal writes, such perspectives are problematic from a disability studies perspective for two primary reasons: (1) they "rest [...] on an individual model of disability, where disability is regarded as a product of biological determinism or 'personal tragedy' in the individual" (91), and (2) such understandings of disability largely consider the medicalized causes as constituting dysfunctions which one simply prefers not to have (89). As explained through Reindal's critique of such arguments, even though practices such as gene therapy generally do not seek to prevent persons with disabilities from reproducing, they *do* seek to prevent the reproduction of the disability in and of itself (89). In short, Reindal argues that such procedures remain irrevocably linked to the practice of eugenics by essentially "mask[ing] eugenics as science" (Miceli and Steele 85). Such distinctions merely subdivide and convolute the concept of eugenics, differentiating between that which sociologist and disability activist Tom Shakespeare designates "weak eugenics," practices that are non-coercive, and "strong eugenics," which eliminate the possibility of choice for persons with disabilities ("Choices," 669).

Disability studies scholars Michael George Miceli and Jason Kenneth Steele, however, deconstruct and problematize this distinction, noting that "the crude racial and class prejudices espoused by early eugenicists are now being replaced by so-called scientific evidence of genetic inequality" (86). As evidence for this claim, Miceli and Steele observe that physicians offering gene manipulation therapies rarely, if ever, discuss the positive effects of disabilities with their patients. This pattern is discussed in further detail by psychologist Katja Boersma, who notes that physicians and other healthcare workers tend to focus on the negative aspects of patients' personalities as related to conditions such as chronic pain; concurrently, they ignore aspects with "potential added value" (226) of accompanying characteristics. In her research into the personalities of persons with chronic pain, Boersma notes that positive traits remain underdiscussed in both research communities and with patients; for example, persons with chronic pain are more likely to avoid self-harming activities while being more self-directed than their largely pain-free peers (226). As a result of this tendency toward erasing positive personality traits and other qualities, disability is understood almost wholly in negative terms, as a condition of being to be avoided if possible. In one particularly notable case that considers the anti-disability rhetoric inherent in such thoughts, popular autism advocate Sarah Kurchak refers to the 2015 measles outbreak in Southern California as stemming from persons against the measles, mumps, and rubella (MMR) vaccine. These persons, also known as "anti-vaxxers," choose not to inoculate their children against the now largely preventable MMR diseases.[3] Because the anti-vaxxer movement believes ASD to be caused by the MMR vaccine, Kurchak argues that anti-vaxxers are essentially demonstrating a preference for children with measles to those with autism. "We're facing a massive public health crisis because a disturbing number of people believe that autism is worse than illness or death." While not overtly or, perhaps, intentionally eugenic, such rhetoric continues to have a hugely negative effect upon the futurity of crip communities. Patterson and Satz particularly highlight why distinguishing between weak and strong eugenics can be deceptive, explaining that

> At the core of the field of genetic counseling lies a paradox epitomized in the injunction that the counselor be nondirective. Ann Platt Walker perhaps unwittingly suggests part of the conflict by her choice of language in *A Guide to Genetic Counseling* (1998): "Adherence to a nonprescriptive (often referred to as 'nondirective') approach is perhaps the most defining feature of genetic counseling. The philosophy stems from a firm belief that genetic

1. Crip Futurity and Literary Utopias

counseling should—insofar as is possible—be devoid of any eugenic motivation" (8). The phrase "insofar as is possible" within the dashes reveals a problem, suggesting its author's concern that the enterprise of genetic counseling may by its nature be unable to free itself totally from a eugenic cast [122].

The tendency to see technology that eliminates disabilities as wholly positive and non-problematic has also been proliferated by speculative fiction through visions of idealized futures. A multitude of authors have implicitly and explicitly considered such issues, with the resulting materials obstructing rather than promoting an agenda that supports persons with disabilities per Kafer's socially conscious eye. Particularly noteworthy among such narratives are considerations of the utopic, the idealized "no place" characterized "as having a perfect social, legal, and political system" (OED, "utopia, n."). Because the utopic seeks to depict the very qualities toward which humanity strives, what is understood to be the best of our species' potential, these narratives are particularly meaningful for analyzing the interrelatedness of disability and societies. Only by understanding the characteristics that our societies deem ideal can we recognize which persons inherently fail to meet that ideal and are thus rendered considered of even striving toward perfection.

The Utopia as a Model for Futurity

Speculative fiction, particularly futuristic science fiction, has long acted as both a mirror of society's values and a place from which ideas for future innovations are incubated. For example, the original *Star Trek* series is often credited with introducing the conceptions from which the actualization of technologies such as automatic doors, cellular phones, tablets, and many other innovations were born. I argue that utopic speculative fiction spaces have a similar effect upon the construction of our societies; the positively depicted aspects and characters included in these narratives also often further the value of those features and persons in our current societies.

However, to investigate utopian tales in the context of disability studies, one must first recognize the diverse definitions of what constitutes a good or perfect life, as such a concept lies at the heart of utopian narratives. In her text critiquing happiness as an idealized model for futurity, intersectional feminist scholar Sara Ahmed further questions when it began to be taken for granted that eudaimonia, the good life or a life worth living, equated to a desire for happiness (*The Promise of Happiness*). Ahmed points out that rarely does a life worth living intersect with one's personal happiness per most traditional philosophical origins, whether Eastern or Western. In fact, a life lived in the pursuit of pleasure or happiness is historically understood as hedonistic and often associated with immorality or a lack of refinement according to such theories. And, although happiness in and of itself is something that is innately immeasurable, many of our most influential figures in terms of philosophy, literature, the arts, and other realms of idea creation have lived remarkably *unhappy* lives. Consider tragic religious figures such as Thích Quảng Đức's self-immolation in protest of prosecution against his religion, Christian martyrs and martyrdom itself as a means of achieving sainthood within Catholicism,[4] or Jewish persons refusing to convert on penalty of death; notably, martyrdom is present among nearly all world religions, including, in addition to Christianity and Buddhism, the Bahá'í Faith, Sikhism, Hinduism, and others. Similarly, major leaders in political thought have often been targeted by assassination efforts while living demonstrably unhappy lives per their own accounts. Revolutionaries such as Malcolm X and Dolores Huerta did not practice contentment in their speeches or personal letters, but rather outrage and restlessness. Even those who considered the foundations of the good life themselves were often persecuted. In fact, such treatment includes the very creator of utopia himself, Saint Thomas More, who was put to death by Henry VIII for his refusal to support the divorce of the king from his then-wife, Catherine of Aragon.

Due to the various and shifting understandings of what a good life or perfect world might look like, some literary representations of utopias are especially conducive to a disability studies reading. While certain texts largely ignore disability, many take a troubling stance on this aspect of humanity. Thomas More's classic work *Utopia* originated an innovative, albeit cruelly worded, idea for treating persons with disabilities that, simply put, does not stand the test of time:

1. Crip Futurity and Literary Utopias

>...there remained nothing but that some public provision might be made for the poor whom sickness or old age had disabled from labour, "Leave that to me," said the Fool, "and I shall take care of them, for there is no sort of people whose sight I abhor more, having been so often vexed with them and with their sad complaints; but as dolefully soever as they have told their tale, they could never prevail so far as to draw one penny from me; for either I had no mind to give them anything, or, when I had a mind to do it, I had nothing to give them; and they now know me so well that they will not lose their labour, but let me pass without giving me any trouble, because they hope for nothing—no more, in faith, than if I were a priest; but I would have a law made for sending all these beggars to monasteries, the men to the Benedictines, to be made lay-brothers, and the women to be nuns."

In one paragraph, More's characters equate persons with illnesses and disabilities to beggars while simultaneously suggesting that they be forced to become nuns, priests, or monks. While not unusual within the context of sixteenth-century England during which he wrote, More's text is noteworthy for considering the disadvantaged place that those who are aged, disabled, or ill inhabit in a perfect world, setting the standard for similar anti-disability practices in subsequent utopic narratives.

Of particular significance for this study are utopic texts developed in overt conversation with the historic contexts in which they were written and what disability historian Kim E. Nielsen terms the "creation" of persons with disabilities as "citizens" within a larger Anglophone, but particularly U.S. American, context (49). As the concept of disability arose through the demarcation of "good" vs. "bad citizens" in the newly independent United States of the late 18th century, solutions for the treatment of those termed "deviant" and "dependent" were sought. As such, literatures with an Anglophone context that strove to address issues of deviance and citizenship during this period to the early 19th century were particularly significant for establishing the manner that persons with disabilities were to be treated in the young country. I argue that such texts formed the basis for and reflect conceptions of disability within the Progressive Era, setting the tone for how disability was historically understood and continues to be viewed by many cultures in the United States and beyond.

Texts such as Edward Bellamy's groundbreaking 1888 novel *Looking Backward*, H.G. Wells's 1895 *The Time Machine*, William Morris's

Disability in Wonderland

1890 *News from Nowhere*, Samuel Butler's 1872 *Erewhon*, Percy Greg's 1880 *Across the Zodiac*, and Charlotte Perkins Gilman's particularly influential *Herland* (1915) offer examples of utopias that are uniquely situated to develop the conception of an U.S.-Americanized or U.S.-influenced idea of perfection. Notably, each example offers a unique glimpse into the manner in which persons with disabilities, illnesses, or the elderly are to be treated within such systems while simultaneously helping create a master narrative that negativizes and stigmatizes disability within the U.S.

Bellamy's especially influential text, *Looking Backwards*, upon which the popular Nationalist Clubs of the late 19th century were based, offers a utopic vision of Boston in the year 2000 in which disability is all but eradicated. One of the novel's primary characters, Dr. Leete, explains the nature of the utopia in which the protagonist, Julian West, finds himself in idyllic but notably anti-disability terms:

> The number of persons, more or less absolutely lost to the working force through physical disability, of the lame, sick, and debilitated, which constituted such a burden on the able-bodied in your day, now that all live under conditions of health and comfort, has shrunk to scarcely perceptible proportions, and with every generation is becoming more completely eliminated.

Julian enters this utopic setting with a kind of disability of his own: he can only sleep when sepulchered within a concrete bunker, suffering from a sleep disorder that would likely now be classified as insomnia (APA, DSM V). Like many cured of disabling conditions in this utopic setting, Julian finds himself able to sleep in the year 2000 without any of his usual aids. Many such conditions are explained by the societal problems of 1887. For instance, a woman's inferiority to man is referred to as a disability that stems from her dependence upon man, while Julian's insomnia is said to result from the stress of capitalism. Those who clearly *do* possess bodies with disabilities are hidden from West's, and thus the larger society's, view and are continuously referred to in terms of their "burden" upon society. While not subject to the same institutionalization of late nineteenth-century Bostonites with intellectual and physical disabilities (Nielsen), persons with disabilities in Bellamy's fictional society are still segregated from the general population. While simultaneously "damning" the increasing reliance upon "insane asylums" in

1. Crip Futurity and Literary Utopias

1887, Julian does little to question where persons with the same disabilities reside in the year 2000 (Bellamy). The decreasing numbers of persons with disabilities in the 21st century also suggests that this utopia practices eugenics, though the exact means by which disability is eradicated in this fictional society is never clarified.

Similarly, Samuel Butler's *Erewhon*, whose title is an adaptation of the word "nowhere" spelled backward in allusion to the etymology of the word "utopia," also stigmatizes persons with disabilities. In the idyllic country of Erewhon, persons with disabilities are delegitimized via their own justice system. In a clear critique of the nineteenth-century British penal system, persons with illnesses and disabling afflictions must go to trial and face sentencing in Erewhon, while those who commit crimes such as theft and murder are instead given bed rest and medicine. As literary critic and scholar Patrick Parrinder explains, this society punishes "physical rather than moral deviations" (19). Parrinder highlights a scene in which an Erewhonian with tuberculosis is sentenced to life imprisonment: "The judge who passes this sentence gives full vent to the eugenic anxieties underlying the Erewhonian persecution of disability, disease and physical weakness. He explains to the unhappy prisoner that, if harsh measures were not taken against disease, 'a time of universal dephysicalisation would ensue'" (19). Butler wrote his novel in 1872, at the beginning of the eugenics movement, a mere decade prior to the coining of the term "eugenics" by Francis Galton (OED, "eugenic, adj. and n."). The troubling suggestion by Butler is that persons who commit crimes are no more to blame for their actions than those who inhabit bodies with disabilities. Butler delineates three separate classes among criminals with illnesses, including "those affecting the head, the trunk, and the lower limb." Higgs, the narrator of this tale, finds such practices inhumane, an idea meant to be transposed upon the treatment of convicted felons within the reader's own late nineteenth-century setting:

> ...the treatment of all convicted invalids had been much more barbarous than now, for no physical remedy was provided, and prisoners were put to the severest labour in all sorts of weather, so that most of them soon succumbed to the extreme hardships which they suffered; this was supposed to be beneficial in some ways, inasmuch as it put the country to less expense for the maintenance of its criminal class ... those who had been imprisoned even for trifling ailments were often permanently disabled by their

imprisonment; and when a man had been once convicted, it was probable that he would seldom afterwards be off the hands of the country.

When Higgs falls ill with a cold, he finds himself stigmatized to the extent that even his fiancée considers telling the authorities of his condition. She believes that his sickness is indicative of a moral defect of some kind and finds even the mention of his illness rude. Fortunately, Higgs recovers quickly, explaining, "I never remember to have lost a cold so rapidly." By putting his mind to it, Higgs is apparently capable of curing himself. This thought depicts both disability and illness as defects not of character, like the Erewhonians surmise, but of will; purely by focusing and trying harder, Higgs is able to become healthy again.

This mindset is particularly troubling in light of contemporary politics of the early 21st century, which often contextualizes disability through such narratives as figure skater and testicular cancer survivor Scott Hamilton's idea that "the only disability in life is a bad attitude" (Ehrenreich). Journalist and breast cancer survivor Barbara Ehrenreich refers to this concept as the "smile or die" rationality, by which persons with cancer are seen to validate and allow their own deaths if they are openly unhappy about being ill. Ehrenreich wrote about this phenomenon in 2010, but this mindset reifies ideas shared by earlier cancer survivors. Scholar and poet Audre Lorde, during her own battle with breast cancer, notes that she "read a letter from a doctor in a medical magazine which said that no truly happy person ever gets cancer." The effect of becoming ill in a culture that perceives illness as the result of negative thinking has a profound effect upon Lorde, who explains:

> Despite my knowing better, and despite my having dealt with this blame-the-victim thinking for years, for a moment this letter hit my guilt button. Had I really been guilty of the crime of not being happy in this best of all possible infernos?
>
> The idea that the cancer patient should be made to feel guilty about having had cancer, as if in some way it were all her fault for not having been in the right psychological frame of mind at all times to prevent cancer, is a monstrous distortion of the idea that we can use our psychic strengths to help heal ourselves.

The idea that disability and illness result from a bad attitude further aligns all disability as mentally derived, curable, and based upon a perceived weakness within the person who has the disability. These narratives

1. Crip Futurity and Literary Utopias

argue that persons with disabilities are in some way inferior as a precursor to becoming disabled, not *because* they have disabilities, in an even further extension of anti-disability rhetoric. Elsewhere, I refer to this understanding as the "downer vibe," whereby persons with disabilities are both perceived as allowing themselves to become disabled and unpleasant to be around as a result of this perceived attitude (Martin Sandino).

Such a narrative is only furthered by texts such as Percy Greg's *Across the Zodiac*. This story follows a young unnamed Englishman who speaks with a military officer, Colonel A, who recounts his voyage to Mars using a mysterious substance called apergy. On Mars, the colonel finds an almost utopic society in which the women are beautiful, nearly all persons are free of disease, and hierarchical structures have been abolished. The persons of Mars are slightly shorter than the humans of Earth, yet the Martians believe that Colonel A is a tall Martian rather than someone from Earth. Despite their relative utopic existence, the Martians are more emotional than their Earthian counterparts, often getting into verbal arguments but rarely engaging in physical confrontations. Near the end of the novel, the colonel's friend becomes ill, an extreme abnormality on Mars:

> ...illness is so rare among a race educated for countless generations on principles scientifically sound and sanitary, inheriting no seeds of disease from their ancestry, and safe from the infection of epidemics long extirpated, that no apprehension of serious physical cause for her changes of temper and complexion entered into my mind...
> "I have never seen illness, but if Eunané is not ill, and very ill, all I have gathered in my father's household from such books as he has allowed me, and from his own conversation, deceives me wholly; and yet no illness of which I have ever heard in the slightest degree resembles this."
> "I take it to be," I said, "what on Earth women call hysteria and men temper."

Eunané's disease proves to be caused by a severe Earth-based virus, likely brought to Mars by the colonel himself, but the association of her illness with hysteria further ties affliction to the concept of mental weakness. Freud describes hysteria, a notably female-associated ailment whose name originates from the Latin and Greek terms for uterus, as an emotionally-driven disease generated from an overabundance of feeling (Webster). Such an illness was believed to result from a female's lack of mental ability, which has led contemporary readers to question the degree to which Greg's Martian society is truly non-hierarchical (McCormack).

These early examples of Anglophone speculative fiction paint a stark picture in terms of disability studies, providing early justification for eugenics, euthanasia, and ostracism based upon a person's perceived mental weakness as the reason for psychological or physical disability. Within these technologically or socially savvy visions of the future, it is reasoned that anyone with good sense and willpower would simply fulfill the role of the normate. Failures to meet these expectations are associated with the choice to fill the role of the madman, the animal, or the overly emotional woman. Similar examples are prevalent in other texts of the time, including William Morris's *News from Nowhere*, a utopic setting in which disability is quite rare but renders one as "less than men and women," Charlotte Perkins Gilman's *Herland* in which disability has been eradicated and purportedly never occurs, and H.G. Wells's *The Time Machine* in which the mentally inferior or "childlike" Eloi are actively preyed upon by the mentally superior Morlocks.

The Wonderland as Utopia for Children

Yet, if utopic Anglophone literature of the late 19th and early 20th century targeting nearly entirely adult readerships offer largely negative understandings of persons with disabilities, so too do those meant for children and those invested in their educations offer an opposite and predominantly positive understanding. In brief, utopias featuring and predominantly for children provide far more diverse artistic representations[5] of disability while often calling into question the nature of normalcy itself. In short, utopic literatures concerned with child readerships eschew Orr's gray utopia for one resplendent with difference. However, despite this marked dissimilarity, seldom do studies of the utopic considerations delve into the realm of children's literature. One reason for this discrepancy in scholarship, according to children's literature professor Catherine Butler, is that people just don't take fiction marketed for juveniles as seriously as they do literature meant to

1. Crip Futurity and Literary Utopias

be consumed by adults. Recent scholarship, however, suggests that literature intended for children can actually be more impactful and thematically meaningful than its adult counterparts (Butler). The reason for this significance draws from the fact that children's literary texts are effectively marketed to and consumed by a dual audience: both children and the adults who care for them act as readers of these literatures. Such texts are just as much for children as they are for the people who surround them, including librarians, teachers, parents, caregivers, and many others. It has further been suggested that such literature may be demeaned because of its intended audience and because the realm of care is "numerically dominated by women"; often the purveyors of juvenile texts include far more female librarians, teachers, and caregivers than male-identifying persons (Butler).

In order to bring children's literature into a more thorough understanding of utopias as depicted during the time period of this study, it is particularly useful to consider the subgenre of children's speculative fiction that is the wonderland.[6] In the introduction to this text, I define this term as referring to a utopic literary place largely created to serve an audience of children; this definition predominantly draws upon such texts as Lewis Carroll's *Alice in Wonderland*, L. Frank Baum's *The Wizard of Oz*, J.M. Barrie's *Peter Pan*, and C.S. Lewis's Narnia series. According to the Oxford English Dictionary (OED), the word "wonderland," from the German "wonderland" actually predates Lewis Carroll's 1865 novel. The term is found to have first appeared in English Satirist John Wolcot's 1790 text, *Complimentary Epistle to James Bruce* under the nom de plume of Peter Pindar. In this poem, the eponymous Scottish traveler is referred to in meritorious terms via his link to the wonderland, "Where other travelers, fraught with terror, roam/ Lo ! Bruce in Wonder-Land is quite at home;/The fame cool eye on Nature's forms looks down/Lions and rats, the courtier and the clown." The definition given by the OED for wonderland based upon this literary text is far from specific, offering merely, "a. An imaginary realm of wonder and faery" and "b. A country, realm, or domain which is full of wonders or marvels."

As a whole, it is difficult, however, to contextualize experiences of wonder as they are applied in texts that create lands built upon the emotion. Sara Ahmed, one of the academics responsible for defining and fleshing out the field of affect studies, argues that "'wonder' is a key affective possibility within the women's studies classroom." On her research blog, Ahmed describes what she refers to as "feminist wonder," expanding on the concept introduced briefly in her pivotal book *The Cultural Politics of Emotion*. In this earlier text, she offers a definition for "wonder" as a key feminist emotion that stems from one of the primary emotions that distinguishes humanity:

> Wonder is an encounter with an object that one does not recognise; or wonder works to transform the ordinary, which is already recognised, into the extraordinary. As such, wonder expands our field of vision and touch. Wonder is the pre-condition of the exposure of the subject to the world: we wonder when we are moved by that which we face [qtd. in "Feminist Wonder"].

Ahmed's understanding of feminist wonder emphasizes the importance of the physical element, explaining that "the surprise of wonder is crucial to how it moves bodies." Thus, her conception of wonder stems from the act of curiosity as explained through the work of psychoanalyst and feminist mythopoesis scholar Clarissa Pinkola Estés. Pinkola Estés, in her reading of classic fairy tales through a feminist lens, notes that such stories tend to punish women who act upon their natural senses of curiosity: "...women's curiosity [i]s given quite a negative connotation [in these fairy tales] ... in reality, the trivialization of women's curiosity so that it seems like nothing more than irksome snooping denies women's insight, hunches, intuition. It denies all her senses." When acted upon, it is curiosity that brings about the sensation of wonder. In fact, it is curiosity that largely spurs the male protagonists of the aforementioned utopic novels to discover places such as Erewhon, Herland, the 21st century, and Mars, forming the basis for their subsequent sense of wonder at such utopias.

It is not surprising that the wonderland genre not only follows a narrative in which children find success by cultivating curiosity, but that such tales tend to feature young female protagonists. These heroines typically adhere to what Pinkola Estés refers to as the "wild woman archetype" by offering deference to female role models, following their intuitions, and taking part in their own journeys as heroines. To understand the deeper connotations of the wonderland and truly unpack the term, it is essential that some models be considered, and a new, more concrete understanding of the wonderland genre be put forward.

1. Crip Futurity and Literary Utopias

Wonderland as a Keyword

To clarify how the term "wonderland" is understood and depicted in feminist and disability studies, I will draw upon key texts essential to the formation of the wonderland concept. In particular, this analysis will consider Carroll's *Alice's Adventures in Wonderland* from 1865, Barrie's *Peter Pan* from 1911, Baum's *The Wonderful Wizard of Oz* from 1900, and Lewis's *The Lion, the Witch, and the Wardrobe* from 1950. These four texts work especially well for this analysis for three reasons: all follow the same essential wonderland narrative, are based in an Anglophone tradition, and were written in the English language. Translation, whether cultural or linguistic, brings in additional considerations, so I have chosen to primarily work with texts written in my primary language for this study. Furthermore, I have chosen to focus on the original stories that are best known and most indicative of the wonderland structure, incorporating details from sequels only when necessary for clarification.

In developing the concept of the wonderland as both a keyword and theme, I argue that such spaces are delineated not only by existing outside of the scientific, moral, and societal rules that govern the outside world and magical creatures, but also by offering a vividly shifting concept of the self, such that Lacan's understanding of the mirror stage is constantly enacted. The mirror stage as a psychological theory refers to that point at which infants look into a mirror and are able to recognize their reflections as images of themselves. By recognizing themselves as depicted in exterior objects, children begin to understand the symbolic order of the world. In the wonderland, the body is constantly in a state of transformation, such that one becomes continuously estranged from oneself and one's physical image, as exemplified in the *Alice in Wonderland* quote: "I knew who I was this morning, but I've changed a few times since then." In addition to this quality, I identify the following primary characteristics that mark a text of the wonderland subgenre:

1. The young heroine's journey: The heroine's path through her novel largely follows mythologist Joseph Campbell's hero's journey, a common narrative framework exemplified drawn from the life stories of Prometheus, Osiris, Jesus, and Buddha Gautama. Such

a progression, Campbell finds, is common across cultures in epic narratives and religious writings alike. More recent examples of the hero's journey, also known as the monomyth, include *Star Wars*, *Harry Potter*, and *The Lord of the Rings*. The journey for the heroines outlined in this study particularly draw upon certain elements of Campbell's monomyth, including the stages:

  i. The ordinary world
  ii. The call to adventure
  iii. Tests, allies, and enemies
  iv. Approach
  v. The ordeal
  vi. The reward
  vii. The road back

Darker characteristics that are more representative of an adult's hero journey, such as the resurrection, are eliminated from this list.[7] Perhaps the authors of the wonderland, largely appealing to children and their caretakers, simply find that such material is too dark for these spaces. However, nonetheless, some wonderlands do maintain these elements; they are eliminated merely because they are not applicable to most wonderland narratives.

    2. Monsters, fairy-folk, and talking animals: Animals may be anthropomorphized or human-like, even if they do not actually talk, such that they are distinct from those encountered in the real world.

    3. A new system of law: The wonderland is governed by rules that largely differ from those of the real world, especially in terms of morality, science, and economics or administration.

    4. Geographic realism: The wonderland physically and literally exists. There may be some initial confusion as to whether or not the space exists merely in dreams, but it is eventually proven to exist as a real place.

    5. The child protagonist: The wonderland is visited by children or child-like figures from our own world, often female, who act as the stories' heroes. These characters largely interrupted everyday life in the wonderland; their arrival decidedly marks the land.

    6. Magic and sorcery: Magic or sorcery truly exists to some extent and is at least partially depicted as non-technological in origin. Notably, the sixth condition will not be given its own section within

1. Crip Futurity and Literary Utopias

this book; simply put, the presence of magic is so inextricably linked to the prior five qualifications as to not require its own section to be demonstrated.

The Young Heroine's Journey

A feminine version of Joseph Campbell's monomyth might be considered appropriate to describe the typical wonderland protagonist, who is often a young female such as Wendy in *Peter Pan*, Alice in *Alice in Wonderland*, Dorothy in *The Wizard of Oz*, and Lucy in *The Lion, the Witch, and the Wardrobe*. However, this model for the heroine's journey is unsuccessful at defining all features of the wonderland protagonist. The predominant reason for such a limitation lay in the fact that the female protagonist in a wonderland setting is largely ageless, while other models of the heroine's journey, such as that of Valerie Estelle Frankel or Maureen Murdock, depend on a female figure aging from childhood to adulthood; thus, another notable feature of the wonderland is agelessness. All citizens of Oz are frozen at whatever age they were when falling under the fairy queen Lurline's spell to counter death:

> From that moment no one in Oz ever died. Those who were old remained old; those who were young and strong did not change as years passed them by; the children remained children always, and played and romped to their hearts' content, while all the babies lived in their cradles and were tenderly cared for and never grew up. So people in Oz stopped counting how old they were in years, for years made no difference in their appearance and could not alter their station [*Tin Woodman of Oz*].

Similarly, Neverland is described as a place where children never grow up. While Alice may not have spent enough time in Wonderland to age significantly, it is noted that age is at least tampered with to the point that one may grow older or younger within a single day. Similarly, while the Pevensies do age within Narnia, they are rendered children again upon returning to the real world. Notably too, in the Narnia series, multiple characters are killed before being resurrected as younger versions of themselves, including Aslan and Caspian X (*The Lion*; *The Silver Chair*). The afterlife too is pictured as a sort of wonderland within a wonderland; Aslan's Country, as it is called, offers an ageless afterlife in which the good may meet again in paradise.

Disability in Wonderland

Frankel and Murdock's models of the heroine's journey also largely exist within a patriarchal framework, while wonderlands often exist in nonpatriarchal or even matriarchal societies. For example, in the land of Oz it is effectively illegal for men to practice magic because only women are given magical permits (Baum, *The Tin Woodman of Oz*). Women can mentor men who want to learn magic, but men are not allowed to practice unsupervised in Oz. Similarly, while co-rulers, the Queen of Hearts demonstrates vastly more power than her husband, the king; she is furthermore feared and seen as a fierce ruler in contrast to her largely impotent husband. Lastly, the narrative across wonderland texts follows the traditional hero's journey more closely than models of the heroine's journey, perhaps because the protagonists themselves are pre-pubescent girls more in line with Campbell's model from infancy to death.

The ordinary world and the call to adventure. Each of these wonderland stories begin in the ordinary world, a place not unlike the one inhabited by us as readers. *The Wizard of Oz* opens with Dorothy going through the motions of a regular day on her aunt and uncle's farm in Kansas. *Peter Pan* begins by giving the exact address at which the Darlings live in average London. *Alice in Wonderland* begins with Alice lazing by her sister's side in a field later identified as located in rural England, and *The Lion, the Witch, and the Wardrobe* opens with the four Pevensie children travelling from London to somewhere "in the heart of the country." The call to adventure occurs when the child protagonists are distracted from the normal world around them, whether by the White Rabbit, a young boy flying around their room, a tornado, or an ancient wardrobe. The children do not usually travel to these wonderlands on purpose, but literally or figuratively fall into them. In this way, the wonderland is similar to the "unknown world" described by Campbell: "...a forest, a kingdom underground, beneath the waves, or above the sky, a secret island, lofty mountaintop, or profound dream state; but it is always a place of strangely fluid and polymorphous beings, unimaginable torments, super human deeds, and impossible delight" (48).

These new worlds have new rules and histories that the child protagonists have to learn in order to be successful on their journeys.

Tests, allies, and enemies. Once transported to the wonderland, the young heroines are made aware of their new situations in a myriad of

1. Crip Futurity and Literary Utopias

ways, but often their first encounters are with friendly, magical figures. In Lucy's first meeting with a Narnian, she encounters the friendly faun, Mr. Tumnus, who invites her home for a dinner during which the pair become friends. Mr. Tumnus is not a mentor figure, but rather a peer who simply makes Lucy aware of the status quo in Narnia.[8] Similarly, when Wendy is struck from the air, her first acquaintances in Neverland are the friendly Lost Boys, who tell her about Neverland before asking for stories. Dorothy first meets the friendly Munchkins in Oz and Alice encounters a speaking Mouse.[9] From that point on, the heroines face minor obstacles and gather allies all while becoming aware of greater enemies whom they know they must eventually fight.

The approach and the ordeal. As the final confrontation approaches, the heroines may prepare by failing or passing minor tests. Perhaps the most concrete example of this phase of the journey is seen in *The Wizard of Oz*, when Dorothy teams up with Toto, the Tin Man, the Cowardly Lion, and the Scarecrow, while clearing obstacles along the Yellow Brick Road and making her way to the Emerald City. There, she learns that she must defeat the Wicked Witch in order to return home, a lie propagated by the eponymous wizard. She approaches the Wicked Witch of the West's castle, where she faces the ordeal of having to kill the Witch. Similarly, Wendy befriends both Pan and the Lost Boys, rises in their esteem through her storytelling abilities, and then goes with them to face the wicked Captain Hook and his crew. Alice befriends the Mad Hatter, the Cheshire Cat, and the March Hare; manages to tie the King and Queen of Hearts in a croquet game; and attempts to defeat the Queen through her testimony at trial. Finally, Lucy and her siblings befriend Aslan and his allies, break the White Witch's spell, and eventually face the Witch's army.

The reward and the road back. Upon successfully defeating their key nemeses, each heroine and her allies are rewarded: Dorothy is told how to return home, Lucy and the other Pevensie children are made Narnian royalty, and Alice and Wendy are finally returned home. Each of the children also expresses a desire to return to the ordinary world throughout the texts. Dorothy famously laments "there's no place like home!"; Lucy tells Mr. Tumnus, "Oh, Mr Tumnus–I'm so sorry to stop you ... but really, I must go home. I only meant to stay for a few minutes" (17); Alice notes that "it was much pleasanter at home"; and the

Disability in Wonderland

Darling children weep, "Let us go home!" In this manner, the reward and the road back are one and the same. By conquering their enemies, the girls are allowed to leave the wonderlands and return to the ordinary world, with the sole exception of Lucy. It is worth noting that Lucy only expresses a desire to return home when she is brought to Narnia alone, but when she is transported back to Narnia with her siblings, she is more than happy to remain in the magical land rather than return to a war-torn World War II England.

This summary does not yet comprise the entirety of the wonderland narrative, but its basis in the Campbell model makes it useful as a primary examination, this visual was removed. In the following sections, this model will be amended to include additional elements common across these wonderland narratives.

Additional similarities exist between the hero's journey and that of the heroine in wonderland. Campbell's monomyth includes the figure of a mentor or protector, generally an elderly person who provides supernatural aid, while the heroines in wonderland tend to encounter similarly innocuous, ageless, and inhuman figures. Glinda the Good Witch in Oz and the talking lion Aslan in Narnia are examples of such characters. As with many classic utopian narratives, these early meetings tend to include in-depth explanations of the status quo (Ferns 38). Because the utopic journey acts as a fictional travel narrative in many ways (Ferns 38), it is essential that readers be made aware of the society into which the protagonists are delivered. Unlike adult-oriented utopic narratives, however, wonderland tales intended for children offer less detail and are less academic in tone. Such exposition is delivered by magical creatures of far more interest to a largely child audience: Lucy is told of Narnia by Mr. Tumnus the fawn, Wendy learns more about Neverland from Peter Pan while they are midflight, Dorothy is made aware of her situation in Oz by Glinda the Good Witch, and Alice receives information throughout the novel from the helpful, friendly, and magical Cheshire Cat.

In addition to providing essential information for the narratives, these creatures make readers aware early on that the story will be filled with monsters, fairy-folk, and talking animals. Strangely, size is also essential to this narrative feature: the fully grown Munchkins whom Dorothy encounters with Glinda are "about as tall as Dorothy," Alice's first adventure in Wonderland has her growing and shrinking in turn,

1. Crip Futurity and Literary Utopias

Wendy notes that Peter Pan is as "tall as herself," and Lucy finds Mr. Tumnus "only a little taller than Lucy herself" (9). The children are particularly normalized in terms of height and, in some cases, age, in their untransformed states. One reason for such a decision may be related to the apparent ease by which these protagonists are elevated to levels of authority unbefitting children in a typical context. For example, Dorothy is crowned a princess of Oz (Baum, *Ozma of Oz*), the Pevensies are made rulers of Narnia (Lewis, *The Lion*), Alice eventually achieves the status of queen (Carroll, *Through the Looking Glass*), and Wendy is made "mother" to all of the lost boys, the highest possible position within the context of Pan's society within Neverland (Barrie).

This elevation may simply be a reestablishment of humans as innate rulers of animals within a typically Judeo-Christian hierarchy of species, but it may also appeal to young readers who typically have little control over their lives (O'Kane 150). Developmental psychologists such as Wray-Lake et al. note that it is generally not until adolescence between the ages of 13–17 that children are offered some agency over their own lives. To bring in some insights from horror studies, the choice of this age group for wonderland authors, particularly with female protagonists, creates a lead female character who is also most likely pre-menstrual. Menstruation within the same Judeo-Christian context is commonly associated with sinfulness; thus, these young women are depicted as the idealized image of the pure, prepubescent child (Briefel; Kissling). As Pinkola Estés notes, the first menstrual blood has significant symbolism within the fairy tale narrative, literally embodying the crossing of the threshold from childhood to adulthood, something that does not occur within the ageless wonderland.

In their roles as young women in positions of power who are nearing adulthood, these female protagonists appear to have no trouble befriending a wide range of magical creatures and anthropomorphized, talking animals. In the Oz books, Dorothy meets the Nome king and his subjects, fairies such as Polychrome and her sisters, numerous species of human-like races across the various countries, and an array of talking animals such as the Cowardly Lion, the Hungry Tiger, Billina the hen, and even the talking Toto.[10] In Wonderland, Alice learns of the monstrous Jabberwocky and speaks with various animals, including the White Rabbit, the March Hare, Absolem the Caterpillar, the Cheshire

Cat, and creatures such as the living playing cards. While having fewer of these characteristics, Neverland also presents Wendy with magical creatures such as fairies, mermaids, and the unseen gnomes. Furthermore, in Narnia, Lucy immediately meets Mr. Tumnus, a talking fawn, upon entering the fantasy world where the land is inhabited by cyclops and other monsters and nearly all of the animals are capable of speech.

A New System of Law

Another marker that differentiates the wonderland from the real world is the overturning of the rules, ethics, and other codes governing the real world. Whether moralistic or scientific, these wonderlands present spaces that are in many ways similar to our own but slightly different. In this manner, wonderlands inhabit the space of the uncanny, which Freud defines as that which "proceeds from something familiar which has been repressed" ("The Uncanny," 16). Many fears associated with the uncanny surround the alteration of one's body, such as the loss of an eye or limb. Often, creatures within these wonderland spaces, fantastic inhabitants and human visitors alike, are liable to undergo extreme physical alteration at a moment's notice in an uncanny manner. In *Alice in Wonderland*, Alice grows both exceptionally large and small, in turn, through the ingestion of various substances (Carroll).

> The Caterpillar and Alice looked at each other for some time in silence: at last the Caterpillar took the hookah out of its mouth, and addressed her in a languid, sleepy voice.
> "Who are *you*?" said the Caterpillar.
> This was not an encouraging opening for a conversation. Alice replied, rather shyly, "I—I hardly know, sir, just at present—at least I know who I *was* when I got up this morning, but I think I must have been changed several times since then."
> "What do you mean by that?" said the Caterpillar sternly. "Explain yourself!"
> "I can't explain *myself*, I'm afraid, sir," said Alice, "because I'm not myself, you see."
> "I don't see," said the Caterpillar.
> "I'm afraid I can't put it more clearly," Alice replied very politely, "for I

1. Crip Futurity and Literary Utopias

can't understand it myself to begin with; and being so many different sizes in a day is very confusing" [Carroll, *Alice in Wonderland*].

Alice notes that she is no longer herself, recognizing that the being who is Alice is no longer be stable within the context of a mirror—she is constantly having to recognize her present state anew, as her body comes to have an uncanny presence in the story and she regularly must engage with Lacan's mirror stage. Similarly, Trot and Cap'n Bill consume Lavender Berries and Dark Purple Berries[11] to grow smaller and larger at various times throughout their own adventures (Baum, *The Scarecrow of Oz*). Even more radical transformations, such as that between living creature and inanimate object, also occur, generally by turning a person to or from stone (Lewis, *The Lion*; Lewis, *The Horse*; Lewis, *The Voyage*; Baum, *The Marvelous Land*; Baum, *The Patchwork Girl*). Characters may also change in terms of sex (Baum, *The Marvelous Land*), coloration (Baum, *The Patchwork Girl of Oz*), and between living and dead (Lewis, *The Lion*; Barrie) through various mechanisms. In this manner, there is no steady state of being; this constant change leads to the creation of an uncanny feeling both meant to set the reader slightly ill at ease and appear eventually rectifiable. The changes are largely meant to evoke wonder, rather than fear.

However, both the concept of the uncanny and mirror theory offer an insightful introduction to disability studies and crip identity. In disability studies, it is often argued that the "able-bodied status is always temporary, disability being the one identity category that all people will embody if they live long enough" (Davis, "Introduction," VII). Thus, it is noteworthy that nearly all bodily conditions within these wonderlands are demonstrably changeable and ephemeral; one will eventually go through the mirror stage again as one must eventually experience the uncanny. As Davis notes, "Disability studies demands a shift from the ideology of normalcy" (Davis, *Bending Over Backward*, 39), a messiness that seems reflected in these wonderland settings. Such an ideological shift seems apparent through the constant bodily transformations within these texts, with the exception of the eternal youth that often occurs.

In addition to differences in physicality, the morality and law within wonderlands also differs from those of the real world. While literary theorist Josephine Ross argues that incarceration exists merely as

Disability in Wonderland

a last resort in Oz, where criminalization is rare even for actions such as kidnapping, assault, and murder (109), punishments such as temporary incarceration and enslavement are present in nearly every book of Baum's contributions to the Oz series. Ross makes much of the jailer installed in *Rinkitink in Oz*, noting in her comment that Ojo is the first person to ever be imprisoned in Oz. In fact, there are dozens of persons imprisoned throughout the Oz books, either by the central government of the Emerald City or another empire. A notable example is Princess Ozma's imprisonment of the Flatheads. Ozma traps this race of angry and violent persons in their mountain home by creating an indestructible, impassable wall. Although the Flatheads are not imprisoned in a traditional jail, they are clearly rendered involuntarily immobilized and confined. Furthermore, Ross fails to acknowledge the Official Wardrobe in the Emerald City prison, described as "a white robe, which cover[s Ojo] from head to foot, but ha[s] two holes just in front of his eyes, so he c[an] see where to go." This robe is problematic in many ways, being uncomfortably similar to the garb of KKK members per some theorists (Bell and Bell, 232) and demonstrating how Emerald City prisoners are dehumanized and standardized. Rather than remaining human while imprisoned, Ojo is literally transformed into a ghostlike figure with this mandatory costume. Ojo eventually receives a positive, albeit not innocent verdict, but his time in prison is notable given his minor crime: picking a rare six-leaved clover. Furthermore, Ojo is only released because of the fortunate connection between himself and the monarch Ozma; he is able to escape a lifelong sentence as a result of nepotism. As the princess of Oz, Ozma alone determines Ojo's culpability and, because she likes him, she allows him to go free without further punishment. However, he is notably not compensated in any way for time already served.

Ojo's story is the only demonstrative instance of an official trial and incarceration process within Oz, even though Ozma unofficially passes judgment and punishment on many others throughout Baum's books. For example, it is noted in *The Patchwork Girl of Oz* that magic is outlawed in Oz except when practiced by either the sorceress Glinda the Good or otherwise sanctioned by her specifically:

"I am not allowed to perform magic, except for my own amusement," he [Dr. Pipt] told his visitors, as he lighted a pipe with a crooked stem and began to

1. Crip Futurity and Literary Utopias

smoke. "Too many people were working magic in the Land of Oz, and so our lovely Princess Ozma put a stop to it. I think she was quite right. There were several wicked Witches who caused a lot of trouble; but now they are all out of business and only the great Sorceress, Glinda the Good, is permitted to practice her arts, which never harm anybody. The Wizard of Oz, who used to be a humbug and knew no magic at all, has been taking lessons of Glinda, and I'm told he is getting to be a pretty good Wizard; but he is merely the assistant of the great Sorceress. I've the right to make a servant girl for my wife, you know, or a Glass Cat to catch our mice—which she refuses to do—but I am forbidden to work magic for others, or to use it as a profession" [Baum, *The Patchwork Girl of Oz*].

Dr. Pipt, also known as the Crooked Magician, practices magic illegally in Oz. When he is caught, he is stripped of his magical powers by Glinda and his body altered so that he is made "a simple Munchkin ... a man like other men." His body is literally altered with the hope that he will be unable to break the law again. This radical and state-sanctioned changing of the body bears eerie parallels with the histories of institutionalized marginalized bodies in the United States, including the forced sterilization, lobotomization, and castration of persons with disabilities or perceived to be infirm in some manner.

The law which finds Ojo imprisoned for plucking a rare clover also marks the world of Oz as a wonderland, however: a place with laws that are radically different from those in the real world. While not terribly onerous when endured by heroic and humanlike creatures in the context of Oz's Emerald City, imprisonment in wonderlands generally follows the rules for a "fantasy land" as defined by famed children's fantasy author Diana Wynne Jones, "Prison is really a lot of DUNGEONS in one place, plus a fairly grisly TORTURE Chamber. The prison will be reached by a stone stair, dampish, lit by torches in brackets on the walls, and guarded by sadistic soldiery" (emphasis in original, 150). For example, when Dorothy is imprisoned by the Wicked Witch, she must watch the torture of her colleagues, including the literal tearing apart of the Scarecrow and denting of the Tin Man.

A similar dichotomy between being tried and/or imprisoned by a "good" character appears across multiple wonderlands. When the Lost Boys and Wendy are captured by Captain Hook and his crew, they are placed in a damp, dirty brig before being forced to walk the plank in punishment. Although no judicial punishment befalls the pirates after

Disability in Wonderland

they are defeated by the protagonists, they too seem to be punished by the rules that bad things must befall the wicked in a wonderland:

> Fifteen paid the penalty for their crimes that night; but two reached the shore: Starkey to be captured by the redskins, who made him nurse for all their papooses, a melancholy come-down for a pirate; and Smee, who henceforth wandered about the world in his spectacles, making a precarious living by saying he was the only man that Jas. Hook had feared.

When such ill befalls a heroine, it is often portrayed as unfair, unlucky, or the result of evil, but both law and punishment do occur across these wonderlands. The conclusion of *Alice in Wonderland* even revolves around a trial during which the Queen of Hearts repeatedly yells, "off with her head!", to punish Alice for breaking "rule 42" by being more than a foot tall. Alice is, in fact, only in court in the first place as a witness to a crime perpetrated by the Knave of Hearts. The Knave is facing judgment for having stolen some tarts, a crime which was punishable by death within the context of Wonderland.

While not quite as silly, the rules within Narnia are equally as fierce when enacted by an evil force, generally a wicked queen, upon a heroine or her allies. When the children arrive in the magical land after Lucy's initial visit, they find the following note on the door of her friend Mr. Tumnus:

> The former occupant of these premises, the Faun Tumnus, is under arrest and awaiting his trial on a charge of High Treason against her Imperial Majesty Jadis, Queen of Narnia, Chatelaine of Cair Paravel, Empress of the Lone Islands, etc. [the evil White Witch], also of comforting her said Majesty's enemies, harbouring spies and fraternizing with Humans.
> signed MAUGRIM, Captain of the Secret Police, LONG LIVE THE QUEEN [Lewis, *The Lion*]

For his sentence, Mr. Tumnus is turned to stone. Likewise, when Aslan goes to the White Witch to accept punishment for Edmund's crimes, sacrificing himself for the young boy, he is summarily and brutally executed. In contrast, when the Pevensies come to power, they show mercy to the cruel Rabadash, who both attempts to blackmail Queen Susan into marrying him and overthrow the rulers of Narnia. The kindhearted Lucy suggests that as long as Rabadash promises not to commit any additional acts of evil, he should be allowed to go free. Rabadash refuses even this condition. However, rather than executing him, it is decided that the young man will be transformed into a donkey. Such unusual punishments are particularly in line with the strange logic and rules that govern wonderlands, where law and order largely follows the whims of various rulers.

Geographic Realism

Although wonderlands initially appear to exist within dream worlds, these lands are proven to exist physically and literally within the contexts of their narratives. Except for the first Wonderland novel, which suggests that Alice may have merely dreamed her experience,[12] each of these four wonderlands exist as accessible locations that are reachable from the real world of the story. Readers are taken, through the vehicle of a young protagonist, to these strange worlds from ones that are similar to our own, lending a level of reproducibility to such adventures. Peter Pan famously offers clear directions for reaching Neverland, "Second [star] to the right, and straight on till morning." Similarly, after accidentally venturing through the wardrobe into Narnia by herself, Lucy is later able to bring her siblings along with her to Narnia using the same method, while the children of the Narnia series find multiple other methods to venture to this wonderland throughout the books.

Unfortunately, the path to wonderland is not as reliable for all protagonists. Dorothy always seems to encounter some sort of natural disaster or other great calamity in order to visit Oz, be it a tornado, a shipwreck, or an earthquake. Similarly, Alice has little control over her own adventures to Wonderland, though it is suggested at the end of the second book that she may be able to travel to the world via mirrors if she wishes.

Many of these books also include maps or are able to be mapped, following the convention of fantasy series. In fact, such a cartographic insert has become so popular as to be considered a genre trope, defined by TV Tropes as the "left-justified fantasy map." As a method of world building, these authors not only imagine new worlds, but literally create geographies for their wonderlands. Whether or not they themselves develop the maps, these lands are described in enough detail to be mapped by illustrators or other fans.

Maps are quite popular in fantasy series set in worlds that are not wonderlands or that are intended for adult audiences. Famously, George R.R. Martin's *A Song of Fire and Ice* novels saw the cartography of Westeros adapted for the opening sequence of the television series *Game of Thrones*, demonstrating the importance of physicality in the fantasy genre. Similarly, Tolkien's iconic *Lord of the Rings* series includes maps in each book of the series, placing not only locations but battles and other significant occurrences in the book. Especially fond of this geographic realism, Baum describes himself in the introductions of Oz texts as the mere "royal historian of Oz," stating that he is receiving these stories via letter and telegraph rather than creating them himself. At some points, likely when Baum grew tired of writing such narratives, he remarks that he has "lost contact" with Oz, but the world never ceases to exist and connection is soon after reestablished.

The Child Protagonist

Wonderland stories tend to be aimed at audiences composed mostly of children and intended to be children's literature, with some exceptions to this general rule. I have previously discussed some of the rationale behind the authors' focus on young female characters, but I have yet to explain why certain texts have been left out of this study based on this rule. After all, *The Lord of the Rings* has been included in other studies of wonderland spaces, *Winnie-the-Pooh* meets many of the rules previously outlined, and even Diana Wynne Jones's *Howl's Moving Castle* series fits these guidelines. However, *The Lord of the Rings* trilogy and *The Hobbit*, while marketed toward children and adults, do not follow either a child protagonist or a character from the real world with whom children can relate. Hobbits are of similar stature to children and fairly innocent compared to the other races in Middle-earth, but they are simply too comfortable with the rules and fantastical creatures of their world to be truly relatable to the average child reader. *Winnie-the-Pooh* has the character of Christopher Robin, who some theorists think may actually identify as female (Shea et al.); however, Christopher Robin is *not* the protagonist of the Pooh books. Instead, he is a side character who occasionally steps from his home into the Hundred Acre Wood. He is not enough of a constant presence in the land to have an overall effect

1. Crip Futurity and Literary Utopias

on its landscape and is understood to be a welcome visitor whose presence is merely celebrated from time to time.

Lastly, *Howl's Moving Castle* and the land therein also fails to offer the age-appropriate outsider insight into the enchanted land. Sophie, the protagonist, is an inhabitant of the wonderland of Ingary and has never lived anywhere else; therefore, she is already comfortable with the rules of this society. Howl,[13] in the context of the novel rather than the film adaptation, turns out to be a young man who has entered the series' magical world via a portal from Wales, but he is not the protagonist of the series. Offering a unique perspective in which Wales is the strange world rather than the wonderland, there is no narrative arc that follows the heroine's journey similar to the manner outlined above. Furthermore, the sequel to the initial novel, 1990's *Castle in the Air*, is set entirely in Ingary with no transition between the real world and the wonderland, which is a key concept in this study. Lastly, 2008's *House of Many Ways* may offer a more wonderland-esque narrative in that a young girl from the real world does venture to the Ingary, but its placement as the third in the series suggests that her story is secondary to that of Sophie and Howl. Furthermore, by this point in the series, most readers are well-acquainted with the rules that govern Ingary, removing the aspect of the uncanny.

These child visitors to wonderlands are largely disruptive to the overall schema of the universe, often filling important positions in their societies, such as royalty, usurpers of evil rulers, and other positions of power and respect. In short, the children's adventures to and from these wonderlands are noticed and have a significant effect on the landscapes and politics surrounding them. For whatever reason, these children become well known within these magical worlds, sometimes even before they come to positions of power. Prior to becoming Narnian royalty, Lucy builds a largely positive reputation across Narnia. She gains the trust of a multitude of different animals through word of mouth, instigated by Mr. Tumnus's appreciation of her kindness. Wendy becomes well known in Neverland after just one evening, so much so that even the pirates know of the Lost Boys' "mother." Similarly, Alice is invited to play croquet with the Queen of Hearts while Dorothy meets the all-powerful Good Witch Glinda after accidentally killing the Wicked Witch of the East.

Disability in Wonderland

As explained in detail via the outline of the heroine's journey through wonderland earlier in this chapter, the protagonist must overcome a great ordeal to fulfill the narrative. Wendy and her brothers must help Peter defeat the pirates, Lucy and her siblings must defeat the White Witch, Alice must call out the Queen and King of Hearts' tyranny, and Dorothy must defeat the Wicked Witch of the West. They are not only noticed within the contexts of these wonderlands, but are also actively shaping their atmospheres such that no history of these various wonderlands would be complete without an overview of these characters' roles in them.

Conclusions

The following chapter will demonstrate, in depth, how one particular wonderland series integrates the conception of crip futurity. The wonderland of Oz, I argue, offers a ripe image of difference as something to be celebrated; no characters are depicted as *dis*abled but rather differently abled in a nonhierarchical manner. As Dorothy wanders through each stage of the heroine's journey, she finds that being a normate in Kansas does not render her in a position of power or privilege within Oz. On the contrary, her companions who would be marked as clearly disabled within the context of Kansas are shown to be superior in many ways, including the Scarecrow's ability to go without food and water, the Tin Man's ability to live without breathing, and the Lion's ability to govern compassionately through his empathy.

In the utopic vision of the wonderland, disabilities are not seen as conditions to be cured. Rather, they are portrayed as contributing to the celebrated uncanniness and continuous metamorphoses taking place within these spaces. While the laws of the lands may provide radical physical alterations as punishments for crimes, even these changes are marked as temporary. Furthermore, it is not these conditions in and of themselves that indicate the prisoners' wickedness; merely punishments that seem far from punitive in lands that might otherwise transfigure such persons in any case.

Chapter 2

Finding Criptopia in Baum's Oz Series

New readings of literatures considered to be cultural classics are valuable because they demonstrate that many contemporary philosophies are actually long grounded and historically present. As such, this chapter will provide an in-depth disability studies reading of *The Wizard of Oz* and Baum's other contributions to the Oz series. By analyzing the texts in this manner, I demonstrate both how Oz offers a quintessential example of the heroine's journey through wonderland while providing a space in which difference is largely seen as a virtue rather than a hindrance. Persons who would been deemed disabled in the real world, such as the armless, legless, headless, and even heartless Tin Man who depends entirely upon tin prostheses, are understood as equal to those who fulfill that role of the normate such as Dorothy. In this utopic vision, the binary between those deemed disabled and those deemed normate simply does not exist; nor does the hierarchy that often accompanies this binary.

Such contemporary readings of historically significant texts have proven particularly useful to both critical literary scholars and persons belonging to marginalized communities alike. These analyses often demonstrate how persons rendered largely invisible in earlier contexts may have still engaged with nineteenth- and twentieth-century movements surrounding feminism, queer studies, critical race studies, and other social justice endeavors. For example, some twentieth and twenty-first-century critics offer feminist readings of William Shakespeare's plays, which reestablish the importance of female representation prior to the feminist rights movements within the U.K. With a deeper understanding of the possibilities for a diversity of thoughts on the role of women, contemporaneous demonstrations of extremely anti-feminist positions are no longer acceptable based upon temporal context. In fact, such historical foundations are far less pronounced than many in the popular culture would like to believe. The argument that things were "simply like that" in a certain age is not so simple and the multifaceted nature of human opinion throughout history is revealed through such deep readings. A recent example of this rhetoric occurs in social media-based conversations surrounding education and literature professor Ebony Elizabeth Thomas's 2019 book on media depictions of race[1] (@ebonyteach, "I'll send my Tweets..."). Her original post responds to *Star Trek* star William Shatner's disagreement with the decision of the Association for Library Service to Children (ALSC) to change the name of its Laura Ingalls Wilder Legacy Award to the Children's Literature Legacy Award in early July 2018 (@WilliamShatner, "Did you hear..."). The basis for this potentially temporary renaming lies in the fact that Ingalls Wilder's books include images of persons in blackface, as well as largely negative portrayals of indigenous peoples. In Shatner's Tweet, he argues that it is "disturbing" to apply a contemporary understanding of race to works published in the past such as Ingalls Wilder's. Arguing against this position, Thomas's response notes that Shatner's position may be influenced by himself participating in a television series that, while "groundbreaking for its time ... is problematic from a 2010s POV, especially on gender" ("1. The tea..."). Shatner then begins a series of tweets questioning Thomas's expertise as a newly tenured professor of children's literature and race, while repeatedly arguing that contemporary 2018 "opinions" cannot be rightly applied to *Star Trek's* original 1966–1969 context ("I actually read," "An expert?").

This incident, covered by *Inside Higher Ed* (Flaherty), demonstrates the tendency for certain persons, particularly White men located outside of academia, to question this type of contemporary reading of historic texts. In Flaherty's article, she includes the tweets of U.S. literature professor Brigitte Fielder, who publicly defends Thomas while explaining the importance of reconsidering texts from other time periods with a critical gaze. In particular, Fielder explains that Shatner repeats a "common (and historically false) argument: that past racism ought not to be judged by 'modern' standards of opposing racism because racism was not objectionable at the time ... there have always been people objecting to racism, even when those people were not in the majority"

2. Finding Criptopia in Baum's Oz Series

(qtd. Flaherty). Contemporary readings from the lenses of gender studies, critical race studies, disability studies, queer studies, other fields concerned with forwarding social justice, and intersectionally thus refocus attention on efforts toward progress within these time periods. Furthermore, these efforts destabilize the historicization of a homogenized normate, an idea that has worked to effectively invisibilize marginalized persons' historical presence.

Secondary, tertiary, and further readings of canonical texts are particularly useful in disability studies as they demonstrate that the normate exists ubiquitously as a shifting social fabrication. Disability theorist and activist Rosemarie Garland-Thomson defines the normate as "the veiled subject position of the cultural self ... outlined by the array of deviant others" (qtd. Linton 231–232), essentially referring to those who are marked as *not* disabled or, in some readings, otherwise rendered queer via race, gender identity, sexuality, or other characteristics. In reality, few texts exist that do not offer some example of an individual who possesses qualities of a disabled mind or body. Some recent contemporary readings of Shakespeare point to the figure of Richard III with his purported humpback, limp, and shortened arm (Siebers 229), while other close readings reexamine characters such as Sherlock Holmes in terms of mental illness, particularly reading him as a person on the autism spectrum (Freeman Loftis).

In this chapter, and along with such useful deep readings, I argue that Oz offers a quintessential criptopic space—a utopia oriented toward children that depicts multiple disabilities in a nonhierarchical manner. Persons with what would be termed disabilities in the real world are neither held as morally superior to the normates through what disability activist Stella Young dubs "inspiration porn" nor marked as inferior or wicked as a result of their differences. Instead, all persons within Oz are marked as being socially disabled within certain settings, while the medicalized model of disability is removed altogether.

The Young Heroine's Journey Through Oz

L. Frank Baum wrote a popular, classic story ripe for analysis and entry into the speculative fiction canon with his 1900–1919 Oz series.

Disability in Wonderland

These tales are also useful for unpacking the heroine's journey, providing a clear example of the various narrative devices discussed in the first chapter. Almost concurrent with the release of the first Oz book, *The (Wonderful) Wizard of Oz* (hereafter *The Wizard*, both the 1900 novel and the 1939 film), came many close readings of this story following a young Kansas girl's adventures through the magical world of Oz. One of the most well-known interpretations is the populist reading offered by historian Henry Littlefield in his 1964 article, "*The Wizard of Oz*: Parable on Populism" (Parker). Littlefield argues that a strong degree of symbolism exists among the various characters and featured elements: the yellow brick road representing the gold standard, the Emerald City representing the dollar, and the silver shoes, which were changed to ruby in the film, representing William Jennings Bryan's plan to add silver to the nation's gold standard (49). Other popular theories suggest fundamentalist Christian themes (Leach) and a reading via Joseph Campbell's theory of the monomyth and the hero's journey (Beebe).

These analyses, however, tend to focus on singular events and characters in the first text of the series, *The Wizard*, rather than considering the Oz series as a continuous whole. Furthermore, their authors often disregard points in the remainder of the series that could easily disprove or at least complicate their readings. In particular, Littlefield fails to account for why Baum would be so invested in late eighteenth-century politics when he was writing from an early twentieth-century perspective, or to consider the clear allusions to Teddy Roosevelt (Baum, *Ozma of Oz*), John D. Rockefeller (Baum's 1908 stage adaptation, qtd. Swartz 34), and Thomas Edison (Baum, *Lost Princess of Oz*). Similarly, Leach compares the thematic progress in the first Oz book to Bunyan's *Pilgrim's Progress*, which Baum likely read, but would have had little to do with the personal philosophies of Baum as a theosophist. While a clear parallel exists between the silver slippers that Dorothy wears throughout *The Wizard* and Bunyan's atheistic "By-ends" who "are always most zealous ... when religion goes in silver slippers" (249–250), he completely overlooks Baum's extremely public agreement with the American theosophical movement and preference for science over religion (Roesch Wagner, qtd. Baum, *The Lost Princess of Oz*). In fact, on the subject of God, Baum raged in *The Aberdeen Daily News* asking, "What good are the Christian teachings?" (qtd. Schwartz 200). Furthermore,

2. Finding Criptopia in Baum's Oz Series

Leach fails to account for the reality that the Emerald City, which he equates to Bunyan's "bejeweled Celestial City" (250), turns out to be as gray as Kansas, with state mandated green-tinted glasses required to merely make the city appear bejeweled. Similarly, Beebe's reading of *The Wizard* focuses largely on the cyclical nature of Dorothy leaving from and returning to Kansas, ignoring Dorothy's permanent move back to Oz as soon as she convinces her aunt and uncle to relocate with her (Baum, *Tik-Tok of Oz*). While the heroine may be said to engage in a series of challenges along her journey, she never actually has much to fear because death is quite uncommon and reversible in Oz.

It is only by drawing and expanding upon each of these readings, while recognizing their relative shortcomings, that a fuller picture of the heroine's journey through wonderland becomes clear. I argue that, although *The Wizard* is the most familiar of the Oz stories, it cannot be properly analyzed without accounting for the context of the whole series. As Baum wrote the Oz books, he continuously drew upon new technologies and utopic visions to develop a detailed picture of Oz as a wonderland. The earliest book in the series focuses primarily on characters in Oz, particularly Dorothy, but the later contributions portray Oz and the Emerald City as characters in and of themselves. This change in attention is evident in the titles of later installments in the series, including 1904's *The Marvelous Land of Oz* and 1910's *The Emerald City of Oz*, which are far more focused on world building than *The Wizard*.

For the sake of brevity, and with the understanding that *The Wizard* is the best-known of the Oz books due to the huge success of the 1939 film adaptation of the same name, this analysis will mostly focus on the first Oz story and bring in essential elements from other texts in the series when necessary. I will provide a brief overview of this original tale, which follows Dorothy Gale's initial trip to Oz, without ignoring contrary and supporting points in the books that follow, detailing Dorothy's heroine's journey through wonderland. I recognize that many readers are more familiar with the film than the original text and will note important differences between the two versions that are critical to fully understanding the significance of disability in *The Wizard*. I argue that *The Wizard* is an essential early text dealing with the presence of disability in utopic settings, which I also contend is incredibly scarce in utopic literature from the time period. In particular, Baum's Oz is a

Disability in Wonderland

crip-friendly utopia because nearly all bodies are presented as malleable or potentially changeable, as demonstrated in the first chapter of this study. Simply put, Oz allows for radical contingency and the "barely acknowledged vertiginous fear [...] of loss of control and of dismemberment" (Quayson). Furthermore, Oz interrogates the tenuous relationship between the social and medical models of disability by directly confronting the possibilities of bodily change inherent in amputation and prosthesis. Unlike utopias such as Bellamy's *Looking Backward* (1888), Butler's *Erewhon* (1872), Perkins Gilman's *Herland* (1915), and Morris's *News from Nowhere* (1890), the Oz utopia does not call for the death of persons with physical or mental disabilities, "euthanize" elderly persons, or eliminate illness and infirmity completely. In fact, as noted in the previous chapter, persons with Oz do not age, though those who were previously elderly at the time of Lurline's spell remain elderly; those who required care at the time of this spell, including some of the aged and children, continue to need such care in a manner simply regarded as the order of life in Oz.

In her critique of futurist visions for queer and disabled persons, theorist Alison Kafer considers the nature of utopias extremely disappointing to persons inhabiting disabled bodies, asking "Why is disability in the present constantly deferred, such that disability often enters critical discourse only as the marker of what must be eliminated in our futures or what was unquestioningly eliminated in our pasts?" (10). She further questions whether, by its social definition, the utopic is understood to entirely remove those with disability and illness. Building on Kafer's work, I argue that, based upon the presence of persons with disabilities in the Oz utopic context, Baum's model offers a profoundly positive answer to this question. Oz exists as a utopia that does not eliminate the subjectivity of the disabled body.

As offered in the previous chapter, the characteristics that define a wonderland, per this study, include:

1. The Heroine's Journey, entailing:
   i. The ordinary world
   ii. The call to adventure
   iii. Tests, allies, and enemies
   iv. Approach

2. Finding Criptopia in Baum's Oz Series

    v. The ordeal
    vi. The reward
    vii. The road back

2. Monsters, fairy-folk, and talking animals
3. A new system of law
4. Geographic realism
5. The child protagonist
6. Magic and sorcery

Thus, throughout this overview of *The Wizard of Oz*, I will denote the appearance of certain characteristics throughout the narrative with an abbreviated "WC" (Wonderland characteristic) with the characteristic's number and title.

A General Overview of *The Wizard of Oz*

In both the original book and film adaptation, *The Wizard of Oz* begins with a young,[2] spirited girl named Dorothy (WC 5: The Child Protagonist). Raised by her Aunt Em (Auntie Em in the film) and Uncle Henry on a farm in Kansas, Dorothy and her faithful dog Toto are carried away from the ordinary world (WC 1: Heroine's Journey [HJ]: The Ordinary World) to Oz by a tornado. In the film version, some parallels are made between the creatures who inhabit Oz and their Kansas-based counterparts, including farmhands and a cruel local woman, but such parallels are notably absent from the books. When Dorothy regains consciousness after the tornado, she finds herself in a strange land that she soon learns is called Oz, finding herself in Munchkin Country in particular. She also learns that she has unintentionally killed the Wicked Witch of the East, sister to the even more sinister Wicked Witch of the West. Glinda, a good witch, tells Dorothy that because she has killed a Wicked Witch, she should take the witch's shoes, which are known to possess magical properties (WC 6: Magic and Sorcery). Upon hearing that Dorothy desires to return home, she tells Dorothy to follow the iconic yellow brick road to the Emerald City to meet the great and terrible wizard who rules over the city (WC 3: A New System of Law); Glinda believes that the Wizard may be able to return Dorothy and Toto to

Disability in Wonderland

Kansas (WC 1, HJ: The Call to Adventure). As they travel toward the Emerald City, Dorothy and Toto meet the Scarecrow who desires a brain, the Tin Woodman (hereafter Tin Man) who desires a heart, and the Cowardly Lion who desires courage (WC 2: Monsters, Fairy-Folk, and Talking Animals). Along the way, they must overcome obstacles such as a field of poppies, which makes all the "meat," or flesh-based life forms in Oz, fall asleep (WC 1, HJ: Tests, Allies, Enemies). When the group finally reaches the Wizard, they are told that they must defeat the Wicked Witch of the West (hereafter the Witch) before he will grant their respective wishes.

The quintet[3] thus depart to find and defeat the Witch. However, having been spying on the group, the Witch instead finds them first and kidnaps them with the help of her winged monkeys (WC 1, HJ: The Approach). The book specifically states that the winged monkeys only work for the Witch because she possesses a magical Golden Cap that enslaves them. While the Tin Man is rendered motionless and trapped due to his need for oil and the Scarecrow's innards are removed and thrown about, Dorothy, Toto, and the Cowardly Lion are captured and forced into slavery (WC 1, HJ : The Ordeal). When she speaks with the Witch, Dorothy is so furious about the fates of her friends that she throws a bucket of water on her, unintentionally causing the villain to melt and die. Once the Tin Man and Scarecrow are restored through oiling and re-stuffing, respectively, the group returns to the Wizard to claim their prizes. However, upon meeting the Wizard face to face, they learn that he is actually a confidence man with tricks that merely make him appear powerful, masking a complete lack of actual magic.[4] Despite the Wizard's assurances that they already possess the traits that they desire, the Tin Man, Scarecrow, and Cowardly Lion continue to demand the promised attributes and are given gifts that are symbolic of these traits instead (WC 1, HJ: The Reward). The Wizard apologizes to Dorothy, however, because he is unable to return her home to Kansas. Dejected, the group returns to Glinda who tells Dorothy that she has had the ability to return home all along through the use of her magic shoes. The shoes will grant Dorothy's wish if she wears them and taps her heels together. Dorothy and Toto bid farewell to their friends and return home to Kansas (WC 1, HJ: The Road Back; and Geographic Realism) via the magic shoes.

2. Finding Criptopia in Baum's Oz Series

Differences Between the Text and the Screen

Perhaps the most notable difference between the film and book versions of *The Wizard* is that the film portrays Dorothy's trip to Oz as a dream or hallucination that occurs as a result of hitting her head, while Oz exists as a real place on earth in the novels. Upon waking and explaining her dream to Aunt Em in the film, Dorothy is depicted as a frivolous young girl overcome by youthful fantasies. This characterization is reinforced throughout the film, which portrays Dorothy as helpless and weepy. In the movie, Dorothy frequently weeps and laments her inability to return home; in contrast, in the book she is determined to go back to Kansas so that her aunt and uncle do not worry about her (Baum, *Annotated Wizard* 47). While the film Dorothy is portrayed as a damsel in distress who needs help from her companions and often screams in fear, the book Dorothy offers a heroine who usually saves both herself and her companions. For example, after melting the Wicked Witch, Dorothy frees Toto and the Cowardly Lion from slavery, refills the Scarecrow with his hay, and hammers the Tin Man back into form before oiling him. Dorothy, however, remains human in the book; she does occasionally cry, but it is often for reasons that are emotionally accessible to adult audiences and in line with the humanist hero. For example, Dorothy cries after killing both of the wicked witches by accident and at the prospect of having to kill the Wicked Witch in order to return home.

Furthermore, neither her youth nor shortness of stature prevent Dorothy from being the principal heroine of the Oz books, despite the fact that shortness is often equated with silliness in the film. The movie offers a troubling depiction of the Munchkins—children and adults with dwarfism who speak almost exclusively through means of song and laughter. In this manner, the Munchkins fulfill the quality referred to as narrative prosthesis by Mitchell and Snyder, wherein "disability pervades literary narrative, first, as a stock feature of characterization and, second, as an opportunistic metaphorical device" (*Narrative* 47). The Munchkins are mere stereotypes in the film, meant to be humorous and silly. In the books, however, the Munchkins are clever farmers and one of the most prosperous races of Oz in terms of innovation and wealth. Furthermore, in the books, Munchkins are nearly average in height because most people in Oz are roughly the same height as Dorothy, who towers above these figures in the film. This difference is explained in the book when Dorothy first encounters the inhabitants of Munchkin Country: "They were not as big as the grown folk she had always been used to; but neither were they very small. In fact, they seemed about as tall as Dorothy, who was a well-grown child for her age, although they were, so far as looks go, many years older" (Baum, *Annotated Wizard* 34). Furthermore, many of the peoples in Oz are of the same or similar stature to the Munchkins, including the first person Dorothy meets in Emerald City: "a little man about the same size as the Munchkins" (Baum, *Annotated Wizard* 170), and the Hammer Heads, who are "quite short and stout" (338). Moreover, as specified in later Oz books, people in Oz do not generally age:

> From that moment [when Queen Lurline enchanted the land] no one in Oz ever died. Those who were old remained old; those who were young and strong did not change as years passed them by; the children remained children always, and played and romped to their hearts' content, while all the babies lived in their cradles and were tenderly cared for and never grew up. So people in Oz stopped counting how old they were in years, for years made no difference in their appearance and could not alter their station [Baum, *The Tin Woodman of Oz* 541].

For this reason, height and size have a different significance in the Oz books. Individuals who are short and small, whatever their age, are not infantilized. Similarly, as evidenced by the child ruler Princess Ozma, a childish appearance and youth are not associated with a lack of wisdom or intelligence. Little People of America, an activist group devoted to the rights of persons with dwarfism as well as education about this condition, notes that negative portrayals of dwarfs have led to an abundance of social stigma against this group. Notably, the filmic version of *The Wizard* largely helped to contribute to such a stereotype, depicting persons with dwarfism as childlike and mentally inferior (Snyder and Mitchell, "Re-engaging the Body").

Bodies in Transition

Despite the relative agelessness of Ozite bodies, their sizes are often in flux. People of Oz can, and often do, pass between animacy and

2. Finding Criptopia in Baum's Oz Series

inanimacy, thinking and lifelessness. In her essential text on the subject, Mel Chen explains animacy as:

> ...described variously as a quality of agency, awareness, mobility, sentience, or liveness. In the last few decades [the 1990s and early 2000s], *animacy* has become a widely debated term within linguistics, and it is in fact within linguistics that animacy has been most extensively developed and applied. A pathbreaking work written in 1976 by the linguistic anthropologist Michael Silverstein suggested that "animacy hierarchies" were an important area of the intersection between meaning and grammar, on the basis of evidence that spanned many languages. Within linguistics today, animacy most generally refers to the grammatical effects of the sentience of liveness of nouns, but this ostensible meaning opens into much wider conversations.

By considering the manner in which all bodies transition between animacy and inanimacy, while questioning the inherent hierarchy that distinguishes between such transformations, Chen effectively introduces the concept of object-oriented ontology (OOO). This philosophical movement specifically rejects placing privilege on living bodies, especially those belonging to humans, over those of non-living objects (Atanasoski and Vora). However, I would argue that such a hierarchical model is nonexistent in Oz due to the consistent transition of bodies between these positions within a non–Ozite hierarchy of animacy. In particular, Tip/Ozma, Jack Pumpkinhead, and the Gump experience significant bodily transformations over the course of the second Oz book, *The Marvelous Land of Oz*.

Tip spends most of this book identified as a young boy, but it is later revealed that he began life as a female, Princess Ozma. As a baby, Tip/Ozma was transformed to prevent them[5] from coming to power in the matriarchal monarchy of Oz. Their transformation back into a girl at the end of the story "demonstrates the ease with which sex and gender roles are swapped in Oz [...] additional examples of gender switching abound" (Pugh 221). Notably, too, this change in biological sex seems to be accompanied by a change in gender; Tip/Ozma both inhabits a body medically defined as one sex and identifies with that sex. The hierarchy of animacy is not the only such social structure undermined in Oz's utopic vision, which reverses the patriarchy against which Baum fought for the entirety of his life. Additionally, the thin line between the living and dead is demonstrated through the characters of Jack Pumpkinhead and the Gump, both of whom are brought to life with the Crooked Magician's Power of Life. After life is bestowed upon him, Jack Pumpkinhead agonizes over the eventual rotting of his pumpkin head and loss of his life, while the Gump, whose body is created of a variety of random items so that the heroes may escape Jinjur's Army of Revolt, begs to be disassembled. The Gump explains, "I did not wish to be brought to life, and I am greatly ashamed of my conglomerate personality" (Baum, *Marvelous Land of Oz*, 386). And, later, when The Gump is disassembled:

> The antlered head [i]s again hung over the mantle-piece in the hall, and the sofas [a]re untied and placed in the reception parlors. The broom tail resume[s] its accustomed duties in the kitchen, and finally, the Scarecrow replace[s] all the clotheslines and ropes on the pegs from which he had taken them on the eventful day when the Thing [the Gump] was constructed [Baum, *Marvelous Land of Oz*, 387].

Death occupies a strange place in Oz because individuals rarely die. Even when villains are accidentally killed, their deaths are greatly lamented; it is thus his call for the murder of the Wicked Witch that marks the Wizard as a non–Ozite most of all. The Gump's body, per his continued requests, is put to death at the end of *The Marvelous Road to Oz*. However, his head remains alive and well, even offering advice and amusing chit chat. Jack Pumpkinhead buries and creates tombstones for each pumpkin as it rots and receives a new pumpkin head inundated with life as soon as it is set upon his shoulders. As noted in Chapter 1, the wonderland is a place in which one's physical form may be in a constant state of flux in a variety of ways. Other characters' bodily transformations include shrinking and growing via the consumption of magical lavender and dark purple berries (Pessim, Trot, and Cap'n Bill in *The Scarecrow of Oz*), transformation into animals (Bibil/Prince Bobo of Boboland in *Rinkitink in Oz* and Coo-ee-oh in *Glinda of Oz*), conversion into inanimate objects (Uncle Nunkie, *The Patchwork Girl of Oz*), changing color (Polychrome, *The Road to Oz*), and metamorphizing between animacy and inanimacy (Tik-Tok and the Tin Man).

Models of Disability in Oz

The radical bodily alterations, the manner in which bodies are constantly transforming, and the marked refusal to accept universal

2. Finding Criptopia in Baum's Oz Series

privileging of one bodily state over another in Oz all work to undermine the medical model of disability. The medical model of disability recognizes the body as a structure that is constantly judged and its perceived defects cured, invisibilized, or, as in many utopic worlds, negated through euthanasia. In this manner, the disabled body is distinguished as the damaged form of a normate body. In contrast, the social model of disability,

> ...interprets disabilities as being an interaction between physical impairment and the social and cultural environment. In other words, the problem for the person with an impairment is not just the struggle with the physical body that this often entails, but the larger and more inchoate struggle with negative and intransigent attitudes toward people with impairments [Quayson].

The Oz books demonstrate a strong preference for the social model of disability by questioning what normal is in terms of height, weakness, and motion, with each character and each condition showing strength. In this manner, the Oz series as a whole presents the possibility of radical contingency, a counter position to the normate described by Donald Davidson that undermines the assumed reality that all persons have "a largely correct, shared, view of how things are" (qtd. Eldridge 488). In disability studies, this concept refers to the presumption that it is better to be a person without disabilities than to be a person with disabilities. Although Dorothy is one of the more normative figures in the novels, she is imperfect in many scenarios, suggesting that normalcy itself can be debilitating in certain circumstances.

Three of Dorothy's four companions, the Scarecrow, the Tin Man, and the Cowardly Lion, are each initially missing an important piece of themselves: a brain, a heart, and courage, respectively. Each character feels that by missing this characteristic or item, he is kept from being a full person—a normate. The trio believe that the Wizard of Oz will not only return Dorothy and Toto to Kansas but will also help the three of them become complete beings by providing them with their missing parts and ameliorating their perceived deficiencies.

Dorothy's weakness is not revealed until later in the book when the group encounters one of the primary obstacles on their journey: the magical poppy field. When the quintet reaches the poppies, only Dorothy, Toto, and the Cowardly Lion fall into endless sleep. This scene is altered in the film version and quite short, as Glinda sends snow to

Disability in Wonderland

counteract the poppies' effects at the behest of the Tin Man and Scarecrow. In the book, however, the Scarecrow and Tin Man's lack of flesh, initially perceived as disabilities, makes them impervious to the flowers' effect on the "meat" or flesh-and-blood creatures (Baum, *Annotated Wizard* 109–10). Thus, the Scarecrow and Tin Man are able to pull Dorothy and Toto out of the flowers, while getting help to save the Cowardly Lion from the queen of the field mice and her subjects. In fact, because Tin Man has previously shown her kindness, the very quality he believes he lacks, the queen agrees to help him save the others.

The group continues on towards the Witch, the primary villain of the story. The Witch, although weathered and ugly in the book, is not green as portrayed in the film. Instead, she has a single eye and is incapable of bleeding, marking her as a character with physical disabilities similar to those of her heroic counterparts (Eyler 330–1). Both she and the non-meat members of the quintet are incapable of bleeding, while another heroic character, Bristle, also has only one eye (Baum, *The Emerald City of Oz*). However, the Witch's most interesting disability, and most significant in terms of disability narratives in Oz, is her vulnerability to water. In W.W. Denslow's illustrations from the original publication of the book, the Witch is consistently pictured holding an umbrella which she is said to always carry (Baum, *Annotated Wizard* 220). Presumably, this umbrella is used to protect her from water, although she also utilizes the item as a weapon to strike heroes like Toto. Rather than being represented with the classic stereotype of a witch on a broomstick with a tall black hat, Denslow, chose to portray the Witch with this umbrella in hand, a flamboyant hat upon her head, and childlike braided pigtails. Furthermore, the stigma attached to the word "witch" is reevaluated in the Land of Oz. Feminist critics have noted that the figure of the witch or crone as a trope in fiction devalues the role of women, but the witches in Oz defy the stereotype of the wicked, elderly, and spinster-esque figure. In addition to the Wicked Witches of the West and East, there are the Good Witch of the North, Locasta, and the Good Witch of the South, Glinda; both of these good witches are described as being young and beautiful.

Readers of *The Wizard* text already know of the Witch's aversion to water, so it is far less surprising when the Witch is melted at the end of the filmic version of the story. The Witch's sensitivity to water, however,

2. Finding Criptopia in Baum's Oz Series

is particularly notable because it is a quality she shares with the Tin Man. This is an essential detail for understanding the text beyond the portrayal of this disabling quality as inherently good or evil. Furthermore, in the film adaptation, the Wicked Witch of the West is the only fully human character presented with non–White skin, presenting a racialized image of wickedness. Alissa Burger argues in her reading of racial representation in the film that the filmmakers' choice for skin tone was designed to position the Wicked Witch with another power deemed "wicked" by U.S. American film audiences at the time: the Japanese government and its people (109).

The Witch's actions to prevent the heroes' success further demonstrate how the Tin Man and Scarecrow's differences can be both disabling and empowering. The Scarecrow has been marked as a disabled character physically, based upon his ability to be set on fire, and socially, due to the value judgment that he is foolish because he does not have a brain (Eyler 324). However, these bodily differences often prove advantageous. Certainly, the Scarecrow may be more easily lit on fire due to his straw innards, but the straw man's fluid physicality allows him to be re-stuffed with new straw as needed, have his straw removed for various purposes, and avoid pain and other negative effects that befall the meat characters. On their journey to the Witch, the group is attacked by a group of black bees, which have been commanded to "go to the strangers and sting them to death" (Baum, *Annotated Wizard* 209). The brainless Scarecrow begs the Tin Man to help him remove his straw innards and use them to cover the meat characters so that they cannot be stung. According to the brainless Scarecrow's clever plan, the Tin Man stands still and allows the bees to sting him so that their stingers break (Baum, *Annotated Wizard* 209). When the Witch sends her flying monkeys to attack the group, the Scarecrow and Tin Man are rendered only temporarily incapacitated when they are unpacked and strewn about, dropped upon sharp rocks, and severely dented (Baum, *Annotated Wizard* 215). These attacks would have killed their meat counterparts, but merely delay the Scarecrow and Tin Man. As soon as Dorothy accidentally melts the Witch, she, Toto, and the Cowardly Lion head off to rescue their companions. With the help of the Winkies, Dorothy recovers the Tin Man and has him repaired "as good as ever" (233). He is so pleased "that he we[eps] tears of joy, and Dorothy ha[s] to wipe

Disability in Wonderland

every tear carefully from his face with her apron, so his joints w[ill] not be rusted" (233), demonstrating a sweet scene that is representative of the caring relationships that exist between the characters and pervade the entire series. The Winkies, Dorothy, and her companions then set to finding the Scarecrow's clothing which they fill with new "nice, clean straw" (234) and the Scarecrow is brought back to life. After each of its members has reestablished his or her autonomy, the group then returns to the Wizard for their rewards.

At this point in the story, the Wizard's role in the disability narrative of Oz becomes complicated. First, the Wizard is proven to be a humbug, a great pretender from the real world utilizing his superior technology to simulate the magical powers inherent to Oz. The Wizard has benefited greatly from the Ozites' fear of him, first commanding that they build him the Emerald City and then ruling over it (Baum, *The Wizard*, 266). Despite knowing he is a fraud, the Cowardly Lion, Tin Man, and Scarecrow still consider the Wizard to be an authority over their bodies and deficiencies, even when he tells them that they have no disabilities. While they are, in fact, already imbued with the qualities they seek, they still feel bound to ask for their missing parts; thus, Ozites, like their contemporary Anglophone counterparts, are driven by some mechanism to normalize. Due to the largely accepting nature of Ozites toward these heroes, the regulating force is clearly not the state, but an internalized power worthy of future research.

The characters' perceived deficiencies are amended in this case; however, this sort of curative behavior is extremely rare in Oz. The Cowardly Lion, Tin Man, and Scarecrow come to the Wizard asking that their respective perceived disabilities be remedied, but the Wizard clearly tells our heroes that they are disabled in name only. To the Scarecrow, he explains, "You don't need them [brains]. You are learning something every day. A baby has brains, but it doesn't know much. Experience is the only thing that brings knowledge, and the longer you are on earth the more experience you are sure to get" (Baum, *Annotated Wizard* 270). To the Cowardly Lion, he explains, "You have plenty of courage, I am sure... All you need is confidence in yourself. There is no living thing that is not afraid when it faces danger. True courage is facing danger when you are afraid, and that kind of courage you have in plenty" (*Annotated Wizard* 271–2). The Wizard does not deny that the

2. Finding Criptopia in Baum's Oz Series

Tin Man embodies a real difference via his missing heart. He merely tells the Tin Man that he is fortunate to be missing the organ, which "makes most people unhappy" (*Annotated Wizard* 272). The Tin Man's role is clearly as a figure disabled through his prostheses as well as his physicality rendering him, in turn, human, cyborg, inanimate object, and robot. This fluidity marks the Tin Man's role as a central figure ripe for the study of disabled bodies in the land of Oz. Some minor narratives surrounding the fragile citizens of China Country and the armless Hammer Heads of Quadling Country, who have large heads but no arms, also speak to the narrative of bodily presence in Oz. However, they are but briefly mentioned as they appear in the remainder of the book as the quintet speeds along toward Dorothy's eventual return to Kansas.

The Tin Man as Crip

Baum's Tin Man began his life as a Munchkin, the race most commonly represented in Oz, working as a woodcutter with the ominous and foreshadowing name of Nick Chopper. He fell in love with a Munchkin girl named Nimmie Amee (*Tin Woodman of Oz* 446), but the jealous Wicked Witch of the East enchanted his axe so that it severed Nick's legs, arms, and head, before splitting his torso in half. Each time a limb was removed, the Tin Man went to the local tinsmith and had the part replaced with one made of tin. Contrary to being displeased by these bodily changes, the Tin Man becomes extremely vain about his new body, polishing its various parts quite often and eventually having them coated in nickel (Baum, *Marvelous Land*, 269).

However, there are a few notable downsides to being made of tin aside from the Tin Man's perceived loss of love due to his lack of heart (see Eyler). His body easily corrodes, which renders him incapable of moving until he is oiled by a companion. This relationship of care ties the narrative to disability activist Christine Miserandino's concept of "Spoon Theory," described on her popular blog as follows:

> Most people start the day with unlimited amount of possibilities, and energy to do whatever they desire, especially young people. For the most part, they do not need to worry about the effects of their actions. So for my

Disability in Wonderland

explanation, I used spoons to convey this point. I wanted something ... to actually hold, for me to then take away, since most people who get sick feel a "loss" of a life they once knew. If I was in control of taking away the spoons, then she would know what it feels like to have someone or something else, in this case Lupus, being in control.

At the beginning of the day, a person with a chronic illness receives a certain number of spoons, or energy, with which they can do a specific number of tasks. Certain tasks may take more spoons, such as cleaning one's house or completing work. Once those spoons are gone, however, a person with a chronic illness, such as Miserandino's Lupus or my own fibromyalgia, simply has no choice but to return to bed. Once there are no spoons, the energy that is necessary to complete one's daily tasks has been completely used. Furthermore, unlike persons without such disabilities, this energy takes much longer to return, sometimes days or even weeks. For the Tin Man, "oil is a source of life" that replaces water as a life-giving source—the energy, or spoons, with which the Tin Man is able to complete his daily activities (Moore 87–88). Water quickly depletes the Tin Man's energy until he is eventually rendered completely inanimate, the condition in which Dorothy first encounters him. The Tin Man, despite having no physical heart, cries quite often, which rusts his jaws so that he is frequently incapable of speech. Only through the care provided by Dorothy and his other companions is the Tin Man able to speak or move again.

It is essential to highlight that the Tin Man is not considered weak due to his need for care. As someone who runs on oil rather than energy, the Tin Man is often described in terms of a beneficial post-human condition: "I was a much better man than ever," the Tin Man explains of his tin body, "for my body could not ache or pain me, and I was so beautiful and bright that I had no need of clothing ... but my tin body only needs to be oiled and polished" (Baum, *Tin Woodman of Oz* 26). This notion that mechanical and magical creatures are superior to their meat counterparts is a theme repeated throughout the Oz books. Because they have no need for food and rest (Wagenkgnecht 27), the mechanical creatures and cyborgs are often depicted as superior to their meat companions, often saving their fleshed companions from biological factors that render them motionless while protecting them from physical pain.

2. Finding Criptopia in Baum's Oz Series

Tik-Tok and Energy

Another character who depends upon oil is Tik-Tok, the clockwork man created by the firm of Smith & Tinker. Tik-Tok is described on his instruction card as a creature who "Thinks, Speaks, Acts, and Does Everything but Live" (Baum, *Ozma of Oz*) and must be both oiled and wound in order to remain animate. "Tik-Tok is produced technologically, even though he exists in a fictional world where most things come about by magic" (Abrahm and Kenter). Notably, Tik-Tok is not nor has ever been alive, distinguishing him from the transhuman Tin Man. In appearance, Tik-Tok is similar to Theodore Roosevelt, one of Baum's heroes. Roosevelt "cut a dashing figure ... posing in a wide-brimmed hat, a fringed buckskin shirt, alligator boots, and all the accouterments of a horseman: the leather belt, the ivory-handled Colt revolver, the Winchester rifle, the bowie knife, the silver spurs, and a belt buckle that shone like justice" (Rogers 116). Many of these features can be found in original illustrator John R. Neill's illustrations of the Tin Man, particularly the hat, Roosevelt-like moustache, and depiction of a shirt strikingly similar to that worn by members of the 1st United States Volunteer Cavalry, also known as the Rough Riders. Tik-Tok has three separate screws, one for thought, speech, and movement, but is entirely dependent on other people to wind these gears as his arms are quite short. When he is occasionally dismantled by his enemies, he must depend on master tinsmiths, such as Smith & Tinker or the Nome King's steward, Kaliko, to replace his various parts (Baum, "Tiktok and the Nome King").

The care narratives of Tik-Tok and the Tin Man emerge through their respective needs for winding and oil. Without support, the mechanical men are rendered incapable of animacy, becoming objects instead of persons in the novels. This ability to be rendered inanimate and non-human was likely something to which Baum could easily relate, as he suffered many health issues related to being born with a weak heart. Baum suffered his first heart attack at age fourteen (Schwartz 174), likely the result of rheumatic fever (Schwartz 324), which left him immobilized for the first time in his life. His family—including his wife, Maud; his mother-in-law, noted suffragist Matilda Joslyn Gage; and his son, Harry—all contributed to his care at various points in his life. They

Disability in Wonderland

supported his ability to write in bed and, in Harry's case, did ghostwriting for Baum when he was incapable of fulfilling his publishing obligations (Rogers 221). Baum also acted as a caregiver at times, tending to Maud when she became chronically ill for two years following the birth of her son Robert, his Uncle Adam who was immobilized for nearly all of his life, and his father who was chronically ill for the remainder of this life after being thrown from a carriage. Baum had a personal, lifelong relationship with the nature of care, provided by both himself and others, which clearly translated into his books.

Baum links energy, specifically mobility, to both politics and technology. He complicates the physicist's definition of the term by applying his understanding to both material and transcendental energy sources. Baum considers science to be invested in culture and context, offering an early cultural studies construction of the terms "energy," "technology," and "science." He practices what Bruce Burgett and Glenn Hendler refer to as a "keyword" approach to defining "energy," which provides context for the use of certain terms over the course of time and in particular contexts. Thus, as demonstrated by his use and explanation of energies and technologies in the land of Oz, Baum offers a "flexible" (Williams qtd. Burgett and Hendler 2) approach to the concept, looking at "energy," "technology," and "science" as words whose meanings are in a flux both with time and between the hard sciences and humanities. Energy, as understood by Baum, is limited for all persons in different ways. One such as Tik-Tok or the Tin Man may continue indefinitely as long as they are, in turn, cranked and oiled. While Dorothy and the Lion simply cannot go as long as their mechanical counterparts due to their need for food, water, and rest, they have an advantage in being able to provide their own sources of power. Similarly, Toto, notably as intelligent as his four counterparts, requires sustenance and rest; yet he sleeps more often than the other flesh-based life forms. Toto provides one of the most heroic and brave characters in the series, remaining fierce and defending his friends despite his need for extra rest and care. In this manner, *The Wizard* offers multiple visions of energy that well depict those offered in the real world. Rather than praising those with a moderate amount of energy or scorning those with excess or a scarcity of energy, Ozites simply accept them for who they are, offering a positive vision of futurity for crip communities.

2. Finding Criptopia in Baum's Oz Series

Finding Criptopia

Baum's contributions to the Oz series offer one example of criptopia. While there is clearly a lack of perfection within Oz due to the presence of villainous figures, I argue that Oz offers a classic example of a U.S. American utopia, or *the* Utopia Americana, as Edward Charles Wagenknecht refers to Oz in one of the earliest critiques of the series (1929). In his analysis of Oz's inherent "utopian tension," Karp notes that Oz fulfills the definition of a utopia for the following reasons: "a communal sharing of food, the elimination of money and poverty, a dearth of punishment, an absence of greed reminiscent of Sir Thomas More, and the virtual elimination of death or disease" (103). Many of these characteristics overlap with Raymond Williams's argument for the four types of utopia, defined as:

> (a) *the paradise*, in which a happier life is described as simply existing elsewhere; (b) *the externally altered world*, in which a new kind of life has been made possible by an unlooked-for natural event; (c) *the willed transformation*, in which a new kind of life has been achieved by human effort; (d) *the technological transformation*, in which a new kind of life has been made possible by a technical discovery ["Utopia and Science Fiction"].

The first definition applies particularly well to Oz in *The Wizard*, though, notably, the three other characteristics do appear throughout the various texts that constitute Baum's contributions to the series.

Baum's Oz creates a world likely based upon the socialist utopias presented in Edward Bellamy's 1888 *Looking Backward* and William Morris's 1890 *News from Nowhere* (*Annotated Wizard* xcvi), but without their harsh treatment of persons with disabilities. The lack of class struggle and hierarchies further aligns Oz with Fredric Jameson's understanding of the utopic, in which non-egalitarian social structures are abandoned (30). Utopia exists in Jameson's understanding as a "form [of] representational meditation on radical difference, radical otherness, and on the systemic nature of the social totality" (xii). The following description of Oz shows the influence of socialism on the creation of this fantasy world and how, despite the royalist system of government in many Ozite nations, the system is quite collectivistic and egalitarian. Furthermore, it demonstrates how these nations abide by a Westphalian

Disability in Wonderland

understanding of the state while consisting almost exclusively of the proletariat. It should also be noted that individuals may become royalty in Oz as a result of possessing a natural instinct to lead, intelligence, and likeability, as in the case of the Tin Man. Furthermore,

> there were no poor people in the Land of Oz, because there was no such thing as money [...] Some tilled the lands and raised great crops of grain, which was divided equally among the entire population, so that all had enough...
> Every one worked half the time and played half the time, and the people enjoyed the work as much as they did the play, because it is good to be occupied and to have something to do. There were no cruel overseers set to watch them, and no one to rebuke them or to find fault with them. So each one was proud to do all he could for his friends and neighbors, and was glad when they would accept the things he produced [Baum, *The Emerald City of Oz*].

Thus, the farmers and manufacturers of Oz are free from the Marxian concept of alienation, the estrangement that occurs in the distancing of the producer/laborer from the product of their work. In terms of the Oz series as an early work of U.S. American speculative fiction, this lack of alienation applies to human, trans-human, and non-human animal figures. While Marx and Engels were generally critical of utopian idealism as a fantastic rather than scientific concept (Engels), the very nature of the duality that exists between the poverty of Dorothy's family in Kansas and the abundance of all persons in Oz offers an area ripe for further Marxist analysis.

The utopian exclusion of illness is initially troubling in the context of a disability studies perspective, but the inclusion of figures such as the Tin Man, Tik-Tok, the Witch, the China people, and the demonstration of weakness inherent in normative bodies actually marks Oz as a criptopia. Individuals do not become sick by means of germs in Oz, but they are still marked by the traditional features of illness in a non-utopian context: various figures in Oz are immobilized or otherwise incapacitated, require care, and must rest for extended periods of time. Furthermore, the nature of care as reciprocal marks these narratives and portrayals far beyond Mitchell and Snyder's concept of the narrative prosthesis. These characters are not mere placeholders for the concept of purity and goodness (i.e., Dickens's Tiny Tim) or wickedness and perversion (i.e., Shakespeare's Richard III), but rather well-developed

2. Finding Criptopia in Baum's Oz Series

characters who both receive care and provide care for others. Additionally, rather than the caregiver's "recipients [being] seen as suffering a socially constructed dependency" (Fine 24), there are specific contexts in which each character in the quintet is rendered weaker or stronger, more caring or less caring, than others. Both wicked and good characters may have the same attributes, including sex, height, ability, and sensitivity, undermining the medical model of disability that ascribes certain attributes as more beneficial or normal than others. Furthermore, it is worth noting that such a reading of the Oz series is greatly compromised via a reading of *The Wizard of Oz* alone; the context of the entire series is necessary to understand the roles that disability and normativity play. Additionally, this reading would be all but negated when applied to the 1939 film adaptation alone.

For example, Toto, perhaps the most underappreciated and dehumanized member of the quintet, demonstrates a particularly powerful reason as to why the Oz series must be considered as a whole and why the series has so much to offer in terms of disability studies. Toto is an odd dog compared to other animals in Oz because all other animals speak in a verbal/auditory manner. Despite this departure from the average Ozite, however animal in appearance, Toto is given great responsibility and no one views Toto's seeming lack of speech as equivalent to a lack of ability. When Ozma explains to Dorothy that Toto has fallen under the same spell that allows all other animals in Oz to talk, she remarks that Toto is "a wise little dog" who simply prefers not to talk; after all, Toto is able to communicate as effectively via nonverbal methods and barking as his companions do via speech. Upon learning of his ability for speech, however, Dorothy asks Toto why he does not talk while in Oz. The scene that depicts this realization and the Ozites' responses to it is perhaps the best demonstration of how Ozites deal with flux and changeability in Oz, as well as Dorothy's slow adaptability to her new socially constructed world from one based on the medical model of disability:

> "Goodness me!" exclaimed Dorothy. "I never s'pected Toto was fooling me all this time." Then she drew a small silver whistle from her pocket and blew a shrill note upon it. A moment later there was a sound of scurrying footsteps, and a shaggy black dog came running up the path.
> Dorothy knelt down before him and shaking her finger just above his nose she said: "Toto, haven't I always been good to you?"

Disability in Wonderland

Toto looked up at her with his bright black eyes and wagged his tail.

"Bow-wow!" he said, and Betsy knew at once that meant yes, as well as Dorothy and Ozma knew it, for there was no mistaking the tone of Toto's voice.

"That's a dog answer," said Dorothy. "How would you like it, Toto, if I said nothing to you but 'bow-wow'?"

Toto's tail was wagging furiously now, but otherwise he was silent.

"Really, Dorothy," said Betsy, "he can talk with his bark and his tail just as well as we can. Don't you understand such dog language?"

"Of course I do," replied Dorothy. "But Toto's got to be more sociable. See here, sir!" she continued, addressing the dog, "I've just learned, for the first time, that you can say words—if you want to. Don't you want to, Toto?"

"Woof!" said Toto, and that meant "no."

"Not just one word, Toto, to prove you're as any other animal in Oz?"

"Woof!"

"Just one word, Toto—and then you may run away."

He looked at her steadily a moment.

"All right. Here I go!" he said, and darted away as swift as an arrow [Baum, *Tik-Tok of Oz* 489–490].

Toto is able to speak from the beginning of the story, but he *chooses* not to talk until the eighth book in the series. Even without speaking, however, he acts as a wise figure who protects Dorothy and contributes to the group's success. Unfortunately, those who have only watched MGM's film adaptation of *The Wizard* are left with only brief introductions to Toto and many other Oz characters. These representations are, unlike the books, based upon a multitude of hierarchical structures, particularly in terms of disability, species, animacy, and gender.

Conclusions

The Oz series contributes to blurring the binary between human and non-human animal (The Cowardly Lion, Toto, The Hungry Tiger, Billina), object and living creature (Pumpkin Jack, The Scarecrow, Bungle, China people), man and woman (Bill/Billina, Tip/Ozma), human and technology (the Tin Man, Tik-Tok), and race/color (Polychrome and the Blueskins, though *not* the Wicked Witches in the canonical Oz books). Baum's contributions to the Oz series are far from perfect in terms of offering a more inclusive utopian methodology as imagined by

2. Finding Criptopia in Baum's Oz Series

such theorists as José Esteban Muñoz, but they do make some significant advances, particularly within the context of the early 20th century. By offering a multitude of queer characters inhabiting a variety of positions within a predominantly egalitarian society (Pugh), Oz disrupts the traditional hierarchy inherent in places such as Kansas, designating where such bodies may exist, or, in Muñoz's terms, sit (124).

Lyman Frank Baum wrote fourteen books set in the utopian world of Oz between 1899 and 1919, drawing upon and critiquing many of the utopic, but ultimately problematic, themes of the era. Beginning with the immensely popular *Wizard of Oz*, perhaps best known by its 1939 film adaptation, the Oz books represent one of the best-selling series of the 20th century (Baum, *Annotated Wizard* xiv-xv), and remain an extremely popular series among children to this day. In addition to the original Baum texts, their canonical sequels by subsequent authors (1921–2014), and the great number of adaptations for screen, stage, and radio, the Oz books have spurred a great number of parallel texts (Gregory Maguire's *Wicked* series and the musical of the same name), retellings (*The Wiz*, SyFy's popular *Tin Man* miniseries), and non-canonical sequels and prequels (Disney's *The Return to Oz* and *Oz the Great and Powerful*).[6] It is due to this astounding popularity that I argue the importance of a disability reading of Oz. By continuing to engage with the wide range of Oz texts, particularly those by Baum, readers and viewers will come to understand one method through which the concept of utopia can transform into an accessible space, a futuristic vision filled with color and difference.

Chapter 2, in part, is a reprint of the material as it appears in *Monsters of Film, Fiction, and Fable: The Cultural Links between the Human and Inhuman*. Martin Sandino, Amanda, Cambridge University Press, 2018. The book author was the primary investigator and author of this paper.

Chapter 3

Middle Era Wonderlands: A Turn to the Dark Side

It has arguably been since the two world wars that popular media in the U.S. has turned toward the dystopic and deeply pessimistic. As political scientists Amy L. Atchison and Shauna L. Shames point out, "the early twentieth century dealt blow after blow to utopian ideals" (8). In the wake of catastrophic warfare, genocide, the Great Depression, nuclear bombs, and seemingly endless war crimes, the very belief in a peaceful world declined. Furthermore, the resulting Cold War between the Eastern and Western Blocs arguably strengthened the concept of duality, specifically good and evil (Maus 108). As such, the concepts of the dystopic and utopic became further solidified, with "a marked increase in new horror tales that depicted impending, terminal disaster" (Sicher and Skradol 167).

Perhaps the clearest shift from the utopian to dystopic in the wonderland genre occurs with L. Frank Baum's final Oz book, *Glinda of Oz*, published in 1920, a year after Baum's death. Given Baum's exceptionally poor health in 1919, it is quite likely that the majority of this book was written prior to the end of World War I in 1918 (Rogers 222, 236). While his previous Oz book, *The Magic of Oz*, was tellingly dedicated to "the Children of our Soldiers, the Americans and their Allies, with unmeasured Pride and Affection," *Glinda of Oz* directly reflects the effects that World War I had on him in particular and literature more broadly. Dedicated to his son, Robert, who fought in the war, *Glinda of Oz* has perhaps the clearest political commentary of any Oz book. His biographer, Katharine M. Rogers, notes that Baum reflected his specific belief that the squabbles of world leaders had led to the war, despite humans being naturally peaceful (234). *Glinda of Oz* follows Dorothy

3. Middle Era Wonderlands: A Turn to the Dark Side

and Ozma as they seek to prevent a war between the tyrannical Queen Coo-ee-oh of the Skeezers and the Supreme Dictator, or Su-Dic, of the Flatheads.

Baum's interest in World War I further stemmed from a personal angle; two of his sons, Robert and Frank, served. In a letter to his son, Frank, Baum specifically wishes for a speedy end to "this terrible war," expressing far more concern for his sons than any global issues at play (Letter to Frank Joslyn Baum). *Glinda of Oz* is specifically dedicated to Robert, who served in the Army Corps of Engineers in France; the concept of one who is innocent venturing far from home to help end the war for foreign others is clearly reflected in *Glinda* with Dorothy and Ozma traveling to the north of Gillikin Country. The princesses only find out about the war through Glinda's magical Great Book of Records, which records all of the happenings in Oz in real time; the suggestion here is again the distance between the battlefields of World War I and the United States, where Baum likely learned details of the war through newspapers. The positioning of two forces against each other also likely echoes the key oppositional forces in World War I, the Triple Entente of Great Britain, France, and Russia vs. the Triple Alliance of Austria-Hungary, Germany, and Italy (which later joined the Entente). Notably, neither side of the conflict in Oz is depicted as virtuous. Similar to his notes in the preface of his 1918 edition of *Aunt Jane's Nieces of the Red Cross*, Baum's heroines are far more concerned with the innocent civilians surrounding the war than the causes and leaders themselves (Tuerk 108). As one of Baum's heroines in *Aunt Jane* clarifies: "It is merely wholesale murder by a band of selfish diplomats" (qtd. Tuerk 109).

However, *Glinda* remains a rather optimistic portrayal of Oz. In the end, Ozma, Glinda, and Dorothy are able to prevent the war and depose both the Sup-Dic and Coo-ee-oh. Yet, there remains a cloud of doubt over the setting as a utopia, for it is merely by accident that the leaders of Oz learn of the situation between the Flatheads and the Skeezers. Imperialist ideology aside, the question remains as to how many conflicts in Oz has Ozma failed to have been made aware of or been able to prevent. While, per this book in the series at least, no one in Oz may die, Ozma worries that those who engage in combat may become dismembered and perhaps even have one's head thrown into a lake. While one would not drown or die in such a state, Ozma imagines that living under such circumstances would be potentially worse than death.

Oz is far from the first wonderland story to begin questioning the feasibility of utopia. While Narnia eventually becomes far more utopic, *The Lion, the Witch, and the Wardrobe* (1950) offers clear parallels to the Second World War and a wonderland dominated by an evil queen. Similarly, texts from the 1940s through 1980s begin setting up a transition to the underland with themes of death, poverty, exile, betrayal, and abandonment. While these stories generally end with good conquering evil and a former wonderland returned to its state of goodness, there remains the reality that these authors are alerting child readers to the realities of a twentieth-century world that often finds itself at war.

McGuire's Multiverse Compass

In order to understand the manner in which many children's wonderlands relate to one another, I suggest using the "Compass of Magical Worlds" presented in Seanan McGuire's popular Wayward Children series. These novellas offer a useful tool for locating wonderlands in relation to one another, beginning with four cardinal directions: Virtue opposite Wicked, Nonsense opposite Logical. Thus, a wonderland or underland may be placed along this Compass in relation to how these four characteristics are read. However, as stated in the novellas themselves, this cartographic method is far from perfect, particularly when dealing with such subjective experiences as good and evil. Yet, the ability for a wonderland to move across such a spectrum between the beginning and ending of a book or series marks this tool as particularly useful to showing how the ability to shift actually acts as a key marker for the time of transition between the wonderland and underland.

For example, the Narnia books as a series offer one of the clearest transitions from a world of high logic, high wickedness to high logic, high virtue. While not entirely wicked when visited by Lucy at the beginning of *The Lion*, Narnia seems almost entirely ruled by evil by the time she returns for a third visit with her siblings. While Narnia is ruled over by the wicked White Witch from her first encounter with it, Lucy sees even the small resistance in the form of Mr. Tumnus and his

3. Middle Era Wonderlands: A Turn to the Dark Side

friends turned to stone. Yet, once they have defeated the White Witch, Narnia is ruled over by Lucy and her siblings in a kindly manner that is high logic, high virtue. While the world again falls to darkness in the subsequent *Prince Caspian* and *The Voyage of the Dawn Treader*, when under the control of Aslan and/or the Pevensies, Narnia is utopic and harmonious.

Tor, the publisher of the Wayward Children series, has also provided some interpretation for this wonderland theory, suggesting that a pure utopian environment must be high virtue, where the land is "Pure and providential, prov[iding] everything you need" (Stubby the Rocket). In contrast, the dystopian high wicked places of this model are nearly apocalyptic or postapocalyptic, with conditions where one may only barely survive and may die at any time. Examples in children's literature are largely absent, as the darkness, violence, and death associated with such a world is often far beyond the maturity level of most children readers. Perhaps the closest we may come to a high wicked world is Spook City in *The Neverending Story*, whose inhabitants have chosen to enter the Nothing in the absence of any hope or happiness. Instead, horror worlds in adult literatures offer the closest examples as a truly wicked world would likely be something akin to a hell universe, simply too scary for most young children.

Whether virtuous, wicked, or neutral, a wonderland is also guided by either nonsense or logic. In a perfectly logical world, everything is explainable, often as a result of the world's creator having a direct impact. A clear example would be a world in which the dreamer, aware that they are dreaming, manipulates the contents of their vision. While existing within a world of high wickedness, Tallyman Holm of *And Then Emily Was Gone* offers a clear example of high logic. Once he has spoken with "Mental" Jimmy about his visions, Greg learns that he is able to control the monsters. Furthermore, the world of Tallyman Holm has specific rules albeit unusual. The laws are so technical that Greg and Bonnie Shaw eventually get into an argument as to whether or not Fiona may be taken as an "abandoned" child. Bonnie argues that, because she is recently orphaned, no one can lay claim to Fiona. Greg counters that he can speak for Fiona and keep her from Bonnie's clutches. Finally, a careful trade is required in order for Greg to free Emily; Greg must offer his own soul in exchange for Emily's as she was given freely by

Disability in Wonderland

her parents. Everything within this world is explainable, whether or not Greg knows the rules, and exceptions are never made.

In contrast, high nonsense worlds are marked by chaos. They may instead be thought of as dreamworlds in which the dreamer has absolutely no control and events may not be linked causally, chronologically, or logically. The poem, "Jabberwocky," from *Through the Looking-Glass* offers one of the clearest examples as it includes nonsense words, a circular plot, and even its having been written in reverse, such that a mirror must be used in order for it to be read. While it initially appears as though the titular beast is slain by the unnamed hero of the poem, the fact that the first and last verse also mirror one another suggests that even linear time may be abandoned in this world.

Places that are neutral in terms of logic/nonsense and wickedness/virtue are generally less interesting and thus not ripe subjects for the wonderland author. For example, Tor's writers define a world that is neutral in terms of logic and nonsense as one in which, "no change occurs." It is a world unaffected by time or marked by anything but complete stasis. An example may be the mythical figure of Sisyphus continuously rolling his boulder up a hill, only to watch it roll back down. There is essentially no object to mark change in time, only the same monotonous task over and over. Similarly, a world devoid of wickedness and virtue is marked by balance but not harmony; it can neither have nor deny human rights and thus likely has no or very few inhabitants. The clearest example may be the Nothing from *The Neverending Story*, which is described by Gmork in the novel as, "the emptiness that's left ... like a despair" (Ende). While one who enters the Nothing emerges into the real world from Fantasia via rebirth, the state of being in Nothing means a complete lack of existence. Thus, the primary antagonist of the book itself is actually neutral, rather than evil.

Most wonderlands in the early period prior to World War I, however, are marked by a particular ability to move between wicked and virtue, with most stories becoming more virtuous as a result of the protagonist's actions. However, I contend that this ability is often removed from wonderland texts of the middle period between World War I and the 1980s, while the underlands of 1980s to present often are marked by movement from wicked to even more wicked in narratives that seem to require murder, or at least death, for the heroines to be happy.

3. Middle Era Wonderlands: A Turn to the Dark Side

Wonderlands, the Middle Period

Two of the key components of the wonderland journey as delineated in this study are approaching and facing a major ordeal followed by the receival of a reward of some kind. Perhaps one of the clearest elements of an underland, along with the influx of pessimism and anti-medicalism, is the possibility that the hero may fail this ordeal or receive a potentially negative reward for their labors. Within the middle period, wonderlands may still become more virtuous as a result of the hero's actions but they remain spaces of trauma as a result of the ordeals through which the hero's must venture. Furthermore, these wonderlands are perhaps those which may be particularly susceptible to the question of whether or not they actually fulfill the components required to *be* wonderlands, particularly *Charlie and the Chocolate Factory* (1964), *Bridge to Terabithia* (1977), *A Wrinkle in Time* (1962), and *The Little Prince* (1943). Both *Charlie* and *Bridge* may arguably take place entirely within the scope of the "real" world, while *The Little Prince* and *A Wrinkle in Time* may not meet our own world at all. In order for these stories to work, one must first demonstrate that *Charlie* and *Bridge* do include movement from the real world to wonderlands, while showing that fantastic visions of space exploration must depict wonderlands.

Charlie is perhaps the easiest to demonstrate as possessing a wonderland setting, as the titular chocolate factory clearly includes magic that does and cannot occur in the outside world. While Willy Wonka is continuously working on seemingly impossible candies that shrink people, provide all the nutrients one needs in a single eating, allow one to fly, etc., the fact that none of these have been released to the public suggests that they may simply rely on the magic of Wonka and the chocolate factory himself to exist. Even when the Great Glass Elevator is separated from the chocolate factory, this magic remains, as Wonka, Charlie, Charlie's parents, and Charlie's grandparents are simultaneously able to use the glass box to travel through the chocolate factory, over the city, and even through space in *Charlie and the Great Glass Elevator* (1972). While in outer space, the elevator's inhabitants are able to breathe and even travel more effectively than their seeming real world astronaut peers, even visiting a space hotel prior to its guests' arrival.

Disability in Wonderland

Similarly, the eponymous prince of *The Little Prince* travels through methods that exist apart from the real world. It is clear that the prince has abilities marking him as a magical being, including his seeming lack of a need to breathe in space and the seeming disappearance of his body upon being bit by the yellow snake. The story takes place in a desert where the unnamed narrator has crashed his plane and is slowly dying of thirst. Thus, when the prince first appears out of nowhere and begins chatting, one might easily assume the small blond to be a hallucination. Yet eventually the prince finds a well, and both he and the pilot are able to quench their thirst. Recovering his energy, the pilot is then able to fix his plane and fly off following the prince's return to his home planet. Because the pilot is healthy and still able to perceive the prince, as well as hearing the human speech of the snake and fox, one may easily conclude that the desert itself is a kind of portal to the wonderland of which the prince speaks. There is simply no logical reason for the young boy appearing in the desert, and thus the story embraces the fantastic.

A Wrinkle in Time and the other books of Madeleine L'Engle's Time Quintet similarly considers space a kind of wonderland, however flawed. Items and people cross the barrier between the space worlds and the real world, generally via the use of an object referred to as a tesseract. Despite Calvin's demands that Mrs. Who, Whatsit, and Which explain how the tesseract works, citing lightspeed as an option, the older women simply explain that they "wrinkle" across the galaxy (58). While the worlds visited by the protagonists vary greatly, the children's overall goal is to defeat IT, a being which seeks to take control over all life in the universe. While a world controlled by such a being, such as Camazotz in the first book, offers a perfect example of high logic, such a vision is deemed evil within the context of the novels. Camazotz is placed in contrast to Uriel, a planet described as "perfectly safe" (59–60) while containing beautiful scenery and loving, peaceful inhabitants who spend their time dancing and singing.

Lastly, *Bridge to Terabithia* acts both as a wonderland narrative and a commentary on wonderlands as a whole, drawing most obviously from the Narnia series. The author, Katherine Paterson, has overtly stated that she was driven to write the book after the sudden death of her son's eight-year-old friend (Kohn). Paterson states that the novel acts as her attempt to answer the difficult question posed to her by her son, "Why

3. Middle Era Wonderlands: A Turn to the Dark Side

do children have to die?" Thus, in *Bridge to Terabithia* we are presented with two children, Jess and Leslie, who meet and become best friends just prior to Leslie dying in an accident. While Terabithia is arguably an unreal space, wholly imagined by the two children, it nonetheless fulfills all characteristics of a wonderland offered earlier in this study. As linguist Norma Bagnall explains, whether or not Terabithia is real to us as external readers hardly matters—what matters is that Terabithia is real to Jess and Leslie who truly accomplish feats and change their lives based on the events that happen there. It may be more of a psychosocial and linguistic space than a literal one, yet Jess is only able to accomplish growth and accept Leslie's death by visiting the literal forest in which they imagine it existing.

In offering this psychosocial space and the wonderland as metaphor for the growth of child narrators, *Bridge to Terabithia* lays out all the complexity that enters into the wonderland in the middle period. In the context of having lived through one or more World War and the stressors of the Cold War, wonderland authors could simply no longer pretend that children would believe in a utopic space any more than their adult counterparts. Many children saw firsthand the brutality of war, either through living in war zones or occupation, witnessing the Holocaust firsthand, participating in youth conscription, or seeing loved ones leave to fight in the war and potentially lose their lives.

One of the clearest examples of this shift occurs with the Narnia series, which C.S. Lewis explicitly explains was influenced by his family taking in three young girls as part of Operation Pied Piper (Ford 21). Essentially, this program saw urban children, predominantly from London, sent to the countryside to live out the war in towns that were not being subjected to attack by German airplanes. The arrival of such children to the English countryside is, in fact, described in detail as the reason behind the Pevensie children's journey to the house of Professor Digory Kirke:

> Once there were four children whose names were Peter, Susan, Edmund and Lucy. This story is about something that happened to them when they were sent away from London during the war because of the air-raids. They were sent to the house of an old Professor who lived in the heart of the country, ten miles from the nearest railway station and two miles from the nearest post office [Lewis, *The Lion*].

Disability in Wonderland

The context of the Second World War also provides a bit more explanation as to why Edmund may seem to have been so easily swayed by the White Witch's promise of Turkish delights; import, food, and, specifically, sugar rationing would likely have left a young child of ten especially ravenous for sweets. The children look forward to their time with Professor Kirke, as they are excited to engage with the features of the countryside, such as the mountains and woods, as well as meet a wide variety of animals.

Yet while the magical land of Narnia seems to fulfill all of these desires and more, it also does not provide a space of reprieve from war as a whole. In actuality, the children are almost immediately faced with the despotic rule of the White Witch upon arriving in Narnia, as well as an endless winter without Christmas. While their presence eventually leads to the failing power of the White Witch, leading to a visit from Father Christmas, even the gifts they receive directly pertain to their inevitable participation in war against the evil queen; they are, as Father Christmas explains, "tools not toys." From Father Christmas, Peter receives a sword and shield, Susan is given a bow and arrows along with an ivory horn to call for help, and Lucy is gifted a potion to heal the wounds of those who are injured. Strangely, it is only Edmund, who has become temporary aligned with the White Witch, who receives a more traditional gift from his queen in the form of candy. Like their parents, who explicitly support England during the war through army service and other war work in early drafts of the text, the Pevensie children are expected to support the cause of good against evil, totalitarian regimes (Glasner 56).

Narnia thus acts as a psychic realm in which the children are able to help their parents and their country. While the specter of death is all but nullified by Aslan's miracles and Lucy's potion, the Pevensie children deal with a lighter sort of temporary death; they witness the physical death of Aslan before his rebirth, as well as many friends temporarily turned to stone. In this realm, the children experience trauma but are able to overcome it, thus marking the wonderland as a space in which to process tragedies, such as the Pevensies' years-long loss of their parents to the war, Jess's loss of Leslie, the Little Prince's loss of his beloved Rose, Charlie's severe poverty and seeming decline into starvation, and Bastian's loss of his mother. Unlike the children of earlier

3. Middle Era Wonderlands: A Turn to the Dark Side

wonderlands, such as *Alice in Wonderland*, the Oz series, and *Peter Pan*, the protagonists in these novels strive to escape from not from boredom but traumatic experiences through which they are living. The desire to return home largely disappears in this middle period, despite the wonderland conditions being far from utopic.

Notably too in these narratives is the continued presence of disability, albeit in a far more easily altered manner than in previous eras. While Mike Teavee is shrunk to the size of a chocolate bar, he is afterward stretched to a more "normal" size of 10 ft. in height by the Oompa-Loompas. Similarly, Violet Beauregarde inflates to an especially large size before being "juiced" by the Oompa-Loompas but retaining a blueish skin tone. Even Grandpa Joe, who is said to have not left his bed for twenty years, is able to leap and run around after learning that Charlie has won a Golden Ticket (Dahl, *Charlie*, 47); even the mere idea of entering Willie Wonka's Chocolate Factory seems to offer a kind of magic that heals disabled bodies. Similar to the children of *Charlie*, Meg of *A Wrinkle in Time* becomes paralyzed as a result of the cold wickedness of IT. However, the tentacled inhabitants of the planet Ixchel are able to heal her through embracing her and seemingly filling her with a sense of security. As in its World War II, so too do those who fight in the war of Narnia suffer life-threatening and disabling injuries. Yet, Lucy is able to use her cordial potion in order to heal most injuries, while even turning those transformed into stone back into flesh. It is psychological disabilities, however, that are most addressed in these middle wonderland spaces, or at least psychological wounds. One of the clearest examples of this tendency occurs at the end of *The Neverending Story* when Bastion must relinquish memories of his parents in order to understand his truest desire: to be loved and to offer love to others. Rather than being a depressed young man, Bastion becomes possessed of a generally joyous demeanor, "even in the hardest moments of his life" (Ende, 434).

In this way, the wonderlands still act as positive spaces for their visitors. They are able to unpack psychological and physical trauma, face their fears, and grow stronger, without the worry of permanence for anything associated with the negative. The wonderlands may begin in a space of high wickedness but, through the interventions of the child protagonists, largely end in states of virtue.

Underlands and High Wickedness

In the next few chapters I will demonstrate how the turn toward the underland, or dark wonderland, in the 1980s offers a marked change from the middle wonderland narratives. Rather than offering a space of change for our heroes, these stories predominantly suggest that, however flawed, traumatized, or unhappy they may be, the protagonists should embrace their current states of existence. With a clear turn toward high wickedness and away from virtue, these more recent narratives particularly work to attack agents of change, with negative portrayals of doctors, psychology, and healing. Rather than suggesting that one may recover from severe trauma, these narratives instead suggest embracing one's trauma and own wicked actions as part of one's more complicated being.

CHAPTER 4

Alienation and *Charlie and the Chocolate Factory*

Charlie and the Chocolate Factory by Roald Dahl offers a quintessential example of both the middle era wonderlands and the shift toward what disability and literary scholar Julie Avril Minich terms "narrative remediation." Popular during the middle period and late periods, narrative remediation refers to the retelling of specific narrative types via new forms of media. Unlike earlier wonderlands which were predominantly written prior to the widespread use of film or television, *Charlie* was published and adapted within the span of a single childhood. Published as a book first in the U.S. in 1964 and the U.K. in 1965, the first film adaptation, *Willie Wonka and the Chocolate Factory*, was released in 1971; by comparison, *The Wonderful Wizard of Oz* was first published in 1900 with its first full-length film adaptation coming nearly a quarter century later in 1925. Even more notably, while *Alice in Wonderland* was first published in 1865, its first film adaptation, a short film of approximately 12 minutes in length, was not released until 1903. With many adaptations in the first half of the 20th century, *Alice*'s early releases were almost universally panned by critics and box office failures. It is this focus on audienceship that truly defines the middle period, and thus when considering wonderlands either constructed or adapted in this time period from approximately 1918 to 1988, it is essential to consider both which forms of media were dominant for the average citizen and what media objects were most popular and unpopular. In brief, while it is meaningful that *Alice* was adapted for the silver screen in 1903, the reality that almost no one outside of the elite and members of the film industry were able to see the film means that this title is far less relevant from a cultural studies perspective.

Disability in Wonderland

In order to better acquaint readers with the middle era wonderlands in this chapter, I will offer an overview of media types and peak periods of popularity, along with popular wonderland titles published during such periods. Furthermore, I will be drawing upon media theory to demonstrate why the shift in dominating medium matters, especially in terms of the wonderland narrative. I will then explain why and how the contexts of various wonderland publications make these works vivid reflections of their specific cultural moments, with a clear emphasis on the negative visions of futurity that emerged surrounding World War I, World War II, and the Cold War. Finally, I will offer a case study demonstrating how *Charlie* brings all of these elements together to offer a wonderland landscape that is shifting in terms of medium, optimism, and disability history.

Wonderlands and Popular Media Platforms

While this study generally understands the wonderland as originating with Lewis Carroll's 1865 *Alice's Adventures in Wonderland*, it is worth acknowledging that many scholars choose not to distinguish between utopia and the wonderland; as such, many of their texts of study predate the printing press or come from predominantly oral cultures. For example, literary journalist Laura Miller's *Literary Wonderlands* includes five subsections of the wonderland: ancient myth and legend; science & romanticism; golden age of fantasy; new world order; and the computer age. As an editor, Miller brings in pieces on such texts as Homer's *The Odyssey* (est. 8th or 7th century BCE), famously descended from an oral tradition, and William Shakespeare's *The Tempest* (est. 1610–1611), which was of course converted from scraps of script and the memories of theatrical contemporaries rather than transmitted to the masses through Shakespeare's original script. In fact, most of the texts in the earliest period of Miller's book date from prior to the 15th century and the Western invention of the printing press by Guttenberg and his colleagues. Yet the proliferation of literacy and reading did not occur until the rise of the middle class during the Renaissance (*Understanding Media and Culture*), meaning that oral cultures would have been

4. *Alienation and* Charlie and the Chocolate Factory

the dominant form of storytelling even after the European invention of the moveable type. This reality makes it appealing to mark this period as the start of the wonderland and is significant in originating the ideas of the fairy tale and bedtime story. Without the influence of the cult of childhood, however, there really would be no need for distinguishing between the wonderland and other utopic spaces; simply put, there was no children's literature and arguably no children in the contemporary sense at all (Gabin and Humphries 1).

Unlike the erasure of childhood in earlier eras, Anglophone cultures in the late 19th and early 20th century saw the clear demarcation between adulthood and childhood: for "the first time it was widely recognized that children ... have different needs, sensibilities, and habits of thinking; that they cannot be educated, worked, or punished like adults; that they have rights of their own independent of their parents" (Rose qtd. Gavin and Humphries 1). Thus, Charles Dodgson's (pseudonym Lewis Carroll) own simultaneous fascination with and construction of this distinction, as well as the emerging field of children's literature, becomes even more significant. Simultaneous to the rise of children's literature is both the creation of the wonderland and rise of the paperback novel as highly popular medium. While newspapers were similarly popular media platforms in the late 19th and early 20th century, they offered far less in terms of content aimed at child readers or children being read to by their others. While literacy rates across Western Europe reached 90 percent by 1890, the vast majority of these readers only learned to read in adulthood (Lyons 311); it was not until this time period that public education even became widely available across Europe, offering literary access to those of the working classes and girls. Notably, because women are traditionally those who read aloud to their families, especially children, rising literacy rates for women generally leads to an increase in the practice of bedtime reading (Lyons 316). While literacy historian Carl F. Kaestle questions these literacy percentages, as one may be deemed literate in many contexts on the mere basis of having the ability to sign one's own name, he also notes that literacy rates were much lower in the United States at the same time period. It is estimated that only 7 percent of enlisted U.S. Army officers were literate in the 1880s, a number that actually decreased from 42 percent in 1800 (Kaestle 23–24). These data provide insight into the unique nature

Disability in Wonderland

of the growing United States at the time and one of the key reasons literacy in the country has been so difficult to determine: skyrocketing immigration levels in the 19th century, specifically from Southern and Eastern Europe toward the end of the century, meant that many people deemed illiterate actually simply did not read or write English.

In any case, the late 19th and early 20th centuries certainly saw a large increase in the number of readers, particularly those of the newly popular children's literature, in the English-speaking world. The shift from the stage, now largely inaccessible to the lower classes, to the page has even been argued to be a defining feature of the early wonderland. In his essential text on Charles Dodgson and the stage, theater historian Richard Foulkes notes that the famed author of the *Alice* books attended over 400 stage performances between 1855 and 1897. Dogdson's theater trips included the 1886 stage adaptation of *Alice in Wonderland*, and a number of J.M. Barrie's pre–*Pan* works, especially those intended for child audiences. Barrie himself was a successful playwright even prior to the first *Pan* performance, and Dogdson tellingly hailed him as one of his favorite dramatists of the 19th century (Foulkes). The fact that *Pan* began as a play before being translated to the book format further demonstrates the influence of theater on the early wonderland, as well as highlighting the growing accessibility of books to stage plays. Rather famously, L. Frank Baum was extremely preoccupied with the theater, first staging a *The Wizard* adaptation in 1902, a mere two years after the book's publication.

In short, each of these early wonderland creators had a long-lived and significant relationship to the stage, and this fascination with intermediality and adaptation is clearly evident in their most popular works. If we return to the implicit argument offered by Miller in *Literary Wonderlands*, we will see that she offers no distinction between early speculative fiction texts meant for adult audiences and those aimed at children. For example, she places *Pan*, Tove Jansson's *The Moomins and the Great Flood* (1945), and Antoine de Saint-Exupéry's *The Little Prince* (1943) in the same Golden Age of Fantasy[1] section as texts largely too advanced or too mature for child readers, including H.P. Lovecraft's Cthulhu mythos, which features such adult themes as human sacrifice, apocalypse, monsters who eat human beings, gore, and mutilation. This section also includes books with extremely complex themes,

4. *Alienation and* Charlie and the Chocolate Factory

such as Franz Kafka's *The Castle* (1926), which offers a harsh, existentialist critique of bureaucracy, and Aldous Huxley's *Brave New World* (1932), which interrogates such concepts as consumerism, fascism, and the nature of truth. Of course, I would argue that these elevated concepts and horrifying images should differentiate all such speculative worlds from those meant to be accessible to young child readers. Yet, apart from this key difference, I also contend that the children's works, whether or not they meet the specifications for wonderlands in this text, are inherently unique from their adult speculative fiction counterparts. And this separation largely results from this intermediality or "the interconnectedness of modern media of communication" (Jensen 1). These early speculative children's works offer a mixture of mediums in their novel forms, from illustrations to maps to poems to drawings and concrete writing in which the novel's words appear on the page in the manner of the very things they are describing. In particular, the visuality of these works differentiates them from their adult counterparts; the highly descriptive language and depth of world building within the early wonderlands are particularly essential in that they are often as detailed as the scenery offered in a script. In his introduction to the first publication of the *Pan* stage play's script, Barrie even admits that he may have "cribbed [...] from some typed copy" of the script the eventual text that became the *Pan* novel (Barrie, *Peter Pan [The Play]*). Apart from his contributions to children's literature, Baum was perhaps most well-known for his influential texts on shop window dressings, including the monthly *The Show Window: A Journal of Practical Window Trimming for the Merchant and the Professional* (under Baum's editorship from 1897 to 1900) and his subsequent book on the subject, *The Art of Decorating Dry Goods Windows and Interiors: A Complete Manual of Window Trimming, Designed as an Educator in All the Details of the Art, According to the Best Accepted Methods, and Treating Fully Every Important Subject* (1900). Folklorist Archie Green specifically notes the ways in which the color schemes and illusions of Oz appear in these earlier texts (28).

As such, the texts are far more concerned with worldbuilding and immersive imagery than many utopic texts not of the wonderland subgenre. For example, Edward Bellamy's 1888 *Looking Backwards* offers a one-paragraph description of twenty-first century Boston; in contrast,

Disability in Wonderland

Carroll offers a one-paragraph description of the rabbit hole through which Alice falls alone, Baum introduces the Emerald City of Oz with four paragraphs, and Barrie's script for *Pan* introduces the Darling children's nursery with a lengthy seven paragraphs. Yet, even these descriptions fall short of the visuality the author's hoped to provide young readers. The original *The Wizard* included drawings throughout by W.W. Denslow, *Pan* was illustrated by F.D. Bedford, and John Tenniel provided wood engravings for *Alice*.

This tradition of looking forward to potential adaptations and in-depth world description continues to this day, yet perhaps came most to fruition during the middle era with the rise of cinema. Like his forebearers, British novelist and memoirist Roald Dahl often wrote for a variety of mediums: he famously wrote the screenplay for the children's classic *Chitty Chitty Bang Bang* (1968), in addition to the James Bond film *You Only Live Twice* (1967). He additionally wrote for television, with his stories featured heavily in the 1979–1988 British anthology series *Tales of the Unexpected*. He furthermore attempted to write the film adaptation for *Charlie* himself, though was replaced by screenwriter David Seltzer when he failed to meet writing deadlines. At the time of *Charlie*'s book publication, Dahl may have even been better known as the host of the speculative fiction anthology series *'Way Out*, or even as the husband of Oscar-winning actress Patricia Neal, than as a novelist.

Charlie as Archetype

Like Narnia, the context for the narrative of the sweets in *Charlie and the Chocolate Factory* is truly essential to understand the appeal to children. While one may initially associate food rationing, especially sugar rationing, with World War II, the rations themselves actually lasted almost a decade after the end of the war. The Records of the Ministry of Food in the U.K. National Archives demonstrate that rations remained in effect until 1954, a mere decade prior to the publication of *Charlie*. While most children in the mid–60s would have no memory of this time period, the reading of *Charlie* would likely have provided many caretakers with the opportunity to share the history of the war.

4. *Alienation and* Charlie and the Chocolate Factory

World War II haunts the text in many ways, essentially asking those older readers to reminisce with the children around them. Charlie himself even seems to act as a counter to the other children visiting Wonka's factory. As a boy raised in poverty and seeming isolation from many of the joys of childhood, he lives in stark contrast to the other four children who live lives of excess in terms of consumption, whether it be television, gum, food, or possessions. In this manner, Charlie seems almost to represent the child raised during wartime, while the other kids demonstrate the relative excess allowed to many children following the war.

In addition to only enjoying a chocolate bar, which he slowly eats over the course of a month, once a year, Charlie often goes hungry. His family initially eats very little, having "bread and margarine for breakfast, boiled potatoes and cabbage for lunch, and cabbage soup for supper" (5). Charlie is also relatively isolated from other children, with no friends mentioned who exist outside of his family. While Charlie is never explicitly said to be lonely, he is certainly depicted as alienated from other kids of his age. Furthermore, while television features prominently in the book, Charlie and his family learn of the news surrounding the Golden Tickets via newspaper; it seems that his family is so destitute that they cannot afford even a radio. Finally, the fear of dying young hangs over not only Charlie but his parents as well, with the tenth chapter tellingly titled, "The Family Begins to Starve." This chapter tells of Mr. Bucket, Charlie's father, losing his job at a factory and finding a new position shoveling snow, which pays significantly less. As a result, the Buckets go from definitively not starving, though going "from morning till night with a horrible empty feeling in their tummies" in chapter 1 (5), to Charlie carefully measuring his energy so as to not pass out from hunger in chapter 10. Fortunately, this starvation is temporarily staved off by Charlie finding a dollar bill in the street and later permanently avoided through Charlie's ownership of the chocolate factory.

Many of these qualities, including hunger, temporary disability, an aching desire for sweets, isolation, and lack of access to new technologies, harken back to Dahl's own childhood and experiences during the war as a young man. Dahl's official biographer, Donald Sturrock, notes that, in many ways, Dahl began conceiving of *Charlie* as a young boy. He notes especially that Dahl and his schoolmates at Repton would act as

Disability in Wonderland

taste testers for Cadbury once a year, each child receiving his own chocolate bar to evaluate. Dahl would later show affection toward his parents by sending them packets of sugar. During the height of World War II, Dahl was stationed at various North American sites and, upon arriving in Halifax and, later, Washington, D.C., "was immediately intrigued by the difference between the culture of plenty he found in North America and the starved, meager life he had left behind in England" (Sturrock). In multiple letters pleading for aid to the average English family, Dahl refers to England as "starving." While raised in an affluent and loving home, Dahl's experiences at particularly violent boarding schools came from both his teachers and fellow students; Dahl notably developed a strong aversion to chewing gum at this time due to other children sticking it in kids' pubic hair as a form of initiation (Sturrock).

While Dahl may have never experienced poverty, especially at the Buckets' level, he certainly would have acutely felt alienation, hunger, and nearness to death in a manner similar to Charlie. In the short story "Beware of the Dog," Dahl famously came close to death during his career as an RAF pilot. Having received poor instructions regarding directions, Dahl ended up crashing his plane in the No Man's Land between Allied and Axis forces in Egypt. As a result of the accident, Dahl was rendered temporarily blind, with a broken nose, concussion, and other injuries. After escaping the flames of his plane, Dahl notes that he fully expected to die in the desert: "All I wanted was to go gently off to sleep and to hell" (qtd. Sturrock). Because he was mistaken for an Italian soldier (Dahl, *Love* 193), Dahl was taken to a hospital meant for Axis casualties (Dahl, *Going Solo* 103–104). While he writes little of this in his nonfiction texts, he at least speculates in "Beware of the Dog" as to what might have happened had Axis soldiers found him and simply pretended to be English; the protagonist of that story is continuously interrogated for privileged Allied intelligence and is only able to learn he is in Vichy France, rather than the U.K., when he spots a sign in French outside his window. During his time as a pilot, Dahl often notes in his journal his efforts to combat not enemy fighters but rather, hunger (Sturrock). He furthermore comments often on his loneliness, largely resulting from his constantly flying a single-seater plane called a Hawker Hurricane (Sturrock). As a single person flying above

4. *Alienation and* Charlie and the Chocolate Factory

the world, "Sometimes he wondered if he was the only living thing left in the world" (Sturrock). His solace seems to have come in the form of writing, both in his journal, yes, but predominantly in constant letters to his mother back home. From the age of nine (1925) until his mother's death in 1967, Roald wrote over 600 letters to his mother, Sofie Dahl (Dahl, *Love from Boy* xvii). As Dahl's father died when he was merely three years of age, it makes sense that Sofie Dahl would have become the person at home to whom he was closest while away at boarding school. And this relationship was nurtured over the years, for while Dahl would see a tumultuous romantic life, his mother would remain a constant companion.

Dahl seems to imbue Charlie Bucket's character with all of these emotions and memories, making him a character who stands in stark contrast to the other children of the novel. The other children at the chocolate factory are memorable mostly due to their excesses, whether it be in the form of chewing gum, watching television, eating, or, in Veruca's case, simply more of everything. Charlie, instead, is notable for what he lacks: access to food, comfort, a healthy body, and seemingly, even friends of his own age. Of course, he does have an abundance of love and kindness; it is often remarked upon that he is a sweet boy, and he is doted upon by his large family, especially his four grandparents. So, while Charlie may have been meant to be a Dickensian youngster who sees severe poverty but triumphs at the end of the tale into wild riches, he never faces his fate without his family's support.

Death and the Threat of Violence

The middle era of the wonderland phase from World War I to the 1980s is rich with Charlie-like figures, over whom the figure of death looms heavily. While the threat of death, as well as actual death, can be found in the earlier wonderlands, the manner in which it is treated is quite unique from that of the middle period. In short, death is often either laughable, reversible, unthinkable, or impossible. This quality is so indicative of an early wonderland story that, I argue, its presence is far more important than actual chronology. For, while the Narnia books were all written after World War I, they remain in the early wonderland

Disability in Wonderland

period because it seems that few, if any, hero who dies in them remains dead. Mr. Tumnus and the other creatures turned to stone are eventually made flesh again. Aslan heroically sacrifices his life to save Edmund, but comes magically back to life the next morning. Those who are brought to the very edge of death in battle are generally returned to health with Lucy's cordial. In such a setting, death becomes far less frightening, clearly something about which children were not to fret. Such is a mainstay of the middle era wonderlands.

In *Peter*, Wendy is shot from the sky by an arrow and appears to perish, yet she seemingly returns to life a mere chapter later when it is revealed that the arrow tip hit a button worn around her neck. Later, Tinker Bell drinks poison-laced medicine meant for Peter and lies down to slowly die. Only by appealing to all children who dream of Neverland, the audience in the original play, and begging them to declare their belief in fairies by applauding, is Peter able to save Tinker Bell. In short, Peter breaks the fourth wall; amusingly, he is said to "almost fill [...] the fourth wall of [Tinker Bell's] little room" (Barrie) in a wink to the ploy that saves her life.

In *Alice*, the heroine almost immediately falls down a seemingly infinite hole; it is only her nonsensical logic that keeps her from worrying about eventually dying from such a drop. Soon after, poor Alice weeps when she grows over nine feet tall and is stuck alone in a great hall, believing that she will likely be there until she dies; upon shrinking again, Alice even remarks "That was a narrow escape!" (Carroll). Alice suffers many near death experiences throughout the novel, yet these occurrences are almost always played for laughs; for example, when Alice escapes from the ocean created from her tears, she exclaims, "I wish I hadn't cried so much! ... I shall be punished for it now, I suppose, by being drowned in my own tears! That will be a queer thing, to be sure! However, everything is queer to-day." And, while the Queen of Hearts is famous for constantly crying, "Off with their heads!," no one appears to be successfully executed by the regent.

Similarly, while the aptly named Wicked Witch of the West does appear to die in *The Wizard*, none of the heroes stay dead. While theoretically no one is meant to die per the laws of Oz, unless murdered, characters do occasionally become inanimate objects. When rusted over or banged out of shape, the Tin Man eventually becomes unconscious,

4. *Alienation and* Charlie and the Chocolate Factory

temporarily dead. When his straw is strewn about, the Scarecrow similarly turns back into lifeless straw and clothes. Both are brought back to life, however; Winkie tinsmiths repair the Tin Man and he comes back to life, though a bit patched up, while the Scarecrow's clothing is recovered and stuffed with fresh straw to bring him back to life.

While there are some deaths able to be reversed in the middle era, the wonderlands of this time period are remarkable in that they are laden with permanence. And oftentimes, such loss is accompanied by severe loneliness and alienation. *The Neverending Story* follows Bastian as he and his father readjust their lives following the death of his mother. At the same time, Bastian is bullied at school and seeks to escape his daily life through books. In the land of Fantastica, creatures are eaten by swamps, disappear into the Nothing, or are otherwise killed, but usually come back to life eventually. In the real world where Bastian's mother died, however, she remains dead. When he returns from Fantastica, Bastian faces the same bullies, strained relationship with his father, and sorrow surrounding the loss of his mother. The book tellingly ends with Bastian, previously branded a coward, facing his fears and admitting to his theft of *The Neverending Story*, before making a friend in the bookseller from whom he stole the book, and going off for a day of leisure with his father. While his friends of the same age remain in Fantastica, Bastian has clearly gained the confidence to build strong relationships in the real world and face his fears, not only those of his bully and guilt, but also that of loss.

Perhaps it is this happy ending as much as loss that most defines the middle era as well, for though our heroes face the glaring threat of if not actual death, they tend to find solace or survival. These books speak specifically from the experiences of those who have faced similar fates. Roald Dahl and Antoine de Saint-Exupéry (*The Little Prince*) both fought in World War II, the latter perishing during the war. Michael Ende (*The Neverending Story*) survived a childhood in Nazi Germany, including the 1943 Hamburg Bombing, with a father blacklisted by the ruling party ("Michael Ende"). Born to a missionary family, Katherine Paterson (*Bridge to Terabithia*) grew up in Huaian, China, until the Japanese invasion in 1937; thereafter, the family repatriated to the United States, where Katherine attended school speaking Huaian Chinese rather than English ("Katherine Paterson"). Madeleine L'Engle (*A

Disability in Wonderland

Wrinkle in Time) is one of the few authors of this time period who did not experience the war or the loss of a loved one firsthand in the Second World War; her father was too old for conscription, having served in World War I, and she had no siblings ("Madeleine L'Engle Biographical Sketch"). However, like Paterson and Dahl, she had a miserable school life. As a young child, L'Engle notes being called "stupid" by her teachers, whom she felt generally disliked her (*A Circle of Quiet* 247). When she was twelve years old, L'Engle was sent to boarding school in Switzerland, "where she felt abandoned, alienated, and shattered by the loss of privacy" ("Madeleine L'Engle Biographical Sketch").

With their own suffering in mind, these authors imbue their stories with suffering as well, but also generally treat their protagonists to happy endings. Ende's Bastian has come back from Fantastica almost unrecognizable to his father for his confidence. Paterson's Jesse saves the life of his sister May Belle, at the very creek where Leslie met her end, and crowns her the new queen of Terabithia. Saint-Exupéry's narrator, the unnamed pilot, is unsure of whether or not he has witnessed the titular prince's death but is able to survive his own plane wreck in the Saharan desert and write down the prince's tale. L'Engle's Meg successfully saves her brother, Charles, before reuniting with her family, including her missing father.

And, finally, Dahl's Charlie goes from a life of starvation to one where he may even have experienced excess, had he been like his peers on the tour. His family is likely rendered free from the threat of starvation from the moment Charlie wins the Golden Ticket and, with it, a lifetime supply of chocolate. Upon becoming the new owner of Willy Wonka's Chocolate Factory, however, Charlie is provided such stability that we, as readers, are likely meant to be amused upon the destruction of Charlie's tiny house. His family is guided into the magical glass elevator for further adventures, an abundance of food, a home large enough for everyone, and a new friend in the form of jolly Wonka himself. And, almost foreshadowing the underland, all trauma that precedes this happy ending for Charlie seems to be completely erased.

CHAPTER 5

Nostalgia, Fan Fiction, and the Wayward Children Series

With the rise of multimedia universes surrounding key popular texts, adaptations of early wonderlands have become especially popular. Any peripheral search on the internet will tell you just how many times and across how many media platforms the founding wonderland texts have been adapted, as well as how incredibly popular many of these adaptations remain. Despite being just over 120 years of age, the land of Oz may comprise one of the largest multimedia universes of all time. While likely impossible to prove, it is also generally accepted that the 1939 film is one of the most viewed films of all time.

While *The Wizard* and *Alice* began as novels, *Peter Pan* was first conceived of as a play; yet all of these stories have been adapted to multiple stage plays and novels. All have been made into radio plays, comic books, films, television series, and video games. A huge, multigenerational fandom has emerged for each text, supported well, in part, by their entry into the public domain. And fan culture has played an essential part in the continuing legacy of wonderland texts, as well as the many continuing additions to the wonderland genre. The ability of creators to legally publish their fan works is essential to the continued success of these texts. It also makes these series fiscally attractive to large storytelling corporations, with Disney perhaps most famously adapting all three works, despite MGM's *The Wizard* remaining the quintessential Oz film.

Thus, many of the underlands act as continuations of the wonderland subgenre and commentary upon these earlier wonderlands by continuing the tradition of adaptation. Yet, I would argue that fan culture plays a huge part of the wonderland's continued cultural proliferation.

While the Oz, Wonderland, and Pan texts all belong to the public domain, making most adaptations free from royalty fees, this legal distinction essentially comes to define wonderland fan fiction as distinct from those of works outside of the public domain. In short, "fan fiction" generally encompasses extralegal, unpublishable works by devotees of a text or series with a copyright holder in place; commercial adaptations, in contrast, are legally publishable, and thus potentially profitable, works by devotees whose works have entered into the public domain or otherwise given to the public for open use. A text may also cross this largely legal and monetary divide if its author receives permission to use a copyrighted text; for example, Orson Scott Card wrote fan stories set in both universes created by Ray Bradbury and Isaac Asimov, which eventually were published in official literary anthologies (qtd. Whitford).

Fan Fiction

In May 2010, author Diana Gabaldon of the popular Outlander fantasy romance series argued the illegality and immorality of fan fiction, building on a 2008 CompuServe post in which she compared the use of her characters by outside authors to "someone selling your children into white slavery." This article on her personal blog, titled "Fan-Fiction and Moral Conundrums," provoked a strong backlash from Outlander fan communities, leading Gabaldon to eventually remove this post and multiple follow-ups related to her disgust for fan fiction (alternatively fanfiction or fan-fiction).[1] The respondents made a clear comparison between fan fiction as a form of writing and the historic use of pastiche, noting that replication and the use of another author's characters has a long history in literature.

Further study into the division between fan fiction and that of the pastiche is clearly merited. In a previous work, I considered the role of Sherlock Holmes adaptations, with the clear use of the Holmes and Watson characters that occurred during and after Conan Doyle's life. Currently, there exist huge fan communities that create literature related to Sherlock Holmes in relation to popular series such as *Elementary* and *Sherlock* or even the original Conan Doyle works. Such texts

5. Nostalgia, Fan Fiction, and the Wayward Children Series

are available online, published to the web via fan fiction communities like Archive of Our Own and Fanfiction.net. But there are also many books published on this popular detective that have merited subsections for Holmes in bookstores and libraries.

Many speculative fiction authors, particularly the original wonderland writers, never live to see the abundance of fan-based adaptations of their works because they come to fruition posthumously, others celebrate the diverse range of co-authoring that their work spawns, while still others have become well-known in fan communities for trying to curtail "fan fiction." Yet, it is essential to note that much writing, specifically in the wonderland subgenre, is based upon, responds to, or otherwise draws deeply from earlier texts.

The primary arguments against the creation of fan fiction, as explained by author George R.R. Martin of the popular Song of Ice and Fire (Game of Thrones) series, include: (1) in order to maintain a copyright, authors must defend their creative work against fan fiction from a legal perspective, and (2) authors are like parents and protectors to their creations—thus, "play[ing] with" an author's children should require an author's permission (Martin). Other authors, including Gabaldon and Harry Potter author J.K. Rowling (Waters), argue specifically against the use of their characters in erotic fan fiction. These arguments are mirrored in the anti-fan fiction stances of authors like speculative fiction author Orson Scott Card and horror author Anne Rice, who consistently refers to fan fiction as equivalent to rape (Irr 9). Interestingly, most speculative fiction authors support fan creations wholeheartedly or otherwise accept them with some limitations, such as the late speculative fiction author Anne McCaffrey who offered general rules for fan fiction ("Anne McCaffrey").

The arguments against fan fiction can largely be summed up in the following statements and categorizations:

1. The Financial Argument: Fan fiction potentially deprives original creators of profit by reducing their creations to, essentially, generic trademarks (i.e., Thermos, Kleenex, Dumpster, Band-Aid).

2. The Legal Argument: Through violation of copyright statutes, fan fiction authors are breaking the law and impeding on the original creators' copyrights.

3. The Rights of the Author Argument: Fan fiction authors are metaphorically kidnapping, robbing, enslaving, and/or raping original authors' creations by using them without consent.
4. The Anti-Smut Argument: Fan fiction authors often bring characters into sexualized settings in which they would not originally exist.

In the following subsections, I will consider each argument before exploring the positive benefits of fan fiction for particular marginalized communities, including persons with disabilities.

The Financial Argument

Multiple authors have argued that "a copyright MUST BE DEFENDED. If someone infringes on your copyright, and you are aware of the infringement, and you do not defend your copyright, the law assumes that you have abandoned it" (Martin). In order to defend one's copyright ownership over a property, as well as the potential financial benefit to one's heirs, authors must keep their intellectual property from entering the public domain at all costs. Essentially, Martin argues, if a copyright is not defended by its intellectual property holder, then it will become a generic trademark or proprietary eponym, suffering from the so-called "genericide" that has affected brand names that now effectively describe entire products, such as Kleenex, Band-Aid, and Dumpster (Wherry 14). Martin's argument brings to mind infamous stories of brands, such as Disney's decision to sue daycare centers that created murals and other artwork featuring Mickey Mouse and friends in the 1980s (Litman 429). As Wayne State University law professor Jessica Litman explained:

> That's a very good business posture. Being known as the company so aggressive about policing its intellectual property that folks write comic strips and late night skits about it is a very cheap method of deterring infringement, once you've invested what you need to set it up [430].

However, as Litman's analysis highlights, such action is incredibly negative for creators, including Disney, in the long term (430). In fact, *not policing* copyright infringement in the arts, per Litman, has proven to both proliferate and expand interest in original works; it actually tends

5. Nostalgia, Fan Fiction, and the Wayward Children Series

to be more profitable to allow the copyright to be used illegally. As Litman points out, copyright is already very long-lasting: copyright ownership now extends for 95 years from the date of publication for work published between 1928 and 1978, while work published following 1977 extends copyright for the entirety of an author's life plus 70 years, with certain exceptions (Stim).

An extension of the copyright, which according to Litman and countless other voices in the fan and legal communities is already too long, offers *"more than enough* protection to the characters embodied in works of authorship" (431, emphasis in original). Her argument depends on the idea that authors, such as Walt Disney in this case, have greatly drawn upon the public domain in ways that they fail to realize or articulate:

> Walt Disney created Mickey Mouse using preexisting elements. Mickey was not the first cartoon mouse, nor the first cute cartoon mouse. He was probably the first cute motion picture cartoon mouse with a squeaky voice, but other characters had had squeaky voices. The elements of Mickey Mouse's character that Walt Disney drew from the public domain belong to us, the public. The Disney Company has been hanging on to a particular combination of them for a time, but it has them *on loan* from us. Unless Disney is to pull up the bridge after itself, those elements, and their combination in the unique character of Mickey Mouse, need to be returned to the public domain so that the Walt Disneys of tomorrow will have raw materials that they can use to draw new characters [433–434].

The same argument might easily be applied to authors such as George R.R. Martin, who openly expresses the influence of previous authors like J.R.R. Tolkien, creator of *The Lord of the Rings* trilogy (Begley). Tolkien was also influenced by authors whose works are completely or mostly based in the public domain, including George MacDonald (1824–1905), William Morris (1834–1896), H. Rider Haggard (1856–1925), E. Nesbit (1858–1924), and L. Frank Baum (1856–1919) (Anderson). By the copyright rules of today, the vast majority of these authors who influenced an author who influenced Martin could have a copyright claim against him because the first Song of Ice and Fire novel was written in 1991. In short, authors' creations now stand to benefit not only them and their potential children, but the entire lives of potential grandchildren as well—a span of time so long as to extend beyond the artistic and innovation merit-based arguments upon which copyright laws are based.

Disability in Wonderland

As Litman explains, there is no creative justification for extending copyright to such a lengthy period of time. Instead, large corporations that have come to represent individual creators, especially Walt Disney and his Disney Co., have dominated courts in order to allow for such endless trademarks:

> There is also good reason for limiting the scope of intellectual property rights even during the limited time period of protection. We don't give out intellectual property rights to encourage authors to appropriate all of the rents that a given creation might yield. What we want, rather, is to assist authors in earning just enough profit to, first, enhance the creative environment enough to stimulate them to create works in the first place, and, second, encourage them to make their works available to us. If they make a killing, that's great, but it isn't the system's purpose. The system incorporates limitations because its purpose is to benefit all of us in a variety of creativity-enhancing ways [434].

The extension of one's copyright thus becomes ambiguous, particularly with iconic figures such as Mickey Mouse. As such, any other cartoon mouse will have difficulty succeeding because Disney now has the resources to prevent such creatures from entering production on the mere basis of being able to hold them up in court indefinitely.

George R.R. Martin's key argument is that fan fiction and other derivative works would cost him and his descendants potential money, arguing that many fan fiction authors aspire to publish their works because they "just want the bucks." For authors of popular series such as A Song of Ice and Fire and The Lord of the Rings, particularly with the rise of film and television adaptations, there does seem to be infinite money at stake. Yet, it is these very lucrative adaptations that themselves undermine Martin's key point. If "no one gets to abuse the people of Westeros but [him]" then how can he be comfortable with the television adaptation, which hands creative powers over to people who are *decidedly not* Martin? Between the actors' portrayals, the many directors and writers, and even showrunners David Benioff and D.B. Weiss, Martin was given only a minor say in the proceedings, not complete creative ownership. As of the sixth season, the television series went even beyond the current scope of the books. One might argue that Martin's future Ice and Fire novels will, in fact, be adaptations of the series rather than the other way around.

5. Nostalgia, Fan Fiction, and the Wayward Children Series

This is where the monetary argument largely falls apart. Simply put, without the television adaptation and various adaptations of other successful texts, the original writings would eventually lose their cultural capital. Even Martin's cherry-picked examples from speculative fiction history demonstrate this point:

> ERB [Edgar Rice Burroughs] created Tarzan and John Carter of Mars. HPL created Cthulhu and his Mythos. ERB, and later his estate, was extremely protective of his creations. Try to use Tarzan, or even an ape man who was suspiciously similar to Tarzan, without his/their permission, and their lawyers would famously descend on you like a ton of bricks. HPL [H.P. Lovecraft] was the complete opposite. The Cthulhu Mythos soon turned into one of our genre's first shared worlds. HPL encouraged writer friends like Robert Bloch and Clark Ashton Smith to borrow elements from his Cthulhu Mythos, and to add elements as well, which HPL himself would borrow in turn. And in time, other writers who were NOT friends of HPL also began to write Cthulhu Mythos stories, which continues to this day.
> Fair enough. Two writers, two different decisions.
> Thing is, ERB died a millionaire many times over, living on a gigantic ranch in a town that was named Tarzana after his creation. HPL lived and died in genteel poverty, and some biographers have suggested that poor diet brought on by poverty may have hastened his death. HPL was a far more beloved figure amongst other writers, but love will only get you so far. Sometimes it's nice to be able to have a steak too. The Burroughs estate was paid handsomely for every Tarzan movie ever made, and collected plenty on the PRINCESS OF MARS movie I worked on during my Hollywood years, and no doubt is still collecting on the one currently in development ... though the book is in the public domain by now. Did the Lovecraft estate make a penny off THE DUNWICH HORROR movie, the HERBERT WEST, REANIMATOR movie, the recent DAGON movie, the internet version of CALL OF CTHULHU? I don't know. I rather doubt it. If they did, I'll betcha it was just chump change. Meanwhile, new writers go right on mining the Cthulhu mythos, writing new stories and novels.
> Cthulhu, like John Carter, is in the public domain by now, I know. But it wouldn't matter. Because HPL let so many others play in his sandbox, he essentially lost control of his own creations ["Someone Is Angry"].

Here is where Martin and many other anti-fan fiction writers miss the point. Consider the cultural impact of Lovecraft vs. Burroughs: a mere Google search of "Lovecraft" vs. "Edgar Rice Burroughs" offers a whopping 31 million to 4.8 million returns and "A Princess of Mars" returns fewer than 500,000 search hits. *Tarzan* returned to the cultural sphere in 1999 through the power of the Disney Company's marketing mechanism and, at the time, a production cost valued higher than any animated film ever before (Rukstad and Collis). I contend that such success stems from Disney shifting its response to copyright infringement in the Second Disney Renaissance era from 2010 to present. Key acquisitions of this time have greatly shaped the company as a whole. In 2006, Disney acquired digital animation studio Pixar, in 2009, Marvel, and in 2012, LucasFilm. During this time period, Disney has become lax in its prosecution of fans who not only create derivative works, but who actively sell them through such venues as comic book conventions, Etsy, and DeviantArt. Animator and writer Katie Cook began her career and achieved acclaim through fan art, including art that depicted characters from Disney Animation, Marvel, and Lucasfilm. Her DeviantArt and personal websites demonstrate the progression of her artistic career, including a note that her fan drawings of the Hasbro-owned My Little Pony series eventually garnered enough attention on Twitter to lead to a deal for a licensed comic book series with the copyright holder.

Proliferation of derivative work by fans, as demonstrated through this and countless other examples, expands the life cycle of an author's creations, keeps these works culturally relevant, helps original artists and corporations find talented collaborators, and even renews interest in the primary texts themselves. The popularity of Stephen Schwartz's *Wicked* musical, based on the Gregory Maguire novel which was itself an adaptation of L. Frank Baum's *The Wizard of Oz*, not only led to increased sales of Maguire's text, but of Baum's works as well (Kelleter). While other creators benefit financially through unlicensed adaptations, the original creators often profit from the continued significance of their creative works.

The Legal Argument

According to Gabaldon and many other authors who are against fan fiction, the practice is indisputably illegal. U.S. law, however, disproves her claim. In the case of *The Wind Done Gone* author Alice Randall, represented by Houghton Mifflin, vs. Suntrust Bank, representing the estate of *Gone with the Wind* author Margaret Mitchell, the injunction against Randall was summarily vacated. Even this monetary

5. Nostalgia, Fan Fiction, and the Wayward Children Series

adaptation of Mitchell's work was found to constitute fair use on the merit of critiquing the original work.

Fan fiction critics argue that some fan fiction authors profit indirectly through platforms like GoFundMe gift-based accounts that may be popularized through fan fiction notes (qtd. in Nepveu). Others question the ethics of Patreon, which provides content to "subscribers" who pay a certain amount of money to artists each month (ChancellorGriffin). However, these donations or patronage-based services do not offer a specific product for a specific price. Per their websites, GoFundMe donations are considered "personal gifts" and Patreon subscriptions are considered "donations." While the distinctions between a product-based model for financial transactions and these models may seem gray, the legal difference is, in fact, quite clear. Any fan adaptation that is not published as a product for direct profit is legal under current U.S. fair use laws. Profit, in terms of a product-purchase relationship, is key for copyright law to be broken and this simply is not true in many fan fiction cases (Chase).

The Rights of the Author Argument

Strangely similar to the conception of biofuturity defined earlier in this book, multiple authors have referred to their creations as surrogate children of sorts. Martin refers to the people of Westeros as though they are his progeny: "My characters are my children, I have been heard to say. I don't want people making off with them, thank you. Even people who say they love my children." Gabaldon refers to fan fiction as "someone selling your children into white slavery." Historically, many authors have referred to their work as their children and the period of writing as a period of gestation, including those who have actual children. As explained in Barthes's essential "Death of the Author" essay:

> The Author, when we believe in him, is always conceived as the past of his own book: the book and the author take their places of their own accord on the same line, cast as a before and an after: the Author is supposed to feed the book—that is, he pre-exists it, thinks, suffers, lives for it; he maintains with his work the same relation of antecedence a father maintains with his child [4].

Even without considering the problematic equation of literary creations with literal human beings, this argument implies an incredibly property-based understanding of one's children. U.S. law is inherently patriarchal and paternalistic, particularly with regard to the role of children, "the law's current approach to paternity disputes reflects a classic model of property rights and ownership rooted in static, rigid, and exclusive claims" (Noble Maillard 3). Even if children are thought to be one's legal property until the age of adulthood, a parent's 18-year-old+ children are under no legal or moral obligation to do as their parents direct. If we are to think of original works as children on which adaptations are based, then the authors should have no right to directly command behavior after 18 years, a far shorter period than a traditional copyright. As a parent, grandparent, or creator, one simply must accept that one will lose ownership of one's creations at some point. Just as one's parents must pass, so too must the author, per Barthes, die and leave her children to carry on her legacy however they see fit.

The Anti-Smut Argument

As an industry, pornography has a long history of depicting popular media in relation to sexual acts. From small Tijuana bibles depicting pornographic comics in the 1920s–1960s to a popular meme, Rule 34, which states that "if it exists, there is porn of it" with no exceptions, pornography has been linked to nearly every popular series and publication in modern history. While cases against pornographic depictions of copyrighted characters have historically sided with original creators, such as in the landmark 1978 *Walt Disney Productions v. Air Pirates* case, there is simply *so much derivative* pornography in the internet age that the law has yet to catch up in a meaningful way to handle the excessive volume of potential claims (Carlisle). The primary function of most pornography is neither social commentary nor humor, and thus, the parody argument simply does not apply to paid pornography.

Free pornography, such as that offered by some DeviantArt creators, is legal for the reasons included in the previous sections. Thus, fan fiction created for mature audiences, particularly slash fiction which features an emphasis on same-queer relationships, often sexual, is perfectly legal. As the following sections will demonstrate, in lieu of actual representation of queer relationships in mainstream series, such content may even constitute a form of activism.

5. *Nostalgia, Fan Fiction, and the Wayward Children Series*

Historical Fiction vs. Fan Fiction

Authors, including Gabaldon herself, seem to have no problem with utilizing *actual* ancestors of living persons to tell their stories. In fact, the historic figures who appear in the Outlander series include Marie Louise de La Tour d'Auvergne, Louis XV, Bonnie Prince Charlie, Simon Fraser, 11th Lord Lovat, the Comte de Saint Germain, and others. Historical fiction has long existed as an acceptable and uncomplicated genre whose popular success is demonstrated through both sales and literary awards. Literary theorist Harry E. Shaw goes so far as to say that "few intellectual developments in the last 200 years [prior to 1983] have affected us more profoundly than the enriched sense of historicity which emerged in the 18th century" (9). While he argues that "the historical novel ... suffers from neglect, even contempt" (9) in some arenas, Shaw demonstrates that the historical novel has a long lifespan, originating from such lauded figures as Balzac, Tolstoy, Scott, Herder, Marx, and Ranke (9).

There are many examples of wildly successful and critically acclaimed historical novels in the twentieth and twenty-first centuries. Margaret Mitchell's Pulitzer and National Book Award winning *Gone with the Wind* is set during the U.S. Civil War, including references and depictions of such characters as Confederate officer Wade Hampton III. Lists of major literary award-winning novels and bestsellers are simultaneously filled with historical fiction, from Edith Wharton's Pulitzer Prize–winning *The Age of Innocence* (published in 1920, referring to and set in the 1870s' so-called Gilded Age) to Colson Whitehead's Pulitzer Prize–winning *The Underground Railroad* (published in 2016, set in an alternate 1800s). The popularity of historical fiction among critics and readers alike is even more profound in children's literature, where the ALA's Phoenix Award and Newbery Medal are sometimes thought to "experience [...] a bias in favor of historical fiction" (Kidd).

Many pop culture critics, including the women at feminist media nonprofit *Feminist Frequency,* have pointed out that the depiction of historic events and historically marginalized persons in these works is often highly problematic. Essentially, significant figures and activists who are women, LGBTQ folk and allies, and persons of color are often shown to support causes they abhorred in life or not shown to support key ideologies. For example, they reviewed Woody Allen's 2011 fantasy comedy *Midnight in Paris*, in which Academy Award-winning actress Kathy Bates portrays Gertrude Stein. In the film, Stein speaks almost entirely to male protagonist Gil, even going so far as to support him in the writing of his first novel. *Feminist Frequency* host Anita Sarkeeshian notes that "one of the most important historical figures that Gil interacts with is Gertrude Stein ... one of the most famous writers *and lesbians* in American history. And Woody Allen has the nerve to not have her speak to another female character in the entire film" ("The 2012 Oscars and the Bechdel Test," emphasis in original). Similarly, openly pansexual feminist icon Frida Kahlo, depicted in the 2017 film *Coco*, only speaks with male characters. In a classic example from feminist film criticism, Disney's *Pocahontas* depicts an adult Powhatan princess who is more concerned with protecting the rights of White settlers than defending her tribe.

Fighting back against these appropriations of marginalized historical figures to reaffirm their legacy is not only ethical but necessary. A much-cited example in fan fiction legal studies is *Suntrust Bank v. Houghton Mifflin Co.* This 2001 legal case, which was overseen by the United States Court of Appeals for the Eleventh Circuit, surrounded a coquel of Margaret Mitchell's 1936 *Gone with the Wind*. The case concerned Alice Randall's *The Wind Done Gone*, which tells the story of *Gone with the Wind* from the perspective of Scarlett O'Hara's mixed-race half-sister, Cynara, and offers a critique of the way that Black and mixed-race characters were portrayed in the original novel. The case was settled prior to an official decision, but the court noted that fair use was found:

> The court held that defendant's borrowing from GWTW was fair use. The court first found that the defendant's novel was in fact a parody because it commented on or criticized an original work by appropriating its elements to create a new artistic work. Specifically, TWDG criticizes GWTW's depiction of slavery and race relations in the antebellum South [U.S. Copyright Office Fair Use Index].

In this case, the distinction between coquel and fan fiction is noticeably blurred. As demonstrated by many of the authors against fan derivatives, not all adaptations are of as high of quality or content as *The Wind Done Gone*. Clearly, one may imagine them arguing, *The Wind Done*

Gone, while focusing on a sex worker, also offers more than simple pleasure reading or pornography. However, as the following section demonstrates, even mundane, hypersexualized, or otherwise poorly written adaptations can be meaningful.

Feminist critic Carole Pateman built her argument in Second Wave Feminism around the very idea that the personal is political (Bargetz), and more recent scholars have built upon this notion to argue that the everyday has a key place within the political sphere (Bargetz). Sexuality has been a key space for activism in many movements, including feminism, LGBTQ rights, and disability rights movements. Finally, any judgment against quality must be dismissed because fan fiction by its very definition builds an ouvre of the *fan*—it is by amateurs and celebrated as such. Alternatively, some fan fiction may be of literary award-winning quality, and some pastiches have been published to awards: the WH Smith Literary Award (Jean Rhys's 1966 *Wide Sargasso Sea*; a parallel tale to *Jane Eyre*), the PEN/Faulkner Award for Fiction (Michael Cunningham's 1998 *The Hours;* a fictional coquel, biography, and response to the impact of *Mrs. Dalloway*), the Tony Award (Tom Stoppard's 1966 *Rosencrantz and Guildenstern Are Dead*; a parallel tale to *Hamlet*), the Pulitzer Price (Geraldine Brooks's 2006 *March*; a parallel tale to *Little Women*), the ALA Alex Award, Huston/Wright Legacy Award, New York Public Library Books for the Teen Age Award (Nancy Rawles's 2005 *My Jim*; a parallel tale to *Huckleberry Finn*), and countless others.

Adaptation as a Tool for Representation

What those decrying fan fiction fail to take into consideration is the ways in which fan adaptations have been utilized as a key point of activism, culture building, and representation for marginalized groups. First, it may be useful to consider the perspectives offered in the adaptive novels and parodies mentioned in the previous paragraph.

Title: *The Wind Done Gone* (2001).
Author and Bio: Alice Randall—"She is a Harvard educated African-American novelist who lives in Nashville and writes country songs" (Randall, "Bio").

Disability in Wonderland

Original Title: *Gone with the Wind* (1936) by Margaret Mitchell.

Abbreviated Adaptation Description: "Alice Randall explodes the world created in *Gone with the Wind*, a work that more than any other has defined our image of the antebellum South. Taking sharp aim at the romanticized, whitewashed mythology perpetrated by this southern classic, Randall has ingeniously conceived a multilayered, emotionally complex tale of her own—that of Cynara, the mulatto half-sister, who, beautiful and brown and born into slavery, manages to break away from the damaging world of the Old South" (Randall, *The Wind Done Gone*, back cover copy).

Title: *Wide Sargasso Sea* (1966).

Author and Bio: "Taunted with the cruel nickname the 'white cockroach' as a child, the author Jean Rhys grew up on the Caribbean island of Dominica. She was the daughter of a Creole mother and a Welsh father and always felt distant from both the black and white communities" (Thorpe).

Original Title: *Jane Eyre* (1847) by Charlotte Brontë.

Abbreviated Adaptation Description: Rhys "ingeniously brings into light one of fiction's most fascinating characters: the madwoman in the attic from Charlotte Brontë's *Jane Eyre*. This mesmerizing work introduces us to Antoinette Cosway, a sensual and protected young woman who is sold into marriage to the prideful Mr. Rochester. Rhys portrays Cosway amidst a society so driven by hatred, so skewed in its sexual relations, that it can literally drive a woman out of her mind" (Rhys, back cover copy).

Title: *The Hours* (1999).

Author and Bio: Michael Cunningham "lives in New York, in the neighbourhood where he set part of *The Hours* ... and five minutes from the loft he shares with his partner of 24 years, Ken Corbett" (Brockes).

Original Title: *Mrs. Dalloway* (1925) by Virginia Woolf.

Abbreviated Adaptation Description: "*The Hours* tells the story of three women: Virginia Woolf, beginning to write *Mrs. Dalloway* as she recuperates in a London suburb with her husband in 1923; Clarissa Vaughan, beloved friend of an acclaimed poet dying from AIDS, who in modern-day New York is planning a party in his honor; and Laura Brown, in a 1949 Los Angeles suburb, who slowly begins to feel the constraints of a perfect family and home" (Cunningham, back cover copy).

5. Nostalgia, Fan Fiction, and the Wayward Children Series

Title: *Rosencrantz and Guildenstern Are Dead* (1966).

Author and Bio: "Playwright Sir Tom Stoppard was born Tomás Straüssler on 3 July 1937 in Zlín, Czechoslovakia. He grew up in Singapore and India during the Second World War and moved to England in 1946 with his mother and stepfather, his own father having been killed in Singapore" (British Council).

Original Title: *Hamlet* (c. 1599–1602) by William Shakespeare.

Abbreviated Adaptation Description: Rosencrantz and Guildenstern are the college chums of Hamlet and their story is what happened behind the scenes in Shakespeare's play. What were they doing there in Elsinore anyway? "I don't know; we were sent for." They are not only anti agents, but also anti sympathy, anti-identification, and in fact anti persons, which is uniquely demonstrated by their having such a hard time recollecting which of them goes by what name. The Players come and go; Prince Hamlet comes through reading words, words, words; foul deeds are done; Hamlet is sent abroad, escapes death; and in turn Rosencrantz and Guildenstern find their "only exit is death" (Stoppard, back cover copy).

Title: *March* (2005) by Geraldine Brooks.

Author and Bio: "Australian-born Geraldine Brooks grew up in Sydney. She worked as a reporter for *The Sydney Morning Herald* and *The Wall Street Journal*, where she covered crises in the mideast, Africa and the Balkans" (Brooks, "Geraldine Brooks").

Original Title: *Little Women* (1868–1869) by Louisa May Alcott.

Abbreviated Adaptation Description: "Geraldine Brooks has animated the character of the absent father, March, and crafted a story 'filled with the ache of love and marriage and with the power of war upon the mind and heart of one unforgettable man'" (Sue Monk Kidd). With "pitch-perfect writing" (*USA Today*), "Brooks follows March as he leaves behind his family to aid the Union cause in the Civil War. His experiences will utterly change his marriage and challenge his most ardently held beliefs" (Brooks, *March*, back cover copy).

Title: *My Jim* (2005) by Nancy Rawles.

Author and Bio: "Nancy Rawles is the author of three critically acclaimed and award-winning novels—*My Jim* (Crown Publishing 2005); *Crawfish Dreams* (Doubleday, 2003), and *Love Like Gumbo* (Fjord

Disability in Wonderland

Press, 1997). All three novels address issues of sexuality, violence, and racial oppression in the lives of their female protagonists" ("The Feminist Sexual Ethics Project").

Original Title: *The Adventures of Huckleberry Finn* (1884) by Mark Twain.

Abbreviated Adaptation Description: "Written in the great literary tradition of novels of American slavery, *My Jim* is told in the incantatory voice of Sadie Watson, an ex-slave who schools her granddaughter with lessons of love she learned in bondage. To help her granddaughter confront the decisions she needs to make, Sadie mines her memory for the tale of the unquenchable love of her life, Jim. Sadie's Jim was an ambitious young slave and seer who, when faced with the prospect of being sold, escaped down the Mississippi with a white boy named Huck. Sadie is suddenly left alone. Worried about her children, convinced her husband is dead, reviled as a witch, and punished for Jim's escape, Sadie's will and her love for Jim, even in absentia, animate her life and see her through. Told with spare eloquence and mirroring the true stories of countless slave women, *My Jim* re-creates one of the most controversial characters in American literature" (Rawles, back cover copy).

This is merely a sampling of fiction that derives elements from earlier texts, but the rationale for revisiting key books and plays is clear. These authors seek to subvert classic narratives by refocusing on key characters, groups, or elements that were mostly invisible or erased from the original text.

Adaptations such as those by Randall and Rawles meaningfully reorient classic narratives that minimize the lives of enslaved persons and the controversial use of Black characters as plot devices to further the key narratives of White protagonists. In a retelling of Shakespeare's *The Tempest*, Nalo Hopkinson's 2002 short story "Shift" focuses on the minor characters of Ariel and Caliban. She explains the motivations for her retelling in an interview with journalist Terry Bisson of *Outspoken* magazine:

> Let's see ... in the play, Prospero is a rich white duke who's been exiled to a small island with his beautiful daughter Miranda. There he finds an ethereal fairy named Ariel who's been trapped inside a split tree by a white Algerian (African) witch named Sycorax. Sycorax had been exiled to the island

5. Nostalgia, Fan Fiction, and the Wayward Children Series

earlier, while pregnant with her son Caliban. Sycorax has died, leaving Ariel imprisoned and Caliban abandoned. Prospero frees Ariel and requires her servitude in return, but promises to release her eventually. Prospero takes Caliban in and teaches him to read, but when Caliban attempts to rape Miranda, Prospero makes him a slave (as in, no promise of release). Ariel gets all the flitting-about jobs and Caliban gets all the hard labour. Prospero repeatedly ridicules Caliban. Ariel helps Prospero and Miranda get off the island, and thus wins freedom. I think we're supposed to identify with Prospero and Miranda, but I was disturbed by Ariel's servitude and Caliban's slavery, and even though Prospero eventually pardons Caliban, I had trouble with the play's relentless mockery of Caliban as a "savage."

A few years ago I was visiting Kamau Brathwaite's literature class at NYU, and they were discussing Caliban. I had the insight that Ariel and Caliban could be seen as the house Negro and the field Negro, and I proceeded to mess with the story from there [*Report from Planet Midnight*, 94].

These narratives seek to interrogate the problematic elements of classic tales by shifting characters of color—who are often derided, written in an attempt at cultural vernacular, and trope-defining—to the center of the stories in which they appear.

Jean Rhys also seeks to refocus the *Jane Eyre* narrative on Mrs. Rochester as someone more than the iconic "madwoman in the attic," critiqued by Gilbert and Gubar in the 1979 book of the same name. Within the context of *Jane Eyre*, Rochester's wife, Bertha Mason, acts as a plot point rather than a full character. Her initial function is to prevent Eyre and Rochester from marrying on the basis of her behavior, while also offering a tragic history to explain and excuse the moody behavior of the arrogant Rochester. Mason is described in animalistic terms as a burden on Rochester rather than a person with intellectual disabilities:

> In the deep shade, at the farther end of the room, a figure ran backwards and forwards. What it was, whether beast or human being, one could not, at first sight, tell: it grovelled, seemingly, on all fours; it snatched and growled like some strange wild animal: but it was covered with clothing, and a quantity of dark, grizzled hair, wild as a mane, hid its head and face.

As noted by Gilbert and Gubar, Mason is marginalized in multiple ways: through her disabilities, her mixed-race heritage, and as a woman within the nineteenth-century context (xxxvi). She is a character "created only to be destroyed" (Gilbert and Gubar 78) until her story is

Disability in Wonderland

expanded upon by Rhys. Rhys places Mason in the center of the narrative, rather than Eyre's relationship with Rochester, as the key romance of his life. In doing so, she explicitly questions the racial hierarchy in *Jane Eyre* while also offering personhood to a character defined solely via her mental illness. Gilbert and Gubar predominantly argue that Mason depicts "madness as rebellion" (Donaldson 100); Mason is not so much mentally ill as she is raging against a deeply racist and patriarchal society in a manner deemed improper. In a recent 2002 critique of the text, medical humanities scholar Elizabeth J. Donaldson argues that Rhys's novel "gives voice to the previously silent madwoman and depicts what some might consider the causes of her madness—a difficult childhood, a dangerous social climate, and her husband's ultimate betrayal" (100). In Rhys's text, Donaldson argues, it is not Mason's madness that leads to her being locked in the attic, but rather her being locked in the attic that drives her mad.

Such marginalized characters have often existed both on the margins of narratives and society. As explained in intermedial literary theorist Caren Irr's pivotal text on the feminist nature of fan fiction, the creative commons, and alternative practices to copyright protection, *Pink Pirates*, women and persons from marginalized groups have historically maintained a less than legitimate and often extralegal writing sphere. Such persons often had no ownership over their own creations or even their own bodies, through enslavement, status as the property of one's husband or father, and laws eliminating personal property. For those working toward grand social change, including persons of color, women, and other marginalized populations, as Irr so poignantly summarizes, "ensuring originality and protecting copyright could be less vital than defending a friend's honor or working for emancipation." Prior to the first official wave of feminist history, few women were published. Yet, Irr notes:

> ...although officially excluded from copyright ownership as individuals, women writers were still active in the market ... some even became notorious and exposed themselves to notorious public attack by flaunting conventions that urged anonymous publication as the most genteel strategy for entering the public sphere. Susana Rowson, for instance, not only published a popular novel [1791's *Charlotte Temple*] under her own name, but also took to the stage and opened her own school for women—activities all

the more notable for her undertaking them in a situation in which she was unable to exercise a full complement of economic rights because of her status as a married woman.

Those who did not have the privilege of being married, have a supportive publisher, or have the patronage of a father or other living relative, however, turned to what Irr terms "pink piracy," the illegal or informal sharing of creative works outside of the realm of a patriarchal copyright structure. Unable to be taken seriously or otherwise dismissed as silly (Petersen 189), women and other marginalized populations were denied access to copyright ownership, and thus created their own spheres of literature. Such literatures were privatized, per Irr's analysis, while their male counterparts were publicized and praised.

Nostalgia and Anti-Utopianism

Many contemporary underlands and even wonderlands are written not only with some understanding of these distinctions but also the failures of earlier utopic idealism in mind. In the next few chapters, I specifically unpack the merging of the so-called "real world" and the wonderland spaces in these postmodern wonderland texts. Yet, it is also useful to consider how the underland, in particular, pokes fun at nostalgia and efforts for utopic spaces in a critical manner; which is to say that the postmodern wonderland often merges the "real world" and the underland with an understanding that the world we inhabit offers many, though perhaps not all, of the characteristics of a wonderland space. Seanan McGuire's Wayward Children series includes a world compass that notably includes Earth, or the "real word," as one of its multiverses; tellingly, she is thus arguing that Earth itself has come to offer many aspects of a wonderland (it is considered a world of mid-level logic, low-level wickedness) (Stubby the Rocket). Notably, the Wayward Children series is extremely steeped in fan community, with the world compass famously mapped out in image form and built upon by Tor.com's Jamie Stafford-Hill. Because Tor is the official publisher of the Wayward Children series, this kind of collective worldbuilding and engagement with fan culture leads to deeper engagement with the texts. Furthermore, such involvement provides open communication

Disability in Wonderland

between author and fans, allows the author to build upon fan ideas, and effectively allows McGuire to share the reigns of creation with her fans. As someone who is clearly drawing upon previous works that happen to be in the public domain, particularly the early wonderlands, as well as drawing inspiration from copyrighted wonderlands, McGuire could easily be called a fan fiction author. In fact, she herself has spoken about beginning her writing practice as a fan fiction author, before turning to original works (Bundel). Incidentally, her familiarity with the wonderland canon may be best displayed in her naming of her cats Alice Price-Healy Liddel Little Abernathy McGuire (presumably for Dodgson's friend, Alice Liddell) and Thomas Price Lin Rhymer Taylor McGuire (possibly for Thomas Taylor, original illustrator for the Harry Potter books). McGuire's blog has a particularly telling "Fifty Thoughts on Writing" post, which clarifies exactly the reality that the author is the god of their text but also an incredibly fallible god who is sometimes overthrown:

> You are the author. That makes you, effectively, God. God created the mosquito. Sometimes, God can screw the pooch in a very big way. Being the author doesn't mean that you're incapable of being wrong. Sometimes, you'll write things that are out of character. Sometimes, you'll write things that are out of place. And sometimes, you'll write things that are just flat-out incorrect and inaccurate and insane and *wrong*. That's not a bad thing. The bad thing is refusing to admit it [emphasis in original].

She further notes that fans are far more likely to notice such things as inconsistencies, out-of-character moments, and other mistakes. In short, in the search for perfection as a writer, one must have the fan's gaze.

As a queer, mixed-race woman Seanan McGuire is also one of the voices from less traditionally published authors to emerge in recent years. The previous lack of legal publication venues for persons of color, persons with disabilities, women and gender minorities, and queer folx make twenty-first century speculative fiction more diverse in terms of both representation and storytelling, but also provide a space for these historically marginalized voices to critique their very marginalization. And, as I'll argue in the following chapters, it is specifically this fictocritical element that makes the underland and contemporary wonderland so essential to literary criticism.

Chapter 6

The Underland and the Rejection of the Medical Model of Disability

The now-popular 1985 Disney film *Return to Oz* marks a notable shift in representations of the literary wonderland. In stark contrast to the sun-filled pastoral scene and chipper music on which the 1939 *Wizard of Oz* opens, *Return to Oz* begins with darkness and an eerie orchestra piece. From the first moments, the film is meant to instill fear in the viewer. The darkness fades and we are given a diagonal shot of Dorothy's room. A sleepless Dorothy stares out at the audience from her bed. Almost immediately, we are then reintroduced to her fretful caretakers, who discuss borrowing money from relatives in order to take Dorothy to a doctor in "electric healing," essentially electroconvulsive therapy (ECT). "It's been six months since the tornado," Aunt Em laments, "and Dorothy hasn't been herself since... All she ever talks about is someplace that just doesn't exist. Talkin' tin men, walkin' scarecrows, ruby slippers." Rather than understood as the dreams of a young girl, as in the 1939 film, Dorothy's visions of Oz are treated as pathological, something inherently seen as negative.

Dorothy is taken to a psychotherapist, Dr. Worley, to whom she describes her experience of Oz. She begins by explaining how the Tin Man lost his flesh parts and had them replaced with prostheses. Unflinchingly she tells of his dismemberment and recreation with tin, a detail tellingly left out of the 1939 film. She goes on to explain experiences shared between the book and film: the talking lion, the living scarecrow, and the magic slippers that brought her back home. Dr.

Disability in Wonderland

Worley quickly diagnoses her and explains her condition to the small girl and her Aunt Em in simple terms: "I know just the thing to cheer Dorothy up," "this electrical marvel will ... get rid of all those bad waking dreams."

Rather than being swept away to Oz by a painless, albeit terrifying, tornado, Dorothy in *Return to Oz* is transported back whilst trying to escape the facility at which she is to receive the ECT treatments; she is led by a young girl to a river in which she seemingly drowns back to Oz. The film continues to portray a dark and disturbing vision of Oz, complete with Mombi, a villain who collects heads to wear; Wheelies, persons with wheels for hands and feet; her friends, the Tin Man and Lion, transformed into stone; and a completely destroyed ruin of the Emerald City. Early reviewers noted the terror imbued in this vision of Oz, calling it "grim" (Maslin), "bleak, creepy, and occasionally terrifying" (Kehr), while noting that it would likely scare most children (Maslin; Siskel). Thirty-five years later, the film is still noted for the negative effect it has on young children, with Common Sense Media suggesting closer to a PG-13 than PG rating.

What is more meaningful in terms of this film's representation of the wonderland, however, is the fact that many of the elements that purportedly make this film scary are actually also those which depict disability. Most clearly depicted through the story of the Tin Man losing his limbs, the three visions of Oz offer three different visions of disability and how it was viewed within U.S. culture as well. In the 1901 novel, the Tin Man's dismemberment is offered in a detached manner, while the 1939 film ignores the character's backstory altogether. When Dorothy relates the tale to Dr. Worley in *Return to Oz*, however, the doctor looks back at her with concern. While Dorothy offers the facts of her friend's past without judgment, the adults in the room with her reinforce the rules of the normate world upon her wonderland. The Tin Man and Wheelie's bodies, in particular, are treated as horrific by the adults because of their prostheses. The inanimacy of the Cowardly Lion and Tin Man are marked as though a permanent death rather than a temporary state of being, despite the Tin Man having been similarly rendered immobile in the first book and film. The removal and replacement of heads, normalized by Jack Pumpkinhead's literal pumpkin heads rotting and being interchanged with fresher pumpkins is simply a matter of fact

6. The Underland and the Rejection of the Medical Model

in *The Marvelous Land of Oz*, one of the texts on which *Return to Oz* is based. Yet, in the film, the loss of his head is treated as though tantamount to death. Jack's adamance in referring to Dorothy as his mother is particularly haunting in this scene; he plaintively cries, "help me, mother!" as his head disappears below the clouds, his lifeless body left behind. The deeply negative and disturbing portrayal of ECT and medicalization of Dorothy's experiences furthers the connection between disability and the wonderland, such that even wonderlands themselves are suggested to be mere hallucinations or the results of psychoses.

Disability, in these underland narratives, becomes a marker for the denial of nostalgia. To be true, the eras in which the original wonderland narratives were written were marked by the institutionalization and sterilization of many persons diagnosed with disabilities. Disability historian Kim E. Nielsen notes that the period in which *Alice's Adventures in Wonderland* (1865) was written saw English Common Law, and the U.S. which adopted it through the reception statute, distinguishing between citizens and non-citizens on the basis of disability, as well as race, gender, and other features. *Peter Pan* (1904) and *The Wizard of Oz* (1901) reached U.S. audiences during the so-called "Progressive Era," most distinguishable by the *Buck v. Bell* (1927) decision that continued the practice of compulsory sterilization for many persons deemed disabled. Nielsen notes that more than 65,000 persons were forcibly sterilized in the United States by the 1960s, mostly women and predominantly persons deemed disabled, racial minorities, and the poor (100). Those texts in the latter period of the wonderland era, such as the Narnia series (1950–1956), are notably affected by both world wars and the increased presence of visible disability on the home front, including protests by disability activists.

In this chapter, I will offer a more in-depth view of the underland as representative of a shift back toward the ableist notions of perfection that initially fell out of favor following the end of World War II and the Holocaust. As the real-life consequences of eugenic practices began to fade from recent history, visions of the "right" kind of utopia, or a utopia populated solely by non-disabled persons, started to gain popularity again. And, as such, wonderlands previously considered utopic were reconsidered and often represented as actually dystopic in nature. Narratives began to suggest that, instead of bodily and mental differences

Disability in Wonderland

being worthy of utopic settings, disabilities were again states that ought to be eliminated in a perfect world. As a direct response to the original Oz books and the 1939 *Wizard of Oz* film, *Return to Oz* offers a clear and useful example of this shift. While released in 1985, rather early in the movement toward genetic personhood or humanity as defined by genes, it well indicates that, with the pushback against progress in the disability rights movements. With the birth of Dolly the Sheep, a cloned ovine, in 1996, I argue, so too returned the idea of some genes being superior to others. This chapter particularly utilizes Jordan Peele's *Us* (2019) as a more recent example of how prevalent the underland has become, in addition to the presence of abilist notions of futurity, and the movement of the wonderland from a child-centered space to one that purposefully denies nostalgia.

Us and the Subversion of the Heroine's Journey

By 2019, the transformation of the wonderland into the underland was complete. Children are no longer filled with awe when they enter into these magical spaces but, instead, terror. Jordan Peele's *Us* was specifically marketed as a horror film while drawing upon imagery associated with Wonderland (a red queen, a white rabbit, mirrors, the descent into another world, and even the protagonist's name, "Adelaide White" echoing the title, *Alice in Wonderland*) and Neverland (whistling, the danger of water, shadow people, people in trees). Furthermore, *Us* offers a clear example of the wonderland narrative cycle, including: (1) a heroine's journey; (2) monsters, fairy folk, or talking animals; (3) rules that differ largely from those of the real world, in terms of morality, science, and economics/government; (4) physicality and literal existence, otherwise known as geographic realism; (5) visited largely by children or child-like figures from our own world, usually female; (6) magic and sorcery; and (6) monarchs and tyrants, (7) interrupted or largely noticed by the visit of a human protagonist. Unlike previous wonderlands, however, much of this narrative occurs interstitially—what goes unsaid or undepicted offers a glimpse into the way magic operates in the underland.

Arguably, the **heroine journeying** (1) in *Us* could be either

6. The Underland and the Rejection of the Medical Model

Adelaide or Red, as both the underground and aboveground worlds constitute wonderlands for those who are outsiders. However, as presented upon its first viewing, one is first drawn to Adelaide as the hero of the film with the belief that she is the young girl who encounters her shadow figure (here called "the Tethered"), an underworld counterpart to herself in **the ordinary world (1.1)**. Without the ending narrative twist, we are provided with Adelaide as clear sympathetic protagonist who ventures into the unknown after an initial refusal of the call. Her initial **call to adventure (1.2)** from the ordinary world occurs at the Santa Monica Pier (**4. Geographic Realism**), where young Adelaide (**5. The Child Protagonist**) is drawn to a funhouse with the sign, "Vision Quest: Find Yourself." Inside the attraction, Adelaide becomes afraid and attempts to escape, only to find herself lost in a hall of mirrors. Eventually, she comes across what appears to be her reflection but which turns out to be her Tethered self. Because the film then abruptly cuts to the opening credits before returning to an adult Adelaide eating with her family, we are led to believe that Adelaide somehow escapes this moment or that it has merely appeared as a dream. Rather than descending into the underland of the Tethered, she is able to stay in the ordinary world.

As the Tethered begin invading the land above, however, Adelaide is rendered unable to ignore the underland, leading her to face **tests (1.3)**. In order to save her son, Adelaide ventures to the land of the Tethered, revisiting the funhouse now rebranded as "Merlin's Forest." As she wanders toward the underland, Adelaide easily traverses the maze and a seemingly infinite number of rabbits; notably, one of these rabbits accompanies Adelaide's son, Jason, as a pet at the end of the film. The vocalizations on the soundtrack over a setting bereft of human life suggests speech on the part of the rabbits, much as the animalistic Tethered themselves prove capable of speech.

The approach (1.4) occurs as Adelaide slowly ventures nearer to Red in order to face the final **ordeal (1.5)** through their violent confrontation. In this final battle, the two face off in a fight scene choreographed over an orchestral version of "Five on It," a theme for the film, made to appear as though a dance. Reunited with her son (**1.6 The Reward**), Adelaide returns with him to the overworld and the other members of their family (**1.7 The Road Back**).

The wonderland story here is truncated, representing around 25 percent of the film's total contents. Yet, still further themes of the wonderland narrative appear, particularly through the dialogue and specific word choices that are utilized in the film; Red's monologue upon invading the Wilsons' summer home is particularly telling as it mirrors the format of a fairytale. For example, while monsters do not literally appear in *Us*, Red describes delivering Umbrae as giving "birth to a monster" (**2. Monsters, Fairy-Folk, and Talking Animals**). Red speaks of the laws that govern the Tethered, including the mirroring of their overland counterparts and being forced to "eat rabbits, raw and bloody" (**3. A New System of Law**).

Furthermore, the existence of magic in the underland is merely subtextual. It is mostly the implausible characteristics of the underland that mark it as a place guided, at least in part, by sorcery (**6. Magic and Sorcery**). While Red does not know the origins of the Tethered, she speculates that these shadow persons were created by the U.S. government in order to achieve control over the populace. Her word choice, however, suggests a more mystical origin. While Red believes that the government "figured out how to make a copy of the body," she does not feel that the soul could be replicated. She speaks of having conversations with God, describing his voice as "the most beautiful sound I've ever heard." Furthermore, many of the qualities of the underland characterized as failures in worldbuilding actually suggest a more mystical origin, including the Tethereds' abilities to know what their overworld counterparts are doing, their capacity to live on seemingly raw rabbit meat alone, the spread of information through the underworld, the creation of the red jumpsuits, the lack of toilet and hygiene facilities, and so on. Magic also appears more explicitly in the text through the rebranding of the funhouse as Merlin's Forest, as well as Jason's continuous use of a spark-producing magic trick.

It is the narrative reveal at the end of the story, however, which specifically marks *Us* as a space in which the underland purposefully undermines the nostalgia of the wonderland. We are introduced to Adelaide as a little girl first meeting Red before cutting to the present and a view of whom we assume to be Adelaide sitting in a car with her family. Through flashbacks, we are made to understand that "Adelaide" has undergone intense therapy following her encounter with Red, and that she temporarily lost her ability to speak as a result. However, the final

6. The Underland and the Rejection of the Medical Model

confrontation between Adelaide and Red offers a twist to this narrative, showing that Red attacked Adelaide and replaced her in the world above, leaving the real Adelaide to grow up among the Tethered.

Similar to the reconsideration of nostalgia demonstrated in *Return to Oz*, *Us* reexamines the very notion of the wonderland and finds the space, in many ways, limiting. Clinical psychologist Sean Scanlan defines nostalgia as a "longing for a time and place that never existed" (3), a definition markedly similar to the idea of "utopia" (Greek for "no place"). The denial of such a desire for that which has never occurred or existed is perhaps best demonstrated through recent critiques of the 2016 Donald Trump campaign slogan, "Make America Great Again." Famed journalist Tavis Smiley notes that such fondness for the past ignores the historic (and ongoing) injustices faced by marginalized populations:

> To what specific period of American greatness are you wanting us to return? When black folk suffered segregation after slavery? When women had no right to vote or control their own bodies? When gay brothers and lesbian sisters felt ceaseless hate? When we stole land from the Native Americans? When we sent Japanese families to internment camps? When America lynched Mexicans? I just need Trump to give me some clarity on the time period he wishes to travel back to.

Along with the resurgence of protest against police violence toward Black, Indigenous, and people of color (BIPOC) in the wake of George Floyd's murder, the denial of nostalgia for racism in the U.S.'s past was, in part, visibly dismantled through the removal of Confederate, colonial, and pro-slavery monuments in 2020.

It is with this critical and postmodern eye that the authors of the underland return to the wonderland model. While the underland as a space may be found across media in seemingly infinite representations, this chapter particularly unpacks the films *Return to Oz* (1985), *Pan's Labyrinth* (2006), *Us* (2019); the comic book *And Then Emily Was Gone* (2015); the video game *American McGee's Alice* (2000); and the television show *Stranger Things* (2016–present). Each of these texts particularly considers previous depictions of wonderlands as spaces that do not seek to alleviate but rather ignore the ills of the world. Whether explicitly critiquing the erasure of race, suffering, trauma, war, or even fascist regimes, these wonderlands set up models of merry monarchies, wars without loss, and unrealistic mental stability in child protagonists, all of which attempt to evade the problems of our lived society.

Disability and Nostalgia Denied

It is only through a post–Disability Rights Movement lens that authors began to critique the very notion of the wonderland while simultaneously attaching disability to wickedness, perversion, and alienness. The remainder of this chapter will particularly consider the place that disability plays in these underland texts, including (1) the portrayals of persons with disabilities themselves, (2) the negativization of medical treatment and attempts not only at cure but maintaining certain fixed levels of disability, as well as (3) the complete erasure of trauma as a reality. The combination of these factors suggests an overall increase in the stigmatization of persons with disabilities, arguably resulting from and causing a decrease in representations of positive crip futurities.

Portrayals of Persons with Disability

With the harsh realism of the underland comes the ableism that persons with disabilities actually face. In Jordan Peele's *Us*, the Tethered live in an underland marked by substandard living conditions that ultimately lead to disability. With no access to education, the Tethered usually lose the ability to speak; notably, Adelaide's ability to learn speech through therapy after coming to the upper world suggests that this is not a physical but rather educational limitation. Yet this kinder reading is almost immediately paired with the presence of visible disabilities represented solely by vilified characters. When Pluto meets the Wilsons, for example, he is covered in burn scars despite his young age.[1] Red speaks in a raspy voice meant to sound like someone with spasmodic dysphonia (qtd. *Variety*), leading to many disability rights organizations speaking out against the film (Sharf). The overall presence of the Tethered presents disability as a sort of playacting at being the normate that fails to find success; this theme is best exemplified by the Tether of the Wilsons' friend, Kitty, attempting to put on lipstick

6. The Underland and the Rejection of the Medical Model

before cutting her face in a parody of plastic surgery. The Tether, Dahlia, may be uneducated, but the element of self-harm suggests uncanniness meant to mark her as different. Similarly, Pluto is made to self-immolate by Jason, who takes advantage of either his need or desire to mirror Jason's actions. When the Tethered attempt to become the normate, they are instead punished with physical harm and violence; yet, simultaneously, they are presented as always already disabled. The Tethered generally come across as persons unconcerned with self-preservation, originality, or even love, as persons inherently living with mental illness. They steadfastly follow Red's plan, despite the possibility that she has experienced arrested development following the point of her capture. The Tethered seem merely to possess the desire to kill their above world counterparts before connecting hands in a gruesome imitation of the 1986 Hands Across America event. Like the recent resurfacing of the 2017 ADAPT protests by disability activists, many visibly disabled, this protest is treated as something odd, inconceivable, childish, and, ultimately, insignificant. During the 2017 protests at the U.S. Capitol by persons with disabilities and allies against potential Medicaid cuts, many persons using wheelchairs, amputees, and persons using canes were dragged from the building by police officers (Stein). Footage of this incident resurfaced with the January 6, 2021, pro–Trump storming of the U.S. Capitol, framed as though these activists were protesting the 2020 U.S. election rather than a loss of access to healthcare. Without the context surrounding the video and images of persons with disabilities being carried and dragged from the Capitol building, many people on Twitter openly mocked the activists (@katimcf; @Planet2kCed). For example, user @Planet2kCed tweeted, "Who done took the special needs folk to the capital?????," suggesting that persons with disabilities are unable to make the choice to protest or engage in activism without the support of non-disabled persons. Others simply posted laughing emojis or images of persons expressing disbelief, a clear real-life parallel of the Tethereds' efforts to draw attention to their own suffering. Yet, the film version goes far further with the Tethereds' extreme violence; suggesting not only that such protests, and by extension those which are far more serious in real life, should not be taken seriously except as potential sites of danger.

Presentations of disability in underlands are far from limited to

Disability in Wonderland

Jordan Peele's film. In actuality, the use of disability as a marker for otherness and uncanniness in horror is so prevalent that literary theorist Michael Bérubé summarizes the trope of disability as a device to "mobilize pity or horror" in narrative (570). When Dorothy makes her *Return to Oz* via ECT, she encounters a multitude of characters with disabilities, as she travels her former wonderland. Surrounded by a deadly desert with sands that kill upon being touched, Oz has fallen into ruin. Dorothy's friends, with the exception of Scarecrow, have been transformed into stone. She is furthermore quickly pursued by the menacing Wheelers, who have wheels in place of hands and feet. Although far more sinister than their book counterparts, Baum's description of the Wheelers via the objective pronoun "it" suggests that their difference has rendered them less-than-human:

> It had the form of a man, except that it walked, or rather rolled, upon all fours, and its legs were the same length as its arms, giving them the appearance of the four legs of a beast ... instead of hands and feet there grew at the end of its arms and legs round wheels, and by means of these wheels it rolled very swiftly over the level ground [*Ozma of Oz*].

Unlike in the novels, the Wheelers in *Return to Oz* appear poorly cared for, with dirty clothing and squeaking, unoiled joints. They laugh almost maniacally as they chase Dorothy and her chicken friend Billina to a dead end. When she is able to escape through a hidden door, one of the Wheelers assures her, "You have to come out sooner or later and, when you do, we'll tear you into little pieces." In short, the most visibly disabled characters are terrifying.

While bodily change and the fluidity of the boundary between animate/inanimate, living/object is constantly traversed in earlier wonderland iterations, the underland finds the uncanniness of the non-normative body something to be feared. While Alice is constantly changing size and the creatures around her shift in corporeality in the original *Wonderland* novels, American McGee's video game adaptations add a clear layer of terror to the effects. Madness is a key component of the game, with the main character, Alice, having a madness or mental health meter rather than physical health meter. Should her mental health reach zero, Alice goes "mad" and the player loses the game. Characters are dissected and bifurcated in turn, while others are killed

6. The Underland and the Rejection of the Medical Model

outright; dis- and re-embodiment become key forms of terror in these games. Proceeding through the first game requires the protagonist to use a knife and other weapons in order to literally slice enemies in half. In an iconic image from the series, Alice's signature white apron becomes drenched in the blood of herself and her enemies. While she has merely acted in self-defense, the larger imagery that remains is a woman who is likely mentally ill, capable of committing severe acts of violence, and likely very dangerous. Such a trope about dangerous persons with disabilities has been represented quite often across media, despite the fact that persons with disabilities are far more likely to be victims of violence than to perpetrate it themselves (The World Health Organization).

The second game focuses even more clearly on disability: its villain is a psychotherapist preying on mentally ill young women and children, using his privilege over them to sexually assault them with the firm belief that no one will believe "mad" youths. As a result of Alice's own diminishing mental capacity, as spurred on by this psychotherapist, Wonderland and all of its inhabitants similarly return to ruin. Wonderland as underland begins infecting the normal world of late 19th century London, beginning with the transformation of humans into monsters before Alice's eyes. Eventually, the two worlds merge altogether, as Alice defeats the all-too-human villain of Dr. Bumby by pushing him before a moving train; she defeats his Wonderland counterpart, the Dollmaker by destroying both him and his vehicle, the Infernal Train. The resulting space, Londerland, suggests a space in which Alice learns to coexist with her trauma, mental illness, and the so-called "real" world. She becomes more someone who has "overcome" her disabilities to the point of seeming to harness magical powers.

This manifestation suggests the usage of a trope known as the supercrip. As explained by disability and sport philosopher Jeffrey J. Martin, the supercrip is "a common stereotype in the disability literature ... someone who overcomes their disability in ways that are often seen by the public as inspiring." Oftentimes, this trope is enacted via a disabled character gaining a compensating superpower of some kind; for example, the blind superhero Daredevil from Marvel Comics gains an in-grown radar similar to echolocation following the onset of his disability. This interplay is often used in fictional scenarios but can further be applied to everyday persons with disabilities performing everyday functions in what has become known as inspiration porn (Young). A key example Stella Young gives in the TED Talk introducing this topic is simply completing the task of getting up in the morning or remembering her own name. Essentially, the supercrip comes in two forms. In the first, a disabled person is lionized for merely completing everyday tasks that are rendered no more difficult or minimally difficult as a result of their disability. A popular example from the winter of 2016–2017 is the viral video of then 10-year-old singer Kaylee Rogers[2] singing "Hallelujah" whilst having autism spectrum disorder (ASD) ("Kaylee Rodgers Singing Hallelujah–Official Video–Full HD"). While persons with ASD certainly can have limitations in terms of back-and-forth verbal communication, memorization, and focusing (U.S. Social Security Administration), difficulty singing is far from associated with this diagnosis. In fact, scientists with the National Institutes of Health (Sharda, et al.) have argued that persons with ASD are *more likely* than those without this condition to be musically skilled. Furthermore, numerous famous vocalists, ranging from Courtney Love to David Byrne to SpaceGhostPurrp have shared their ASD diagnoses, often as factors related to their music only insofar as their entire identities are a part of their creations. The point is not that Rogers is unexceptional for her superior singing ability but, rather, her superior singing is formulated by the media as exceptional *only because of* her ASD diagnosis, translating her into a figure of the supercrip.

The second definition of the supercrip finds persons with disabilities developing almost superhuman abilities; in response to a perceived deficit in one area (i.e., sight), one is believed to develop above average abilities in another area (i.e., hearing). While often personified via the superhero Daredevil, the belief that persons who become blind develop above average hearing ability is common enough to have been the subject of multiple scientific studies. In short, they have found that, while the rewiring of the brain that does occur with blindness can lead to improved localization of sound (being able to tell where sounds are coming from), such changes do not occur on a "supranormal" level ("Loss of Sight and Enhanced Hearing").

Stranger Things provides one of the clearest underland depictions of the supercrip according to both definitions. Both Dustin and his

6. The Underland and the Rejection of the Medical Model

actor Gaten Matarazzo openly have cleidocranial dysplasia (CCD), a condition which affects the development of the bones, generally leading to a shorter-than-average height and narrow shoulders (National Institutes of Health). Yet, while much of the buzz surrounding Dustin and Matrazzo focuses on his excellence in being able to defy stereotypes and be a hero within the show and a successful actor in real life, these narratives actually work to position both as supercrips while distracting from inherent systemic ableism. In brief, there's no reason why someone with CCD should not be able to be a successful actor; it is merely ableist casting directors and a larger normate-centered film industry that makes persons with visible disabilities seem exceptional within a Hollywood context. Narratively speaking, Dustin further offers little originality as a person with disabilities; as a nerd who is bullied merely for his CCD, he ends up becoming very invested in more geekish activities, such as science, proving a boon for his companions. As Bérubé notes in his piece on narrative and disability in speculative fiction, disability is in and of itself rendered as exceptional. Similar to his friend Lucas, one of the few Black characters in *Stranger Things*, Dustin is not drawn to his friend group due to an inherent lack of popularity but, rather, one that results from systemic biases. He is always already an outsider and thus becomes an outsider in tendency, even within his group of misfits. It is thus unsurprising that he demonstrates appreciation for the late middle wonderland film, *The NeverEnding Story*, in season three.

Similarly, but more in line with the second definition of the supercrip, Eleven and the previous members of Project MKUltra experiments, are at once portrayed in the context of both disability and superability. The women of Project MKUltra were essentially tortured between the 1960s and 1970s, using methods from psychedelic drugs to sleep deprivation, starvation, and severe abuse of multiple kinds, with the hopes of provoking extrasensory perception (ESP), particularly mind control. As the daughter of one of the original test subjects, Eleven is raised within this heavily medicalized and abusive environment, thus rending her socially disabled as she simply has not had the opportunity to develop relationships beyond those of the subject-observer.

Yet, within *Stranger Things*, and both *Return to Oz* and the *Alice* games more broadly, these experiments actually *are successful*. Eleven does, in fact, develop ESP, including telepathy and telekinesis, the ability to communicate and move objects using her mind. And it is especially telling that Eleven is not only placed within the sensory-deprivation tank that most elevates her powers by the medical establishment alone; Eleven is placed within a makeshift isolation chamber by her friends in order to access the underland of the *Stranger Things* narrative known as the Upside Down. Similarly, Alice and Dorothy, as a result of psychological torture, do return to their underlands. Alice gains the ability to traverse Wonderland and London simultaneously. Dorothy is able to defeat both Mombi and Nurse Wilson, while also gaining the ability to speak with those from Oz through her mirror.

And Then Emily Was Gone more clearly looks at the seeming super crip-ification of heroes as an aftereffect of encountering the underland. The comic's protagonist, ex-detective Greg Hellinger, seems to gain specific special abilities as a result of his experience with the creatures of Tallyman Holm and the Circus of the Night. While the exact details of his interaction with the underland are somewhat ambiguous, we do know explicitly that Greg has previously encountered the seeming leader of this place, Bonnie Shaw. This creature, who appears as a deformed human with fangs, a furry torso, and belted blue jeans, takes away children when their parents offer them in trade for a miracle of some kind. The titular Emily is traded to Bonnie Shaw so that her father may survive an incurable illness, while Billy from issue zero is traded to Bonnie Shaw for money due to his parents' disappointment with his illness and lack of traditional masculine qualities.

When Greg finally approaches Bonnie Shaw in the comic book, Bonnie greets him with open arms, saying, "Greg. Nice to see you again." We know that Greg has been having continuous visions of monsters since finding the remains of a young girl named Emma Lindon during a case five years previously. Explaining what occurred to a young girl named Fiona Tulloch seeking his help in finding Emily, Greg merely states that "all they could tell me was that I'd had a spectacular nervous breakdown." In flashback sequence, Greg remembers talking to detectives outside where Emma's body lies and learning that she's been held in a room belonging to a "sick bastard" for over a year. While we never see Emma's remains or are explicitly told what happened to her, Greg constantly worries that Emily is dead, "just like her," clearly referencing Emma. Furthermore, a painting he remembers from the room in which

6. The Underland and the Rejection of the Medical Model

Emma's body was found seems to act as a portal bringing Greg into the underland that coexists with Scotland. Arguably, from this point of his mental breakdown onward, Greg cannot leave the underland except when in the presence of Fiona; he lives in between both worlds as a disabled supercrip.

Though his ability to see the underland costs Greg both his career and sobriety, his talent for seeing monsters actually mark him as the hero *And Then Emily Was Gone* must rely upon. While understood by most as madness, Greg learns to use his abilities during the narrative, such that he is also able to control the participants of the Circus of the Night and even negotiate with Bonnie Shaw to trade places with Emily as his ward.

However, given the nature of the wonderland and her broader presence within the comic book series, Fiona becomes an even more significant character for our study. At age seventeen and read as female, Fiona fits more of the characteristics of the wonderland protagonist. Furthermore, like Greg, she gains the ability to see the monsters of the underland after encountering Bonnie Shaw. Unlike Greg, however, she has purposefully sought him out and bravely come to demand that Emily be released. Her encounter, however, initially leaves her facially disfigured. When Greg is able to negotiate her and Emily's freedom, the experience with the underland appears to alter Fiona even more significantly. When Emily explains to Fiona that rather than run away with her friend as she'd hoped to do prior to Bonnie Shaw kidnapping her, she wishes to return to the parents who traded her away, Fiona seems to snap. In a scene that can be read a multitude of ways, Fiona decides that the girl beside her cannot possibly by Emily but, rather, a changeling, or evil creature switched in for Emily from the underland. Despite the young girl's claims that she is Emily, Fiona douses her companion with gasoline and lights her on fire until she is seemingly burned to death.

From early on in this tale, we learn that fire is the only sure way to prove that someone is a changeling, though we are given few other details. However, Yeats's essential *Fairy and Folk Tales of the Irish Peasantry* offers a more in-depth description:

Sometimes the fairies fancy mortals, and carry them away into their own country, leaving instead some sickly fairy child, or a log of wood so bewitched that it seems to be a mortal pining away, and dying, and being

Disability in Wonderland

buried. Most commonly they steal children. If you "over look a child," that is look on it with envy, the fairies have it in their power. Many things can be done to find out in a child a changeling, but there is one infallible thing—lay it on the fire with this formula, "Burn, burn, burn—if of the devil, burn; but if of God and the saints, be safe from harm" (given by Lady Wilde). Then if it be a changeling it will rush up the chimney with a cry, for, according to Giraldus Cambrensis, "fire is the greatest of enemies to every sort of phantom, in so much that those who have seen apparitions fall into a swoon as soon as they are sensible of the brightness of fire."

Because we do not see anything clearly non-human in Emily's final actions, it may be interpreted that she has proven herself to truly be Fiona's beloved friend. However, as the fire does, in fact, harm her, the story may instead be suggesting that Celtic folklore itself is ineffective in the context of the underland. Thus we are left with two clear possibilities: either Fiona has gone mad and burned her best friend to death or she has gained essential insights from the underland and can now spot the difference between monster and human. As a result, Fiona, as a character, finds her narrative ending with the same conundrum affecting Greg: she is either insane or gifted. Given that Greg's encounter allows him to become a hero who negotiates this boundary, drawing upon both his madness and superabilities to save Emily, the suggestion is thus that Fiona has become another young woman of the underland who has gained superpowers through her experiences as a person with disabilities. As a result, she, like Greg, must either die or face some worse-than-death ending; for the supercrip, simply put, cannot live peaceably in the normate world.

This negotiation between the mad, the experimented upon, and the person with super abilities is clarified even more overtly in Guillermo del Toro's 2006 film *Pan's Labyrinth*. Following the life of ten-year-old Ofelia in Spain under Franco's regime, much of this tale takes place in the titular labyrinth filled with fantastic and magical creatures. While Ofelia's pregnant mother, Carmen, is clearly marked as chronically ill with an unnamed condition, it is Ofelia who is deemed delusional by her mother and stepfather as a result of her belief that she is travelling between the underworld and the Spanish countryside. In particular, it is notable that Ofelia provokes the most anger when trying to help her mother by placing a mandrake root under Carmen's bed and keeping

6. The Underland and the Rejection of the Medical Model

it watered with milk and blood. For it is pointedly shown that Ofelia's remedy is successful when tended to; Carmen becomes markedly healthier with the root beneath her bed and dies in childbirth almost immediately upon its removal. The suggestion here is that the underworld and its inhabitants are, in fact, real, despite the inability of Ofelia's stepfather to see either.

Interestingly, del Toro has further offered that, while the realness of the underworld should be left to the viewer's interpretation, he believes Ofelia to be experiencing a real underland (Guillen). He notes that there are three explicit clues that the underland is real. Presumably, a minor clue is the effectiveness of the mandrake root in terms of healing Carmen temporarily, and her death upon its destruction. However, del Toro furthermore notes the three biggest hints: (1) a flower blossoming from a dead tree at the end, accompanied by the narrator explaining that "she left behind small traces of her time on earth visible only to those who know where to look," (2) the walls of the labyrinth opening a dead end to allow for Ofelia escape before closing to show her stepfather stuck, and (3) Ofelia's ability to enter her stepfather's locked office by drawing a door with a piece of chalk given to her by the Faun.

Madness, trauma, and superability, particularly the gift of seeing and visiting another world, play key roles in the underland narrative. Women must lean into visions, memories, dreams, and hallucinations in order to become empowered and transgress the boundary between the underland and normal world. "She wasn't a reflection, she was real," Adelaide must tell herself in order to find the pathway to the Tethered world. And by embracing the madness, she becomes both extraordinary and cursed. The final shot of her son, having seen her kill her Tethered counterpart whilst yelling in a manner that mirrors that of the Tethereds' vocals, suggests that Adelaide no longer belongs with her family.

Trauma and Treatment

The medical establishment, especially psychotherapy, also play a key role in these adaptations that transform the wonderland to underland. Many of our heroes survive with severe trauma of some kind, such as the experience in wonderland for Dorothy or the loss of someone in

Disability in Wonderland

Alice, Stranger Things and *And Then Emily Was Gone*. When they turn or are made to rely on the medical establishment, however, health care workers prove largely negative in their portrayals, from predominantly ineffective to embodying actual evil forces. Psychotherapists are particularly negativized in these portrayals, whether set in the past (*Return to Oz, Alice*) or present (*Stranger Things*). The role of psychotherapy in the underland is such a predominant force, in fact, that it is a key component of Eleanor West's School for Wayward Children in Seanan McGuire's series about children returned from wonderlands.

Like *Return to Oz, Alice*'s narrative is framed around her experiences with psychotherapists. At the beginning of the game, Alice wakes to find her house on fire; while she is saved from the flames by her friends from Wonderland, her parents perish in the fire, leaving her severely traumatized and housed within a psychiatric clinic in London called Rutledge Asylum. When she returns to Wonderland, Alice, like Dorothy, finds it a macabre and deeply disturbing iteration of the place she remembers. While this change is partially due to the influence of the Queen of Hearts, Alice is told that much of Wonderland's downfall has resulted from Alice's own mental illness. For ten years following the fire that kills her parents, Alice is treated by Doctor Heironymous "Harry" Q. Wilson, a psychotherapist whose notes suggest pleasure at the idea of Alice never healing from her trauma to the point of being able to leave his care. Alice's hallucinations of Harry suggests that she feels her treatment equivalent to that of a dog's; that she is merely locked in a kennel and fed to be kept alive. Harry's notes further suggest that he may be the very reason for Alice's inability to heal. While the game leaves this cryptic note unanalyzed, the suggestion in the context of the games' broader narratives hints that Harry may be purposefully preventing Alice's recovery, such that she is in catatonia for the vast majority of her time at Rutledge. In the sequel, Alice's psychotherapist, Dr. Bumby, is overtly coded as evil, purposefully pushing mentally ill children and young women into sex slavery by impeding, rather than supporting, their healing. It is only by killing Dr. Bumby and his Wonderland counterpart that the player is able to complete *Alice: Madness Returns*.

Similarly, the television series *Stranger Things*, ongoing as of the time of publication, heavily features the medical establishment in a largely negative role. Initially following the recent disappearance of

6. The Underland and the Rejection of the Medical Model

Will Byers, we see his friends search for him as his mother, Joyce, both grieves his loss and disputes his death. Simultaneously, a young woman with telekinesis, known only as "Eleven," escapes from her "father," a doctor at a National Laboratory in Hawkins, Indiana, who is performing tests on her against her will. While Joyce seems to lack to the resources or incentive to visit a psychotherapist during the week her son is missing, her belief that she is talking to her son, first via disjointed phone calls and then Christmas lights, leads many around her to believe she is mentally unstable. In response to those asking that she remove the Christmas lights used as a makeshift Ouija board for letter-by-letter communication, Joyce tellingly says, "Maybe I am a mess, maybe I'm crazy, maybe I'm out of my mind! But, God help me, I will keep these lights up until the day I die, if I think there's a chance that Will's still out there!" (Season 1, Episode 5).

While *Stranger Things* includes the physical presence of monsters in its underland, they are notably not positioned as the primary villains of the series. Instead, it is those who work at the Hawkins Laboratory who fill this role. Like D'Artagnan, the young demogorgan initially kept as a pet by Dustin before eventually eating the family cat, the monsters of the Upside Down are understood as frightening but not intentionally evil, with few exceptions over the series' five seasons. Conversely, those at the Hawkins Laboratory, particularly the persons in positions of power, purposefully put young women and children at serious risk despite having the advantage of human intelligence. Furthermore, by continuing to open gates between Earth and the Upside Down, the medical scientists at Hawkins Laboratory are knowingly providing access to the extremely dangerous Mind Flayer. In brief, the Laboratory is responsible for torturing the subjects of Project MKUltra, kidnapping Eleven, covering up the disappearance of Will and death of Barb, and ultimately continuing to open portals between the Upside Down and Earth that led to dozens of deaths. While the facility may close following the severe loss of staff in the season three finale, we are also shown that the Russian scientists have successfully reached the Upside Down via a second pathway in the Kamchatka Peninsula and will likely continue allowing the Mind Flayer access to Earth.

Rather than filling the role of antagonist, however, underland narratives often depict medical professionals as simply incorrect or largely

Disability in Wonderland

ineffective. While *Us* largely features scenes of Adelaide's parents speaking with her seemingly bumbling and ignorant psychotherapist, *Pan's Labyrinth*'s Doctor Ferreiro fails at both treating Carmen and hiding his rebel allegiance. While completely absent from the pages of the scant five issues of *And Then Emily Was Gone*, the diagnoses of psychotherapists permeate the pages as Greg explains that "they" said he'd had a massive mental breakdown upon finding Emma's body.

Taken as a whole, the medical establishment is treated as far too limited in perspective to understand the truths behind what the protagonists of these underland tales have and are continuing to go through. The doctors' inability to imagine the existence of the underworld end up causing great harm to their patients or preventing actual healing of any kind to occur. Instead, the largely young female protagonists are left feeling as though they have gone through some sort of psychotic break or are mentally ill to the point of being incurable. The trauma of both having experienced the wonderland and being disbelieved helps to create an underland, a space of recurring trauma. However, while the critique of the medical establishment, particularly in terms of the disabilities each of these protagonists is thought to embody, can be useful in terms of providing a vehicle for self-belief and autonomy in crip communities, the supercrip model works to undermine this success. Rather than being left with rage at those who have pushed them to overperform or gaslit them, the protagonists largely blame themselves and their own weaknesses for their new abilities, which come as more of an additional burden than a blessing for them personally. Meanwhile, narratively, these new abilities mark them as able to become true heroes; just those who will never be recognized in the "real" world, itself another wonderland, from which they will now be forever alienated.

Chapter 7

Alice in the Underland

At the end of Grant Morrison and Dave McKean's acclaimed 1989 graphic novel *Arkham Asylum: A Serious House on Serious Earth*, the Joker makes a statement to Batman that encapsulates the future of the wonderland: "Enjoy yourself out there. In the asylum." Throughout the comic, the distinction between sane and insane, abled and disabled, is consistently blurred. Echoing the findings of Nellie Bly in her essential 1887 *Ten Days in a Mad-House*, the inmates of Arkham find the difference between those within and outside of the asylum to largely result from societal norms and power. In her text, Bly notes the presence of German woman being denied treatment or any representation in her sole and native language; Mrs. Louise Schanz, she argues, is most likely as sane, if not *saner*, than those who are questioning her in English, a language which she clearly cannot speak. In *Arkham Asylum*, the eponymous psychiatrist, Amadeus Arkham kills the murderer of his family, Martin "Mad Dog" Hawkins, using an overabundance of electroshock therapy. When he first takes Hawkins as a patient, following the death of wife and daughter, Arkham is "praised for [his] course and compassion"; when he electrocutes Hawkins to death, the incident "is treated as an accident" and he is told that "these things happen."

Perhaps understanding *Arkham Asylum*'s context, as a piece written by celebrated comic writer Grant Morrison, who is also openly non-binary and gender queer, is most essential to grasping the underland. In interviews with *Mondo 2000* and *Rolling Stone*, Morrison notes how, while they had their "sexuality shit figured out a long time ago!" (Hiatt), they didn't know how to self-identify. They explain that:

> I've been non-binary, cross-dressing, "gender queer" since I was 10 years old, but the available terms for what I was doing and how I felt were few and far between. We had "transsexual" and "transvestite" both of which sounded

like DSM [*Diagnostic and Statistical Manual of Mental Disorders*] classifications rather than lifestyle choices! I didn't want to be labelled as medical aberration because that's not how it felt, nor was it something cut-and-dried and done. I didn't want to "transition" or embody my "female" side exclusively, so I had no idea where I fit in [Prop Anon].

An increase in access to traditional publication venues meant that the voices and stories of those marginalized from popular media avenues began to move to the center. As noted by speculative fiction critic Sheree Thomas and writer/activist Onnesha Roychoudhuri, these voices traditionally silenced in U.S. American cultural production actually represent the majority of U.S. Americans. Thomas uses the metaphor of "dark matter," the invisible force in astronomy which has huge gravitational effect but is imperceivable by humans, to describe speculative fiction works created by Black writers (x). Roychoudhuri goes further to argue that the majority of persons in the United States are in some way marginalized; as the term "minority" has largely disappeared from diversity and equity work, the "marginalized majority" as a term recognizes that the voices most often heard in U.S. society, and heard the loudest, come from those with the most power rather than those who exist in greatest numbers or have the most to contribute. The dark matter metaphor is specific to and essential for analyzing speculative fiction works by Black authors; in this chapter, I will draw upon this theory to provide a more detailed commentary on Jordan Peele's 2019 film *Us* and how it acts as a response to *Alice in Wonderland*. I will furthermore bring this film into conversation with other dark *Alice* interpretations of the underland era, namely Jan Švankmajer's 1988 film *Alice* and Grant Morrison and Dave McKean's 1989 *Arkham Asylum*.

Visibilizing Dark Matter

As clarified by Thomas, Black creators have been contributing to speculative fiction since the genre emerged. Yet, these contributions have largely been erased from the canon, such that only Samuel Delany, Octavia Butler, and postmillennial Black authors are generally included. Even early in the film *Us*, Jordan Peele marks upon this erasure by putting a Michael Jackson *Thriller* t-shirt on young Adelaide.

7. Alice in the Underland

While Jackson's music video had a profound impact on early 1980s culture, it is hardly considered part of the speculative fiction canon, despite having multiple horror and science fiction elements. The video notably opens with Jackson's own understanding of the time in which he worked, with the message, "Due to my strong personal convictions, I wish to stress that this film in no way endorses a belief in the occult." The nearly 14-minute film includes references to horror films, as well as the presence of a werecat and zombies. In choosing these two specific characters, Jackson is himself drawing attention to the presence of Black artists in horror history. The zombies are clearly reminiscent of George A. Romero's 1968 *Night of the Living Dead* in which Black actor Duane Jones plays Ben; tellingly, Ben is assumed to be a zombie and killed by an armed posse of predominantly if not all White men at the end of this iconic film, also highlighting the continued violence against Black men in the United States. The werecat offers a bit of a less obvious reference, though I would argue that Jackson is drawing upon Eartha Kitt's performance as Catwoman in the *Batman* television series in 1967. Replacing Julie Newmar for the third and final season, Eartha Kitt's portrayal of a sexually confident, powerful, and predatory Catwoman was revolutionary in speculative fiction, specifically comic book adaptations. Yet, despite being sexy, Kitt's Catwoman is far less interested in sex and romance than Newmar's; as noted in fashion historian Joseph H. Hancock's overview of Kitt's portrayal, all Newmar's Catwoman seemed to do was "try to seduce Batman" (4). Kitt's Catwoman, on the other hand, was interested in fashion and looking good for her own sake.

Kitt's daughter, Kitt Shapiro, notes particularly how the Catwoman character created space for Black female attractiveness without relying on such tropes as the explicitly promiscuous Jezebel or overbearing Sapphire stereotype. While a seductress when played by Newmar, Kitt's Catwoman seemed a bit more interested in her own career than Batman. Shapiro explains that:

> there were no women of color at that time wearing skintight bodysuits, playing opposite a white male with sexual tension between them! She knew the importance of the role and she was proud of it. She really is a part of history. She was one of the first really beautiful black women—her, Lena Horne, Dorothy Dandridge—who were allowed to be sexy without being stereotyped.

Disability in Wonderland

Unlike her predecessor as Catwoman on the show, Kitt's rendition of the villain exists as more than a villainous counterpart to Batman. Whether or not one agrees with this read of Kitt's Catwoman, the *Thriller* video is essential in and of itself in that it includes an image of a desirable, beautiful Black woman who is not hypersexualized. In fact, the young woman played by Ola Ray in *Thriller* is explicitly trying to *avoid* sex in the film-within-the-film, initially believing Jackson's character to have lied about running out of gas in order to make sexual advances. Her character outside of the film-within-the-film is also given agency; though Jackson wants to continue watching a horror movie she tells him that she, at least, is leaving. When Jackson follows her out and teases her however, she seems fine admitting her emotions with a shy smile. She is refreshingly fleshed out, something severely lacking in earlier portrayals of Black women, particularly in media produced by White men. She is not a man-eating Jezebel, she does not figure as an emasculating counter to Jackson, and she is not hypersexualized. She is happy to dance with Jackson down the street even as he continues joking with her, laughing and even stroking Jackson's chin; this young woman is in on the joke.

Adelaide, especially the original Adelaide who becomes trapped in the world of the Tethered, has much in common with the heroine of *Thriller*. While she is far less overtly happy, she also has a sense of whimsy. In the beginning of the film, we see her not only put on the *Thriller* t-shirt, but notably put it on *over* a t-shirt for Hands Across America. The two t-shirts demonstrate the divisive pivot from idealism in the mid–1980s to mid–1990s in the United States. For Hands Across America is tied to Jackson in two key ways. Firstly, the artist recreated the visual for his December 2001 music video, "Cry."[1] The song was tellingly released not only in a post 9/11 landscape but after the first allegations of sexual misconduct against Jackson in 1993 and after he had repeatedly modified his body through surgery and skin bleaching, purportedly to pass as White (Davis). Interestingly, the song claims that "when that flag glows there'll be no more wars"; in the context of the U.S. entering Afghanistan the same October for what would become a twenty-year long campaign, the song largely fails. All of this background makes it clear that the idealism that made Jackson's similarly themed "Man in the Mirror" a hit in 1988 no longer existed in 2001. Secondly, through the opening video within the film, Peele puts Hands Across America

7. Alice in the Underland

in clear connection with Farm Aid, Live Aid, USA for Africa, and Band Aid. And Hands Across America was, indeed, planned by organizer Ken Kragen, who orchestrated USA for Africa's "We Are the World" in 1985. "We Are the World" was notably written by Jackson and Lionel Richie, espousing the same idealism found in "Man in the Mirror" and "Cry." Notably, Hands Across America asked that participants pay $10 toward charities that sought to end homelessness, raising $15 million after fees (Hassan). In contrast, Band Aid and USA for Africa sought to provide food for the 18 countries most affected by the 1983–1985 drought in Eastern Africa (Weinraub), with the group raising an estimated $75 million per *Rolling Stone*. Interestingly, Spain's *MARCA* magazine estimates that this is likely close to Michael Jackson's net worth at the time (estimated at between $50–100 million).

The fact that most of the performers with USA for Africa were millionaires even in the 1985 context largely demonstrates that similar works, including the 2010 "We Are the World 25 for Haiti," actually work to demonstrate the growing income gap and reality of differentiation between the haves and have nots in the United States. "We Are the World 25 for Haiti" was largely ignored by music critics and would-be donors alike, such that a thorough search made it difficult to even learn how much the charity single earned for relief to Haiti following the devastating 2010 earthquake. Yet, knowing that multiple artists involved with the project were not merely millionaires but billionaires at the time highlights a clear reason why the idealism of the 1980s celebrity-fueled charity efforts has faded: the average person being asked to donate money to a cause by a person who belongs to the top 1 percent of income earners is simply far less tenable in a more contemporary, post–Occupy Wall Street environment.

The depictions of celebrity-driven charity events in the context of Adelaide experiencing them in 1986 are markedly different from how these and similar events are experienced in 2019, when the film *Us* was released. For the idealism of the 1980s has faded, perhaps a result of the culture wars or further divisiveness instilled through the policies of Ronald Reagan, George H.W. Bush, and Bill Clinton. Rhetorician Kem Roper notes that Reagan and Bush's "new right" specifically worked to further the divide between those in the hegemonic class and those in positions of marginality, predominantly through the weaponization of

Disability in Wonderland

"whiteness" and the metaphor of the "Welfare Queen." Within the political discourse of the mid–1980s to early 1990s, Roper explains:

> the very concept of "whiteness" can only exist in contrast to the construction of "blackness," thus, "whiteness" is everything that "blackness" isn't. On one hand, "whiteness" is obvious. It is the ideology of the power structures which are controlled by white men and which hold wealth accumulation, white male dominance, European characteristics of beauty and a particular form of Christian morality in high esteem. In this way, "whiteness" is in direct contrast to poverty, non-white, non-male dominance, non–European characteristics and moral values that differ from the oppressive and judgmental forms of Christianity [43].

This rhetorical separation between those belonging to the hegemonic classes and those who are marginalized is further clarified in Reagan's 1989 Farewell Address. Reagan recalls attending a transnational 1983 economic summit and, supposedly, having a foreign leader lean toward him and say, "Tell us about the American miracle.'" Reagan celebrates the fact that "real family income [is] up, the poverty rate down, entrepreneurship booming, and an explosion in research and new technology." He talks of reifying the image of the United States as "the city on the hill" per John Winthrop.

At the same time, he mentions nothing about the growing number of AIDS-related deaths, estimated at upward of 100,777 U.S. Americans by 1990 (CDC), "Current Trends..." He does not mention that the populations most negatively impacted are Black and Brown, queer, trans or nonbinary, young, immigrants, poor, and/or IV drug users. These populations do not live within his vision of whiteness; they are not residents of the U.S. American "city on the hill." In *Cruising Utopia*, José Esteban Muñoz discusses the safety that comes from passing, whether it be passing as straight, as White, or as a member of the hegemonic elite. An empathetic queer theorist as always, Muñoz kindly notes, "imagine how hard it must be to try to look and act so butch all the time" (79). Yet passing is exactly what Adelaide is trying to do in *Us*, a film heavily influenced by the reality that the idealism, utopianism even, of the Reagan and Bush Sr., eras was matched by a harsh reality facing the marginalized classes. From increased likelihood of infection with HIV and death from AIDS to the stigmatization of Black and single-parent families to the coining and proliferation of the term "reverse racism," the city

7. Alice in the Underland

on a hill became less a goal and more of a weight to bear for many marginalized persons.

The main character of *Us*, whom I will refer to as Adelaide 1, the original Red, spends her entire life passing. She belongs to those on the other side of the so-called "American Miracle." It makes sense that the U.S. government has likely created the Tethereds, these metaphorical stand-ins for the perpetual underclass constructed in opposition to Reagan's "whiteness-as-framework" for the hegemonic class. It makes sense that Adelaide 2, the new Red, clarifies that "what" she is is an American. The Tethered are the twins to their upperworld counterparts, those who would be the same if given the same level of privilege. After all, once she is given the resources Adelaide 2 received, including access to medical care, loving parents, and wealth, she thrives, even outshining Adelaide 1.

Yet, Adelaide and her family remain removed from the hegemonic elite because of their race; despite their wealth and education, they clearly see themselves as less than their White neighbors at the beach house, the Tylers. Gabe's education is telegraphed by his Howard University sweatshirt, suggesting that he not only attended a prestigious university but is well-aware of how his positionality is affected by his Blackness. At a screening at the historically Black university, Winston Duke, who portrays Gabe, explained that "the alma mater symbolize[s] the family's attachment to Blackness" in the film (Freeman). Unlike stereotypes surrounding Black persons in positions of privilege "pretending to be White" or, as worded by feminist scholar Koa Beck, "aspir[ing] to whiteness" (186), the Wilsons celebrate their Blackness while recognizing how it renders them apart from the hegemonic elite. Gabe lovingly sings Luniz's 1995 West Coast hip hop classic "I Got 5 on It" with his family. He later refers to his family's hide-a-key as "white shit," not initially understanding to what his wife is referring.

Yet, Gabe and Adelaide are within the same social circle as the Tylers. They too own a vacation house, even if it was inherited from Adelaide's mother. The Wilsons are further planning to sell the house, not because they are hurting for money, but because they want to continue sending their children to private school. Additionally, without consulting his wife, Gabe purchases a used motorboat. While far from a static statistic, popular boating blog *Quicknav* estimates that, in 2022, an average second-hand 20-foot motorboat would cost between $10,000 and $20,000; the fact that Gabe is able to make such a large purchase without consulting his wife, and without even seeming to irritate her, suggests that the family must be fairly affluent. Additionally, this purchase suggests that the children's private school costs must be quite a bit higher than the price of the boat.

While Gabe's success is suggested by his purchasing power and Howard sweatshirt, Adelaide's history demonstrates that she, too, comes from privilege. While her parents eventually divorced, they at least at some point owned both a home and a vacation house. After the incident at the Santa Monica Pier, Adelaide 1 is sent to see a mental health specialist; in the script, this specialist is clarified to be Dr. Foster, a child psychiatrist. The few scenes in Dr. Foster's office suggest that, not only do Adelaide's parents have access to health care, but that they can afford to see specialists who often charge especially high fees. The large size of Dr. Foster's office further suggests that Adelaide's parents have sent her to a high-cost facility. Her wealth is also displayed through her initial passion for and eventual abandonment of ballet. Misty Copeland, the historic first Black woman to make the rank of principal dancer at the American Ballet Theatre, has noted that the cost of ballet equipment and classes often makes it prohibitively expensive. In an interview with the African American Literature Book Club, Copeland explains, "It takes a lot of money to be a part of the ballet world. Both the training and the supplies are expensive, the shoes, the leotards and the tights" (Williams). Copeland famously began ballet at the relatively late age of 13, learning first at the local Boys and Girls Club (Copeland 24). Because she could not afford a leotard or tights, she wore her drill-team practice clothing, and did not receive the proper ballet equipment and training until she was already discovered to be a prodigy (Copeland). Adelaide clearly does not have the same financial issues when she takes up ballet, wearing a full ballerina's garb complete with tutu. She competes in dance competitions and, per the script, even has her own small private dance studio.

Still, the Wilsons feel less than the Tylers. Their wealth is not enough to erase their Blackness, and they can never be part of the hegemonic elite. The Tylers are said to have a larger boat than the one Gabe purchased; when chased by the Tethered from the Tylers' house, Gabe

7. Alice in the Underland

significantly runs past his own boat and takes Josh's in order to attempt his escape. Josh Tyler has recently purchased an expensive new car. The Tylers clearly have a larger beach house with two rather than one story. Smaller signs of wealth, such as Kitty's plastic surgery and the fine liquor brands in the Tylers' home demonstrate their privilege as well. Kitty casually mentions studying at Stella Adler, whose two-year acting school program cost $35,900 in 2022 (*The Stella Adler Academy of Acting and Theatre*). All of this seems to irritate Gabe, in particular. Gabe feels that Josh at least partially purchased the new car to annoy him, telling his wife, "He had to do it. He just had to get that thing to fuck with me too." Josh jokes about the size of Gabe's boat compared to his own, making a lewd phallic joke that he then repeats loudly to his wife. Yet, Adelaide also notes that she isn't especially fond of Josh and Kitty, while Zora clearly dislikes the two Tyler daughters. They seem keenly aware of their positionality in relation to the Tylers, and this additional aspect of marginality within the wonderland context is what makes the underland such a pivot from earlier iterations.

Death, Disability, and Oppression

Within the above-ground world of *Us*, the Wilsons are clearly privileged; their Tethered counterparts seem drawn together rather by their excessive oppression rather than other communal identity indicators. Their imprisonment in the underground world likely results from a program either created or at least supported by the U.S. government; Red suggests that "they created the Tethered so they could use them to control the ones above. Like puppets." Who "they" refers to is unclear, yet the opening text explains the Underpass as this world is called, in terms of a project clearly linked to the U.S. government: "There are thousands of miles of tunnels beneath the continental United States… Abandoned subway systems, unused service routes, and deserted mine shafts… Many have no known purpose at all." Red's statement of her Americanness also suggests that she understands and respects the state; however downtrodden, Red understands that the Tethered are at least theoretically entitled to all the benefits afforded a person with U.S. citizenship. The dichotomy between the above-ground privileged versus the below-ground disenfranchised is reminiscent of H.G. Wells's *The Time Machine*, with the above-ground Eloi provided with all they need and living a relatively utopian life at the expense of the Morlocks, the below-ground inhabitants of the future who slave away to support their Eloi counterparts. The Morlocks are almost instantly detested by the Time Traveler, who notes, "there was an altogether new element in the sickening quality of the Morlocks—a something inhuman and malign. Instinctively I loathed them." Yet, the Time Traveler soon after posits that the Eloi are descended from the aristocracy while the Morlocks are also human, simply descended from those of the working class. And, similar to the Tethered, the Morlocks turn homicidal as a result of their oppression.

Simultaneously, Adelaide 2 becomes Alice; even her name is similar. Much like her wonderland counterparts, this regular world heroine ventures below ground. Yet, while the usual heroine completely subverts/undermines the power hierarchy within the traditional wonderland narrative, *Us*'s Adelaide 2 is instead subsumed by it. In the Underpass, the disenfranchised have become more powerful than their above-ground counterparts. It is power and privilege, not meritocracy, that forces them below ground. In many ways, the Tethered are even superior to their counterparts. Zora's Tethered, Umbrae, runs faster than her, having practiced in the harshness of the tunnels. Jason spends most of the movie attempting to get his "magic trick," which appears to be some sort of snap-based lighter, to work; his Tethered, Pluto, not only knows how to do the "magic trick" but also has experience with fire itself. Pluto's face is severely burned as a result, yet he is said to have been "born to love fire" by his mother. Adelaide 2 learns ballet, like Adelaide 1, but does so without the proper equipment and on the hard pavement of the Underpass. She gives birth without medical care. In a physical confrontation, she is stronger than Adelaide 1, while her planning abilities suggest a genius level of intelligence. As for Gabe, simply put, his Tethered, Abraham, is stronger than him; the script specifically notes that "he's [Gabe's] simply not as strong" as Abraham. When Abraham grabs and carries Gabe, the movement is compared to that of an adult moving a toddler. While most of the Tethered are unable to speak, they are physically more powerful than their above-ground counterparts because they have had to be to survive.

7. Alice in the Underland

With the clear inclusion of allusions to *Alice in Wonderland* and *Peter Pan*, Peele offers both empathy toward those whose worlds are literally turned upside down by the wonderland heroines and a critique of the very idea of a wonderland vs. a real world. As in *Arkham Asylum*, the very idea of one world being superior, stranger, or more wonderful than the other is turned on its head. Referring to the Tethered as the "shadows" of their above-ground counterparts, Peele asks us to consider what *Peter Pan* might have looked like from the perspective of Peter's shadow. In the Barrie text, the shadow is forcibly reattached to Peter against its will, and then forced to do more or less what Peter does. The fact that Wendy sews the shadow back on suggests both a sewing kit and scissors, images that figure heavily in *Us* as well. Like *Alice in Wonderland*, *Us* features a White Rabbit; in fact, the only rabbit explicitly given a color in the *Us* script is a white rabbit. Like Alice, Adelaide travels underground to a strange new world with new and seemingly impossible rules.

The use of scissors as a weapon specifically seems to harken to the 1988 Jan Švankmajer Czech adaptation of *Alice*. Scissors and sewing feature heavily in this film, as the White Rabbit is a taxidermized rabbit come to life, who must consistently restuff himself much like the Scarecrow of Oz. The beheading at the bequest of the Red Queen actually occurs in this horror adaptation, with the White Rabbit using his scissors to snip the tops off of the animate playing cards who displease the monarch. He later uses the scissors again to decapitate the Mad Hatter and March Hare, who then exchange heads. Švankmajer's adaptation pulls in ideas from other wonderlands, including the transformation of Alice into a fragile China doll much like those depicted in *The Wizard of Oz* book. While Peele has not explicitly noted Švankmajer's *Alice* as an influence for *Us*, it seems that even this cross-wonderland exchange is replicated. Like *Alice* too, food in the Underpass is often disgusting and insufficient. There is the threat of actual death and proof that creatures of the wonderland can die in both texts, both through us witnessing deaths and the presence of corpses. Both *Alice's* wonderland and the Underpass are accessed via modern machinery: an elevator and an escalator, respectively. Both worlds appear as though extensive labyrinths with no maps available and physically difficult spaces to traverse. And both those who live in *Alice's* wonderland and the Underpass are mere counterparts to above-ground figures. In *Us*, the Tethered must mirror the Untethered, while *Alice*'s creatures are all based on everyday items in Alice's room. Because she has stuffed the rabbit, so too is the living White Rabbit of wonderland stuffed. In this manner, the underland becomes a social construction of disability specifically at the hands of those of the privileged classes. Without the upper classes, those in the underland would not only be considered non-disabled but perhaps even superabled.

Finally, and most significantly perhaps, both stories end with a twist which makes the heroine appear to switch places with the villain. We learn near the end of *Us* that Adelaide 1 was originally a Tethered who replaced her above-world counterpart in a violent manner that seems to have permanently disabled Red. One of the last lines of 1988's *Alice* has Alice thinking about the White Rabbit and reflecting, "He's late, as usual. I think I'll cut his head off." If the Red Queen is the wonderland villain, then this Alice is surely her above-ground counterpart.

Conclusions

As the Reagan and Bush Sr. administrations specifically targeted persons of color, queer folk, persons with disabilities, and others belonging to marginalized groups, the utopic vision presented by them became increasingly dystopic in the eyes of the marginalized. This pessimism was specifically cast upon pre-existing wonderlands, rethinking key texts through a postmodern lens simultaneously more aware of issues related to diversity. Critics began looking both at the earliest wonderlands and their authors, noting the far-from-perfect realities surrounding these child utopias. Charles Dodgson was reinterpreted in three biographies from 1995 to 1996 as likely being a pedophile due to his predilection for photographing nude children (Cohen, Thomas, Bakeswell); notably, Morrison's Mad Hatter of *Arkham Asylum* similarly appears to be a pedophile. The character notes: "children interest me ... little girls, especially. Little blonde girls. Little shameless bitches!," suggesting Morrison's familiarity with Dodgson's reputation even before the three biographies. Barrie similarly was thought to be a pedophile in his time, with such speculation reemerging upon a reconsideration of his relationship with the Davies family in Andrew Birkin's popular

7. Alice in the Underland

1979 biography. Children's literary scholar Ebony Thomas notes that *Peter Pan* likely furthered negative stereotypes about Indigenous peoples in the Americas well into the 20th century. Baum similarly has a troubled history when it comes to U.S. government policy and Indigenous populations, advocating, possibly sarcastically, that the U.S. government would do best to literally commit genocide against Indigenous populations to the last person rather than risk vengeance. And, despite his self-identification as a feminist, Baum's letters offer overtly misogynist ideas, including him directly expressing pity toward a friend who has only had daughters.

While extremely useful in terms of understanding disability, the early wonderland narratives, as well as those of the middle period in many cases, simply reinforce powerful narratives that have dispossessed persons of other marginalized groups. The melding of the wonderland and the real world, as so often happens in the underland narrative, clearly notes this tendency and how such a distinction in and of itself works to dichotomize society. By breaking down the barriers between the real world and the underland, these later narratives clarify that, as Joker notes in *Arkham Asylum*, that, without those interred in Arkham Asylum for the Criminally Insane, there would be no Batman. Without the comic book villain, there could be no superhero. And the only factor determining the difference between violence for good and violence for wickedness, in the end, is power.

Conclusions

Following the release of the Rian Johnson-helmed *Star Wars* film, *Episode VIII: The Last Jedi* in 2017, a much-propagated fan campaign began in hopes of creating a replacement eighth installment in the film series. Aptly titled "Remake the Last Jedi," this effort gained widespread media attention in late June 2018 following the group's Twitter-based announcement that $200 million dollars had been pledged to the campaign; largely, Remake the Last Jedi seeks to offset the cost it would take for Disney to produce a new Episode VIII. While far from an actual possibility,[1] the effort to recreate this film in the popular *Star Wars* franchise demonstrates a continued effort to equate speculative fiction with what author N.K. Jemisin terms "Tolkien clones" (Sarkeesian): literatures and fans who at least appear to believe that Tolkien's *Lord of the Rings* was successful because it largely focused on cisgender, White, male, heterosexual, normate characters rather than succeeding *despite* the characters' limited relatability.

Like Tolkien's work, the original *Star Wars* trilogy followed a male protagonist as he predominantly encountered a similarly cis, White, male, heterosexual, normate cast, with a handful of women, droids, and persons of color thrown in to keep things interesting.[2] Despite this reality, Remake the Last Jedi purports to be more concerned with narrative than representation. As explained on their website:

> The more relate-able a hero is to human nature, the more compelling the story because people begin to see themselves in these heroes. This is imperative to storytelling because if you don't care about the characters then you don't care to see where their story goes.
>
> When we decide to edit out the human element from within a story then the story becomes no longer compelling.
>
> This is why many of us tend to point at The Last Jedi [sic] as having a bad story. The characters have lost their relatability…

7. Conclusions

The hero archetype's of the original films is what made these so great, it made characters that everyone could relate to regardless of their background and beliefs.

Despite this analysis, however, one of the largest critiques of *Episode VII: The Force Awakens* is that the story yet again follows the same hero's journey as the original *Star Wars, Episode IV: A New Hope*. What makes these characters lose their "relatability" then, seems merely to be their lack of normativity in terms of positionality: of the ten characters with the most speaking time, in *The Last Jedi* three are portrayed by White males, three by White females, two by men of color, one by a woman of color, and two by technology overtly coded as male.

Furthermore, the model of Campbell's monomyth continues to apply, most clearly through the appearance of the same protagonist as the original series, Luke. Luke Skywalker is called to adventure by Rey's arrival at his self-imposed exile, while he receives mentorship yet again from Yoda, faces the trial of encountering (and fighting) his disciple Kylo Ren, projects himself via the Force despite knowing it may cause his death, succeeds in his showdown against Kylo Ren, is killed, and is resurrected as a Force projection to mentor Rey. In terms of narrative, little has altered: the hero archetype is clearly featured within this film. And thus, one must question what "relatability" actually means in this campaign. Most likely, and as largely suggested by supporters via social media, it is rather non-dominant positionality that makes normate groups uncomfortable rather than the composition of these stories themselves that lead fans to demean such series additions.

While explicitly placed in "a galaxy far, far away," the *Star Wars* films offer a vision of the future that well resonates with many viewers, making it one of the most lucrative and popular franchises in history. And, following the fall of the Empire or New Order in the various trilogies, we are left with a futuristic vision nearing the utopic—not only a world but an entire galaxy free of war. Yet, for many fans, this future must still be homogenous while upholding both White supremacy and the cisheteropatriarchy in order to be truly utopic.

This effort demonstrates yet another move toward a less diversified model of perfection—the gray world exemplified also through groups such as the Sad and Rabid Puppies, as well as cultural moments like RaceFail and Gamergate. Whether based in the future or an idealized present, the key question of "whose utopia" has again come under fierce debate. As I have contended in this book, the role of the person with disability within such spaces has become even more murky despite us being actually better suited to a utopic environment. As science progresses to develop technologies, such as the prenatal gene-modifying CRISPR-Cas9, that may eliminate entire categories of persons with disabilities, debates of ethics ensue. Arguably eugenics-based practices, such as the abortion of fetuses known to have disabilities, have also become divisive issues. For example, in June 2018, when Pope Francis spoke against disability-based abortion at a speech, it was his opposition to abortion as a whole rather than eugenics as a practice that became the subject of widespread news coverage. In this speech, Pope Francis explained his, and the Catholic Church's, position: "It is fashionable, or at least usual, that when in the first few months of a pregnancy doctors do studies to see if the child is healthy or has something, the first idea is: 'Let's send it away.' We do the same as the Nazis to maintain the purity of the race, but with white gloves on" (qtd. Lyman). A brief perusal of highly viewed newspaper coverage demonstrates that many publications, including *USA Today* (Lyman), *The New York Times* ("Pope"), and *The Wall Street Journal* (Rocca) do little to focus on the particular *kind* of abortion to which Francis refers. Instead, the headlines suggest a more wide-ranging anti-abortion platform, with, respectively, "Pope: Abortion is 'white glove' equivalent to Nazi crimes," "Pope Calls Abortion 'White Glove' Equivalent of Nazi Crimes," "Pope Francis Likens Abortion to Nazi Eugenics." Yet, while Pope Francis's comments may initially seem to follow under the auspices of the logical fallacy Reductio ad Hitlerum, also known as "playing the Nazi card," the practice of aborting fetuses that may become chronically ill or disabled infants does actually bear similarity to eugenics practices working to eliminate disability and crip futurity as practiced under the Nazi regime.

While this particular episode may simply demonstrate a journalistic tendency toward the sensational and overly simplistic, it also reiterates the continuation of a perceived limited biofuturity for persons with disabilities. Lee et al. recently reported in *Nature* that scientists have effectively utilized CRISPR-Gold, "a nonviral delivery vehicle for the CRISPR–Cas9 ribonucleoprotein" to decrease instances of "exaggerated repetitive behaviours" in mice. Notably, and as confirmed in Lee et al.'s

7. Conclusions

findings, repetitive behavior is one of the key symptoms of autism spectrum disorder. However, as discussed in Chapter 1 of this study, persons with ASD, researchers, and other invested parties continue to question whether this condition ethically *should* be eliminated, thus limiting the biofuturity of an entire population characterized by a broad spectrum of disabilities or, as argued by some, simple differences. Furthermore, as argued in Chapter 3 of this study, such scientists may actually be working toward eliminating ideal utopians.

The inherent question proposed by the potential elimination of certain disabilities and, thus, their future populations, asks: "What *should* the people of the future be like?" Or, more simply, "in a perfect world, which people should remain?" Yet, an analysis of both the history of conditions considered disabilities and idealized figures demonstrates that even our models of normalcy and superiority have altered over time. In fact, disability theorist and historian Douglas C. Baynton argues that disability has actively been used as a category by which to subjugate other marginalized persons across times. He contends that "disability has been one of prevalent justifications for inequality in American history," particularly injustices against immigrants, Black persons, and women. Similarly, queer and genderqueer persons have been subjugated via the medicalizations of states now considered perfectly healthy, however marginalized.

Nevertheless, despite various disabilities depending wholly or at least partially on a social model of normality, efforts to eliminate disabling conditions altogether continue. Simultaneously, models of idealized communities have and continue to portray utopic spaces as largely absent of persons with identifiable disabilities of all kinds despite persons with many disabilities actually offering ideal bodies to inhabit the mundaneness of a utopic setting. As demonstrated in Chapter 3 of this study, as conditions which, conversely, have been previously understood to be normative have come to be marked as disabling, so too have contemporary readings of past idealized spaces demonstrated the persistence of disabled utopic citizens. Thus, re-readings of traditional consummate figures tellingly show that even allegedly prototypical bodies can often contain disabilities: for example, it is argued by surgeon Hutan Ashrafian that Leonardo da Vinci's idealized figure of the *Vitruvian Man* appears to be suffering from a left inguinal hernia which could easily have led to the model becoming disabled before dying. Similarly, as shown in Chapter 3 of this study, the venerated figure of the highly logical consulting detective, Sherlock Holmes, has been read as depicting disabilities, both consistent with the time of Conan Doyle's writing and through the lens of a contemporary gaze.

Readings with a current understanding of science, disability, and culture, have allowed many marginalized groups to recognize themselves within the typically White and usually male texts that have been canonized and archived while writing themselves into these environments through derivative works. Whether through online communities, contemporary scholarship, fan fiction, or other mechanisms, activists, whether intentional or not, are particularly working against the homogenized agenda of a potentially gray world. While the corporatization and potential end of net neutrality continue to limit online reading and writing spaces, the potentialities for activism and self-representation via the internet remain significant, particularly for persons with disabilities. Debates, such as 2009's RaceFail and discussions surrounding 2014's Gamergate simply would have been made far less effective and instantaneous without such technologies as Tumblr, blogging, YouTube and other video hosting sites, and other digital tools. Efforts for reestablishing a White, male, cis, hetero, normate-centric model of storytelling represented by the Rabid and Sad Puppies, as well as the Remake The Last Jedi campaign, may offer a contrary point showing how these tools can be used against social justice efforts. Yet, I argue that, just as commonly, one can see efforts against such attempts to reestablish the status quo gain momentum and further social progress. As progressive online communities, particularly those working to connect persons with disabilities, continue to grow and achieve influence, one may expect their depictions of multifaceted futures and utopic spaces to continue proliferating as well.

Chapter Notes

Introduction

1. Notably, the film's new release was rerated in 2013 and given a PG rating. As such, *The Wizard of Oz* is now noted to include material that may "not be suitable for children." However, the MPAA does not offer a suggested age range with this new rating.

2. Some have argued that the reappropriation of the term "crip" to refer to disabled communities may be confusing as because of the Crips or Original Crip Homies adopting this name for their street gang. However, as that organization was established in the late 1960s, I argue that the term "crip" can and should continue to be applied to disabled communities, to whom the term "cripple" has been applied since around the 10th century CE.

Chapter 1

1. According to Amazon.com's bestsellers list on October 27, 2017.

2. Tellingly, this piece was included in the 2017 disability studies primer *Beginning with Disability*, edited by Lennard J. Davis.

3. Notably, persons with disabilities and illnesses are one group often disproportionately affected by measles outbreaks, as many persons with compromised immune systems are recommended against receiving the MMR vaccine (U.S. Centers for Disease Control and Prevention, "Who Should NOT Get Vaccinated with these Vaccines?").

4. Notably, martyrdom may take the place of a proven miracle in terms of the steps to become canonized within Catholicism.

5. Throughout this book, the term "representation" will be used in an aesthetic sense, referring to depictions, or lack thereof, of certain groups across artistic mediums.

6. Throughout this study, "Wonderland" as capitalized will refer to the magical world created by Lewis Carroll, while "wonderland" lowercased will refer to such fantasy realms as a whole.

7. Elsewhere, I refer to this space in children's literature as the "underland," a notably dystopic place marked by largely negative emotions.

8. While Mr. Tumnus does turn out to be a spy for the White Witch, his inability to betray Lucy marks him as a friend clearly aligned with Aslan's "good" within the Narnian binary.

9. Capitalization from original text.

10. In the context of Oz, all animals are capable of talking, though some, such as Toto, generally choose to abstain. While Toto is unable to speak "human" in Kansas, he can do so in Oz, but sees no reason to do so unless prompted.

11. Capitalization in original.

12. In *Alice's Adventures Through the Looking Glass and What She Found There* (*Through the Looking Glass*), the sequel to *Alice's Adventures in Wonderland*, Alice questions whether her whole experience in Wonderland is a dream. The final poem of the text, however, demonstrates that these experiences are as meaningful and legitimate as those in the real world: "Life, what is it but a dream?"

Chapter Notes

13. Otherwise known as the far commoner "Howell" when he is in the U.K.

Chapter 2

1. The book to which Thomas refers is entitled, *Toward a Theory of the Dark Fantastic: The Role of Racial Difference in Young Adult Speculative Fiction and Media*.
2. Baum never specifies Dorothy's age, but she is said to be a year older than Trot (*The Lost Princess of Oz*). In the canonical sequels by Ruth Plumly Thompson, Trot's age is given to be ten, making Dorothy approximately eleven years old (*The Giant Horse of Oz*).
3. Despite his relative lack of character in the film, Toto is, after Dorothy, one of the Oz books' primary protagonists.
4. This moment offers an early consideration of speculative fiction author Arthur C. Clarke's Third Law that "any sufficiently advanced technology is indistinguishable from magic."
5. Because Tip/Ozma, in turn, identifies both as male and female, sometimes both simultaneously, I have chosen to utilize gender neutral pronouns when referring to them as a united whole/single person.
6. Canonical texts are generally differentiated from non-canonical Oz works based on their recognition as such by the L. Frank Baum Family Trust.

Chapter 4

1. While the Golden Age of Fantasy is generally understood to have occurred between the late–1930s and mid–1940s, Miller's section on this period spans from 1906 to 1945.

Chapter 5

1. These posts were screen captured and saved for posterity by numerous fan communities, including those cited in this work.

Chapter 6

1. The characters' actor, Evan Alex, would have been around 11 years of age at the time of the film's release.
2. Kaylee is often listed with the misspelled last name of "Rodgers," though she is tellingly much easier to find online via the search terms "autistic girl singing."

Chapter 7

1. Notably co-written by R. Kelly, who has since been convicted of multiple cases of child sexual abuse himself.

Conclusion

1. Apart from copyright and other legal issues, the money "pledged" can hardly be said to represent an actual possibility of recreating *The Last Jedi*, or even actual funds. To contribute to the campaign, one must simply provide an email address, which need not be verified, along with a monetary pledge up to $10,000 in value. Thus, supporters of the campaign's ideas may simply promise an amount of money not represented by their actual bank account holdings.
2. Notably, while the initial trilogy has *two* droid characters, only one person of color (Billy Dee Williams's Baron Landonis "Lando" Calrissian) and one woman (Carrie Fisher as Princess Leia Organa of Alderaan) are represented among the main cast of the original films.

Works Cited

@Planet2kCed [N/A]. "Who done took the special needs folk to the capital????? How they get in?? I AM NOT OK ENOUGH! [Loudly Crying Face]." *Twitter*, 6 Jan. 2021, 1:44 p.m., https://twitter.com/Planet2kCed/status/1346935728308150276.

@katimcf [Kati]. "someone posted video of a protest of proposed Medicaid cuts that I got arrested at in 2017 saying it's from yesterday. Replies full of ableist rhetoric, folks saying they'd push us down the Capitol steps if they'd been there." *Twitter*, 7 Jan. 2021, 9:35 a.m., https://twitter.com/katimcf/status/1347235482867011585.

@WilliamShatner [William Shatner]. "An expert? How is any of this 'expert'? She's taking 2018 opinions and applying them to 50yo TV and making condemnations? This is pseudo intelligent bragging at best." *Twitter*, 4 July 2018, 7:27 a.m., https://twitter.com/williamshatner/status/1014516012224401409?lang=en.

———. "That's not what she said. And where can I see this "enduring quality" work? She said she has a book coming out. BTW on the 'racist stuff' I participated in; I assume you meant Star Trek? I'm sorry that Star Trek upset you. I'd encourage you not to watch. Good enough apology?" *Twitter*, 5 July 2018, 9:21 a.m., https://twitter.com/williamshatner/status/1014907231584698370?lang=en.

———. "Did you hear about the Laura Ingalls Wilder award being renamed over negative lines on the indigenous people of America? Laura changed the lines in the 50's. I find it disturbing that some take modern opinion & obliterate the past. Isn't progress @ learning from our mistakes?" *Twitter*, 30 June 2018, 7:34 p.m., https://twitter.com/williamshatner/status/1013249513757159426?lang=en.

———. "I actually read her diatribe of opinion. How can you claim 'takedown' when she uses current opinions on 50 year old TV episodes & then says I need to stay in my lane? She is so far out of her "lane" that it's sad to see that she is an educator comparing Peter Pan to LHOTP." *Twitter*, 4 July 2018, 7:16 a.m., https://twitter.com/williamshatner/status/1014513255685939200?lang=en.

Abrahm, Paul A., and Stuart Kenter. "Tik-Tok and the Three Laws of Robotics." *Science Fiction Studies*, vol. 14, no. 5.1, 1978.

Ahmed, Sara. *The Cultural Politics of Emotion*. 1st ed. Routledge, 2004.

———. "Feminist Wonder." *Feminist Killjoys*, 28 July 2014, https://feministkilljoys.com/2014/07/28/feminist-wonder/. Accessed 21 Nov. 2017.

———. *Living a Feminist Life*. Kindle ed., Duke University Press, 2017.

———. *The Promise of Happiness*. Kindle ed., Duke University Press, 2010.

———. "Snap!" *Feminist Killjoys*, 21 May 2017, https://feministkilljoys.com/2017/05/21/snap/. Accessed 21 Nov. 2017.

Alice. Directed by Jan Švankmajer, Film Four, 1988.

Works Cited

Alice: Madness Returns. Spicy Horse, 2011.

American McGee's Alice. Rogue Entertainment, 2000.

American Psychiatric Association [APA]. *Diagnostic and Statistical Manual of Mental Disorders*. 4th ed. American Psychiatric Association, 1994.

———. *Diagnostic and Statistical Manual of Mental Disorders*. 5th ed., American Psychiatric Association, 2013. DSM-V, doi.org/10.1176/appi.books.9780890425596. Accessed 8 Feb. 2018.

Anderson, Douglas A. *Tales Before Tolkien: The Roots of Modern Fantasy*. Del Rey, 2003.

"Ann McCaffrey." *Fanlore*, 6 Apr. 2018, https://fanlore.org/wiki/Anne_McCaffrey. Accessed 25 June 2018.

Ashrafian, Hutan. "Leonardo Da Vinci's Vitruvian Man: A Renaissance for Inguinal Hernias." *Hernia*, vol. 25, 2011, pp. 593–594.

Atanasoski, Neda, and Kalindi Vora. "Surrogate Humanity: Posthuman Networks and the (Racialized) Obsolescence of Labor." *Catalyst*, vol. 1, no. 1, 2015.

Atchison, Amy L., and Shauna L. Shames. *Survive and Resist: The Definitive Guide to Dystopian Politics*. Columbia University Press, 2019. JSTOR, www.jstor.org/stable/10.7312/atch18890. Accessed 28 Dec. 2020.

Bagnall, Norma. "Terabithia: Bridge to a Better World." *Language Arts*, vol. 56, no. 4, 1979, pp. 429–431. JSTOR, www.jstor.org/stable/41404823. Accessed 28 Dec. 2020.

Bakewell, Michael. *Lewis Carroll: A Biography*. Mandarin, 1997.

Bakhtin, Mikhail. *Problems of Dostoevsky's Poetics*. Ed. and trans. Caryl Emerson. *Archive.org*, 1984, https://archive.org/details/problemsofdostoe00bakh. Accessed 28 Dec. 2020.

Bargetz, Brigitte. "The Politics of the Everyday: A Feminist Revision of the Public/Private Frame." *Institute for Human Sciences*, 2009, http://www.iwm.at/publications/5-junior-visiting-fellows-conferences/vol-xxiv/the-politics-of-the-everyday/. Accessed 25 June 2018.

Barrie, J.M. *Peter Pan*. 1911. *Project Gutenberg*, 2008, http://www.gutenberg.org/files/16/16-h/16-h.htm. Accessed 15 July 2018.

———. *Peter Pan or the Boy Who Would Not Grow Up (The Play)*. Project Gutenberg Australia, Feb. 2003, http://gutenberg.net.au/ebooks03/0300081h.html. Accessed 20 Sept. 2022.

Barthes, Roland. *Image—Music—Text*. Trans. Stephen Heath. Hill and Wang, 1977.

Baum, L. Frank. *The Annotated Wizard of Oz*. 1900. Edited by Michael Patrick Hearn. Centennial Edition, Norton, 2000.

———. *The Emerald City of Oz*. 1910. In The Complete Wizard of Oz Collection. Middleton Classics, 2010.

———. *Glinda of Oz*. 1920. *Project Gutenberg*, 2009, http://www.gutenberg.org/files/961/961-h/961-h.htm. Accessed 27 Dec. 2020.

———. L. Frank Baum Papers. Special Collections Research Center, Syracuse University, Syracuse, NY. 1900–1942.

———. *The Lost Princess of Oz*. 1917. In The Complete Wizard of Oz Collection. Middleton Classics, 2010.

———. *The Magic of Oz*. 1919. *Project Gutenberg*, 2008, http://www.gutenberg.org/files/419/419-h/419-h.htm. Accessed 27 Dec. 2020.

———. *The Marvelous Land of Oz*. 1904. In The Complete Wizard of Oz Collection. Middleton Classics, 2010.

———. *Ozma of Oz*. 1907. Illustrated by John R. Neill. *Project Gutenberg*, 2008, http://www.gutenberg.org/files/486/486-h/486-h.htm. Accessed 15 July 2018.

———. *The Patchwork Girl of Oz*. 1913. *Project Gutenberg*, 2009, http://www.gutenberg.org/files/955/955-h/955-h.htm. Accessed 15 July 2018.

———. *Rinkitink in Oz*. 1916. *Project Gutenberg*, 2009, http://www.gutenberg.org/files/958/958-h/958-h.htm. Accessed 27 Dec. 2020.

Works Cited

———. *The Road to Oz.* 1909. In *The Complete Wizard of Oz Collection.* Middleton Classics, 2010.

———. *The Scarecrow of Oz.* 1915. Project Gutenberg, 2009, http://www.gutenberg.org/files/957/957-h/957-h.htm. Accessed 15 July 2018.

———. "Tiktok and the Nome King." *Little Wizard Stories of Oz.* Reilly & Britton, 1904.

———. *Tik-Tok of Oz.* 1914. In *The Complete Wizard of Oz Collection.* Middleton Classics, 2010.

———. *The Tin Woodman of Oz.* 1918. In *The Complete Wizard of Oz Collection.* Middleton Classics, 2010.

Baynton, Douglas C. "Disability and the Justification of Inequality in American History." *The Disability Studies Reader*, 5th Kindle ed., ed. Lennard J. Davis, Routledge, 2017.

Beck, Koa. *White Feminism: From the Suffragettes to Influencers and Who They Leave Behind.* Kindle ed., Atria, 2021.

Beebe, John. "The Wizard of Oz: A Vision of Development in the American Political Psyche." *The Vision Thing: Myth, Politics and Psyche in the World*, ed. Thomas Singer, Routledge, 2000. Print.

Begley, Sarah. "5 Books That Influenced How George R.R. Martin Wrote Game of Thrones." *Time*, 30 May 2017, http://time.com/4769331/game-of-thrones-books-george-rr-martin/. Accessed 25 June 2018.

Bellamy, Edward. *Looking Backward, 2000 to 1887.* 1888. Project Gutenberg, 2008, http://www.gutenberg.org/files/624/624-h/624-h.htm. Accessed 17 Feb. 2017.

Bérubé, Michael. "Disability and Narrative." *PLMA*, vol. 120, no. 2, March 2005, pp. 568–576.

"Biography." *MadeleineLEngle.Com*, https://www.madeleinelengle.com/madeleine-lengle/madeleine-lengle-biography-1/. Accessed 20 Sept. 2022.

"Biography." *MichaelEnde.De*, https://michaelende.de/en/author/biography. Accessed 20 Sept. 2022.

Birkin, Andrew. *J.M. Barrie and the Lost Boys: The Real Story Behind Peter Pan.* Yale University Press, 2003.

Bly, Nellie. *Ten Days in a Mad-House.* Munro, 1877. University Pressenn Library, http://digital.library.upenn.edu/women/bly/madhouse/madhouse.html. Accessed 20 Sept. 2022.

Boersma, Katja. "Is the Search for a 'Pain Personality' of Added Value to the Fear-Avoidance-Model (FAM) of Chronic Pain?" *Scandinavian Journal of Pain*, vol. 17, 2017, pp. 226–227.

Brandt, Nicholas, director. *Cry.* Performance by Michael Jackson, MJJ Productions, 2001.

Briefel, Aviva. "Monster Pains: Masochism, Menstruation, and Identification in the Horror Film." *Film Quarterly*, vol. 58, no. 3, Spring 2005, pp. 16–27.

British Council. "Tom Stoppard." *British Council*, 2018, https://literature.britishcouncil.org/writer/tom-stoppard. Accessed 25 June 2018.

Brockes, Emma. "Michael Cunningham: A Life in Writing." *The Guardian*, 7 Feb. 2011, https://www.theguardian.com/culture/2011/feb/07/michael-cunningham-life-writing. Accessed 25 June 2018.

Brockington, Ian F., E. Macdonald, and G. Wainscott. "Anxiety, Obsessions and Morbid Preoccupations in Pregnancy and the Puerperium." *Archives of Women's Mental Health*, vol. 9, no. 5, 2006, pp. 253–263, https://link.springer.com/article/10.1007%2Fs00737-006-0134-z?LI=true. Accessed 8 Feb. 2018.

Brooks, Geraldine. *GeraldineBrooks.com*, 2008, http://geraldinebrooks.com/. Accessed 25 June 2018.

———. *March.* 2005. 2nd ed., Penguin, 2006.

brown, adrienne maree. *Emergent Strategy: Shaping Change, Changing Worlds.* Kindle ed., AK Press, 2017.

Brown, Jax Jacki. "Why I'm Boycotting 'Me Before You' and Why You Should Too." *Junkee*, 15 June 2016, http://junkee.com/why-im-protesting-me-before-you-and-why-you-should-too/80828. Accessed 3 July 2018.

Bundel, Ani. "SDCC '22: How to Create

Works Cited

Your Own Novel Tackles a Complex Issue." *Comic Beats*, 24 Jul. 2022, https://www.comicsbeat.com/sdcc-22-how-to-create-your-own-novel-tackles-a-complex-issue/. Accessed 20 Sept. 2022.

Burger, Alissa. *The Wizard of Oz as American Myth: A Critical Study of Six Versions of the Story, 1900–2007.* McFarland, 2012.

Burgett, Bruce, and Glenn Hendler. "Keywords: An Introduction." *Keywords for American Cultural Studies*, ed. Bruce Burgett and Glenn Hendler, New York University Press, 2007, pp. 1–6.

Butler, Catherine. "Taking Children's Literature Seriously." 2013, http://www.academia.edu/8491847/Taking_Childrens_Literature_Seriously. 15 July 2018.

Butler, Samuel. *Erewhon; Or, Over the Range.* 1872. Project Gutenberg, 2005, http://www.gutenberg.org/files/1906/1906-h/1906-h.htm. Accessed 17 Feb. 2017.

Byzek, Josie. "Criptopia." *New Mobility: The Magazine for Active Wheelchair Users*, 1 Aug. 2013, http://www.newmobility.com/2013/08/criptopia/. Accessed 8 Feb. 2018.

Campbell, Joseph. *The Hero with a Thousand Faces.* 1949. New World Library, 2008.

Carlisle, Stephen. "If You Make It 'Porn,' Does that Make it a Parody?" *Nova Southeastern University*, 9 June 2016, http://copyright.nova.edu/porn-parody/. Accessed 20 Sept. 2022.

Carroll, Lewis. *Alice's Adventures in Wonderland.* 1865. Project Gutenberg, 2008, http://www.gutenberg.org/files/11/11-h/11-h.htm. Accessed 15 Oct. 2016.

———. *Through the Looking-Glass.* 1871. Project Gutenberg, 1991, http://www.gutenberg.org/files/12/12-h/12-h.htm. Accessed 14 Oct. 2016.

ChancellorGriffin. "Legal Disclaimer!" *Patreon*, 31 Aug. 2016, https://www.patreon.com/posts/legal-disclaimer-6659845. Accessed 25 June 2018.

Chase, Darren. "Copyright, Fair Use & the Creative Commons." *Stony Brook University Libraries*, 2018, http://guides.library.stonybrook.edu/copyright. Accessed 25 June 2018.

Chen, Mel. *Animacies: Biopolitics, Racial Mattering, and Queer Affect.* Kindle ed., Duke University Press, 2012.

Clarke, Arthur C. "Hazards of Prophecy." *The Futurists*, Kindle ed., ed. Alvin Toffler, Random House, 1972, pp. 133–150.

Clare, Eli. *Brilliant Imperfection: Grappling with Cure.* Kindle ed., Duke University Press, 2017.

Cohen, Morton N. *Lewis Carroll: A Biography.* Vintage, 1996.

Common Sense Media. "The Wizard of Oz Movie Review—Common Sense Media." *Common Sense Media*, https://www.commonsensemedia.org/moviereviews/the-wizard-of-oz. Accessed 13 June 2018.

Copeland, Misty. *Life in Motion: An Unlikely Ballerina.* Kindle ed., Touchstone, 2014.

Cordero, Rosy. "The NeverEnding Story Oral History: How 3 Brave Kids Helped Save the World by Using Their Imaginations." *Entertainment Weekly*, 18 Dec. 2019, https://ew.com/movies/2019/12/18/the-neverending-story-oral-history/. Accessed 28 Dec. 2020.

"Crip Theory." Breaking Silences, Demanding Crip Justice Conferences, Sept. 2017, Wright State University, https://www.wright.edu/eve.

Cuningham, Henry. "Sherlock Holmes and the Case of Race." *The Journal of Popular Culture*, vol. 48, no. 1, Fall 1994, pp. 44–58.

Dahl, Roald. *Charlie and the Chocolate Factory.* 1964. Kindle ed., Puffin, 1998.

———. *Going Solo.* 1986. Kindle ed., Viking Books, 2009.

———. *Over to You: Ten Stories of Flyers and Flying.* 1946. Kindle ed., Penguin, 1990.

Davidson, Michael. "Pregnant Men: Modernism, Disability, and Biofuturity in Djuna Barnes." *Novel*, vol. 43, no. 2, 2010, pp. 207–226.

———. *Concerto for the Left Hand: Disability and the Defamiliar Body.* University of Michigan Press, 2008.

Works Cited

Davis, Kathy. "Surgical Passing: Or Why Michael Jackson's Nose Makes 'Us' Uneasy." *Feminist Theory*, vol. 4, no. 1, 2003, pp. 73–92.

Davis, Lennard. *Bending Over Backwards: Essays on Disability and the Body*. New York University Press, 2002.

——. "The End of Identity Politics and the Beginning of Dismodernism." *The Disability Studies Reader*, 4th Kindle ed., ed. Lennard Davis, Routledge, 2013, pp. 255–279.

——. "Introduction." *The Disability Studies Reader*, 4th Kindle ed., ed. Lennard Davis, Routledge, 2013, pp. 1–13.

Donaldson, Elizabeth J. "The Corpus of the Madwoman: Toward a Feminist Disability Studies Theory of Embodiment and Mental Illness." *NWSA Journal*, vol. 14, no. 3, Fall 2002, pp. 99–119.

Dreisbach, Shaun. "Top 14 Pregnancy Fears (and Why You Shouldn't Worry)." *Parents*, https://www.parents.com/pregnancy/complications/health-and-safety-issues/top-pregnancy-fears/. Accessed 8 Feb. 2018.

Duffer Brothers, creators. *Stranger Things*. Netflix, 2016–2019.

"Eartha Kitt's Daughter Says Her Late Mother Left Her 'The Ability to Find Laughter.'" *Closer*, 14 Jan. 2018, https://www.closerweekly.com/posts/eartha-kitt-daughter-laughter-after-death-151168. 20 Sept. 2020.

@Ebonyteach [Ebony Elizabeth Thomas]. "1. The tea is that Star Trek TOS was groundbreaking for its time, but is problematic from a 2010s POV, especially on gender. 2. Bill Seriously needs to stay in his lane. 3. There are many racist Trek fans (& SF Fans), hence the # of RTs. They want progress only on their terms." *Twitter*, 4 July 2018, 6:12 a.m., https://twitter.com/ebonyteach/status/1014497207821787136.

——. "I'll send my Tweets to @Penn myself, @WilliamShatner. They tenured me for this work. This is my lane—I have a book coming out in the spring on this very topic. Go ahead & block me like everyone else you disagree with. I'll still be a #StarTrek fan." *Twitter*, 4 July 2018, 10:24 a.m., https://twitter.com/ebonyteach/status/1014560713287917568?lang=en.

Edelman, Lee. *No Future: Queer Theory and the Death Drive*. Duke University Press, 2004.

Edwards, Gavin, "'We Are the World': A Minute-by-Minute Breakdown." *Rolling Stone*, 6 March 2020, https://www.rollingstone.com/music/music-features/we-are-the-world-a-minute-by-minute-breakdown-54619/. 20 Sept. 2022.

Ehrenreich, Barbara. *Smile or Die: How Positive Thinking Fooled America and the World*. Granta, 2010.

Eldridge, Richard. "Metaphysics and the Interpretation of Persons: Davidson on Thinking and Conceptual Schemes." *Synthese*, vol. 66, no. 3, March 1986, pp. 477–503.

Ende, Michael. *The Neverending Story*. 1979. Translated by Ralph Manheim. Kindle ed. Puffin, 2018.

Engels, Freidrich. "Socialism: Utopian and Scientific." 1876. *Marx/Engels Selected Works*, Vol. III, trans. Edward Aveling. Kindle ed., Marxists.org, 1970.

"Eugenic, Adj. and N." *OED Online*, Oxford University Press, January 2018, www.oed.com/view/Entry/64958. Accessed 8 Feb. 2018.

Eyler, Joshua R. "Disability and Prosthesis in L. Frank Baum's the Wonderful Wizard of Oz." *Children's Literature Association Quarterly*, vol. 38, no. 3, Fall 2013, pp. 219–334.

Feminist Frequency. "The 2012 Oscars and the Bechdel Test." *YouTube*, uploaded by Feminist Frequency, 15 Feb. 2012, https://www.youtube.com/watch?time_continue=2&v=PH8JuizIXw8. Accessed 25 June 2018.

"The Feminist Sexual Ethics Project." *Brandeis University*, https://www.brandeis.edu/projects/fse/about/contributors.html#rawles. Accessed 25 June 2018.

Ferns, Christopher S. *Narrating Utopia: Ideology, Gender, Form in Utopian Lit-*

Works Cited

erature. Liverpool University Press, 1999.

Flaherty, Colleen. "Captain Kirk Vs. 2 Professors." *Inside Higher Ed*, 6 July 2018, https://www.insidehighered.com/news/2018/07/06/william-shatner-unleashes-academics-twitter-after-he-criticizes-librarians-over. Accessed 11 July 2018.

Ford, Paul F. *Pocket Companion to Narnia*. Kindle ed. Harper, 2009.

Foulkes, Richard. *Lewis Carroll and the Victorian Stage: Theatricals in a Quiet Life*. Kindle ed., Routledge, 2019.

Frankel, Valerie Estelle. *From Girl to Goddess: The Heroine's Journey Through Myth and Legend*. McFarland, 2010.

Free, Elise. "The Phrase We Should Say Instead of 'As Long as It's Healthy.'" *The Mighty*, 16 July 2015, https://themighty.com/2015/07/what-to-say-to-mothers-instead-of-as-long-as-its-healthy/. Accessed 16 June 2017.

Freeman, Sholnn Z. "Jordan Peele Brings 'Us' Screening to Howard University." *The Dig*, 22 March 2019, https://thedig.howard.edu/all-stories/jordan-peele-brings-us-screening-howard-university. Accessed 20 Sept. 2022.

Freeman Loftis, Sonya. *Fiction and Stereotypes on the Spectrum*. Indiana University Press, 2015.

Freud, Sigmund. "Mourning and Melancholia." *The Standard Edition of the Complete Psychological Works of Sigmund Freud*, vol. XIV, ed. James Strachey, Anna Freud, Alix Strachey, and Alan Tyson, trans. James Strachey, Anna Freud, Alix Strachey, and Alan Tyson, 1917–1919, Hogarth Press, pp. 243–258.

———. "The 'Uncanny.'" *The Standard Edition of the Complete Psychological Works of Sigmund Freud*, vol. XVI, ed. James Strachey, Anna Freud, Alix Strachey, and Alan Tyson, trans. James Strachey, Anna Freud, Alix Strachey, and Alan Tyson, 1917–1919, Hogarth Press, pp. 217–256.

Gabaldon, Diana. "Fan-Fiction and Moral Conundrums." *Voyages of the Artemis*, 3 May 2010, http://voyagesoftheartemis.blogspot.com/2010/05/fan-fiction-and-moral-conundrums.html. Accessed 14 June 2018.

Garland-Thomson, Rosemarie. "Integrating Disability, Transforming Feminist Theory." *The Disability Studies Reader*, 4th Kindle ed., ed. Lennard J. Davis, Routledge, 2013.

Gavin, Adrienne E., and Humphries, Andrew F. *Worlds Enough and Time: The Cult of Childhood in Edwardian Fiction*, ed. Adrienne E. Gavin and Andrew F. Humphries, Palgrave Macmillan, 2009, 1–20. https://doi.org/10.1057/9780230595132_1.

Gibson, Charity. "*The Wizard of Oz* as a Modernist Work." *The Universe of Oz: Essays on Baum's Series and Its Progeny*. Eds. Kevin K. Durand and Mary K. Leigh. Jefferson, NC: McFarland & Co., 2010. 107–118. Print.

Gilbert, Sandra M., and Susan Gubar. *The Madwoman in the Attic: The Woman Writer and the Nineteenth-Century Literary Imagination*. 1979. Subsequent ed., Yale University Press, 2000.

Green, Archie. *Tin Men*. Kindle ed., University of Illinois Press, 2006.

Greg, Percy. *Across the Zodiac*. 1880. *Project Gutenberg*, 2003, http://www.gutenberg.org/cache/epub/10165/pg10165-images.html. Accessed 22 Feb. 2017.

Guillen, Michael. "Pan's Labyrinth—Interview with Guillermo Del Toro." *Twitch*, 17 Dec. 2006, https://web.archive.org/web/20120929100112/http:/twitchfilm.com/2006/12/pans-labyrinthinterview-with-guillermo-del-toro.html. Accessed 28 Dec. 2020.

Hancock, Joseph H., II. "Why Differences Matter to Me." *Fashion, Style & Popular Culture*, vol. 8, no. 11, 2021, pp. 3–11.

Hands Across America. Hands Across America, 2022, https://www.handsacrossamerica.org/. Accessed 20 Sept. 2022.

Hansen, Randall, and Desmond King. *Sterilized by the State: Eugenics, Race, and the Population Scare in Twentieth-Century North America*. Cambridge University Press, 2013.

Works Cited

Hassan, Adeel. "Your Wednesday Briefing." *The New York Times*, 26 May 2016, https://archive.nytimes.com/www.nytimes.com/indexes/2016/05/25/nytnow/nytnow-email/index.html. 20 Sept. 2022.

Hennelly, Mark M. "Alice's Adventures at the Carnival." *Victorian Literature and Culture*, vol. 37, no. 1, 2009, pp. 103–128. *JSTOR*, www.jstor.org/stable/40347216. Accessed 28 Dec. 2020.

Hiatt, Brian, "Exclusive: Comic-Book Superstar Grant Morrison Channeled John Lennon. Hear the Song They Wrote." *RollingStone*, 14 June 2022, https://www.rollingstone.com/music/music-features/grant-morrison-ezra-miller-john-lennon-superman-1367662/. 20 Sept. 2022.

Hopkinson, Nalo. *Report from Planet Midnight*. PM Press, 2012.

"Hugo Award Nominations Spark Criticism Over Diversity in Sci-Fi: Sci-Fi Awards Have Been Roped Into a Furor." *The Telegraph*, 8 Apr. 2015, http://www.telegraph.co.uk/culture/books/booknews/11517920/Hugo-Award-nominations-spark-criticism-over-diversity-in-sci-fi.html. Accessed 14 Nov. 2017.

"Hysteria, N." *OED Online*. Oxford University Press, December 2017, www.oed.com/view/Entry/90638. Accessed 16 June 2017.

Irr, Caren. *Pink Pirates: Contemporary American Women Writers and Copyright*. Kindle ed., University of Iowa Press, 2010.

Jameson, Fredric. *Archaeologies of the Future: The Desire Called Utopia and Other Science Fiction*. Verso, 2005.

Jensen, Klaus Bruhn. "Intermediality." *The International Encyclopedia of Communication*, International Communication Association, 1 Dec. 2015, https://onlinelibrary.wiley.com/doi/pdf/10.1002/9781118766804.wbiect170. Accessed 20 Sept. 2022.

Jones, Diana Wynne. *The Tough Guide to Fantasyland*. 1996. Revised and updated ed., Penguin, 2006.

Kaestle, Carl F., et al. *Literacy in the United States: Readers and Reading Since 1880*. New Haven and London, Yale University Press, 1991.

Kafer, Alison. *Feminist, Queer, Crip*. Kindle ed., Indiana University Press, 2013.

Karp, Andrew. "Utopian Tension in L. Frank Baum's Oz." *Utopian Studies*, vol. 9, no. 2, 1998, pp. 103–121.

Kashdan, Todd B. "The Problem with Happiness." *Psychology Today*, 29 Sept. 2010, https://www.psychologytoday.com/blog/curious/201009/the-problem-happiness. Accessed 8 Feb. 2018.

"Katherine Paterson: Laureate of the 2007 NSK Neustadt Prize for Children's Literature." *World Literature Today*, vol. 82, no. 3, 2008, pp. 18–18. *JSTOR*, http://www.jstor.org/stable/40159722. Accessed 28 Sep. 2022.

"Kaylee Rodgers Singing Hallelujah—Official Video—Full HD." *Beefy TV*, 21 Dec. 2016, https://www.youtube.com/watch?v=Bmx—WjeN7o.

Kehr, Dave. "Return to Oz." *Chicago Reader*, 1985, https://www.chicagoreader.com/chicago/return-to-oz/Film?oid=1073337. Accessed 28 Dec. 2020.

Kelleter, Frank. "'Toto, I Think We're in Oz Again' (and Again and Again): Remakes and Popular Seriality." *Film Remakes, Adaptations and Fan Productions*, ed. Kathleen Lock and Constantine Verevis, Palgrave, 2012, pp. 19–44.

Kidd, Kenneth B., and Joseph T. Thomas, Jr. "A Prize-Losing Introduction." *Prizing Children's Literature: The Cultural Politics of Children's Books*, ed. Kenneth B. Kidd and Joseph T. Thomas, Jr., Kindle ed., Taylor & Francis, 2017.

Kindergarde: Avant-garde Poems, Plays, Stories, and Songs for Children. Ed. Dana Teen Lomax. Black Radish Books, 2013. Print.

Kissling, Elizabeth Arveda. "On the Rag on Screen: Menarche in Film and Television." *Sex Roles*, vol. 46, no. 1, January 2002, pp. 5–12.

Kohn, Diana. "Lisa Hill and the Bridge to Terabithia." *Takoma Voice*, June 2005,

Works Cited

https://web.archive.org/web/20090412030815/http:/www.takoma.com/archives/copy/2005/06/features_takomaarchives0605.html. Accessed 28 Dec. 2020.

Kurchak, Sarah. "I'm Autistic, and Believe Me, It's a Lot Better Than Measles." *Medium*, 26 Feb. 2015, https://medium.com/the-archipelago/im-autistic-and-believe-me-its-a-lot-better-than-measles-78cb039f4bea. Accessed 15 July 2018.

Lacan, Jacques. "The Mirror Stage as Formative of the Function of the I as Revealed in Psychoanalytic Experience." *Écrits: A Selection*, 1966, trans. Alan Sheridan, Routledge, 1977, pp. 1–8.

Landis, John, director. *Thriller*. Performance by Michael Jackson, MJJ Productions, 1983.

Lee, Bumwhee, et al. "Nanoparticle Delivery of CRISPR Into the Brain Rescues a Mouse Model of Fragile X Syndrome from Exaggerated Repetitive Behaviors." *Nature Biomedical Engineering*, 2018, https://www.nature.com/articles/s41551-018-0252-8. Accessed 30 June 2018.

Lees, John, et al. *And Then Emily Was Gone: Issue Zero*. Free Comic Book Day Special Ed., Comix Tribe, 2015.

Lees, John, et al. *And Then Emily Was Gone*. Comix Tribe, 2015.

"Left-Justified Fantasy Map." *TV Tropes*, https://tvtropes.org/pmwiki/pmwiki.php/Main/LeftJustifiedFantasyMap. Accessed 15 July 2018.

Le Guin, Ursula K. *The Lathe of Heaven*. 1971. Ebook ed. Scribner's, 2008.

L'Engle, Madeleine. *A Circle of Quiet*. Kindle ed., Harper, 1984.

———. *A Wrinkle in Time*. 1962. Kindle ed. Square Fish, 2007.

Lewis, C.S. *The Horse and His Boy*. 1954. Archive.org, 2017, https://archive.org/details/narniahorsehisbo00csle. 15 July 2018.

———. *The Last Battle*. 1956. Project Gutenberg Canada, 2013, https://gutenberg.ca/ebooks/lewiscs-lastbattle/lewiscs-lastbattle-00-h.html. Accessed 27 December 2020.

———. *The Lion, the Witch, and the Wardrobe: A Story for Children*. 1950. Project Gutenberg Canada, 2014, https://gutenberg.ca/ebooks/lewiscs-thelionthewitchandthewardrobe/lewiscs-thelionthewitchandthewardrobe-00-h.html. Accessed 15 July 2018.

Litman, Jessica. "Mickey Mouse Emeritus: Character Protection and the Public Domain." *University of Miami Entertainment & Sports Law Review*, vol. 429, 1994.

Little People of America. *Little People of America*, 2013, http://www.lpaonline.org/. Accessed 14 June 2018.

Littlefield, Henry M. (1964). "The Wizard of Oz: Parable on Populism." *American Quarterly*, vol. 16, no. 1, pp. 47–58.

Lorde, Audre. *The Cancer Journals*. 1980. Special Kindle ed. Aunt Lute, 1997.

Los Angeles Stella Adler Academy of Acting and Theatre. "Two-Year Program." *Stella Adler*, https://stellaadler.la/courses/two-year-program/. Accessed 20 Sept. 2022.

"Loss of Sight and Enhanced Hearing: A Neural Picture." *PLoS Biology*, vol. 3, no. 2, 2005, https://www.ncbi.nlm.nih.gov/pmc/articles/PMC544930/. Accessed 28 Dec. 2020.

Lyman, Eric J. "Pope: Abortion Is 'White Glove' Equivalent to Nazi Crimes." *USA Today*, 16 June 2018, https://www.usatoday.com/story/news/world/2018/06/16/pope-francis-abortion-equivalent-nazi-eugenics-crimes/707661002/. Accessed 30 June 2018.

Lyons, Martyn. "New Readers in the Nineteenth Century: Women, Children, Workers." *A History of Reading in the West*, ed. Guglielmo Cavallo and Roger Chartier, trans. Lydia G. Cochrane, U of Massachusetts Press 1999, 313–344.

Martin, George R.R. *A Game of Thrones*. Bantam, 1996.

———. "Someone Is Angry on the Internet." *Not a Blog*, 7 May 2010, https://grrm.livejournal.com/151914.html. Accessed 14 June 2018.

Martin, Jeffrey J. *Handbook of Disability Sport and Exercise Psychology*. Kindle ed. Oxford University Press, 2017.

Works Cited

Martin, Philip. "Trends in Migration to the U.S." Population Reference Bureau, 18 May 2013, https://www.prb.org/resources/trends-in-migration-to-the-u-s/. Accessed 20 Sept. 2022.

Martin Sandino, Amanda. *The Usual Head/ache: Building Empathy for Physical Suffering Through the Use of Poetry*. MA thesis. University of Washington Bothell, 2011.

Maslin, Janet. "Film: A New 'Oz' Gives Dorothy New Friends." *The New York Times*, 21 June 1985, https://www.nytimes.com/1985/06/21/movies/film-a-new-oz-gives-dorothy-new-friends.html. 28 Dec. 2020.

Maus, Derek C. *Unvarnishing Reality: Subversive Russian and American Cold War Satire*. U of South Carolina Press, 2011. *JSTOR*, www.jstor.org/stable/j.ctv6wgcs0. Accessed 28 Dec. 2020.

McCormack, Kathleen. "George Eliot and Victorian Science Fiction: Daniel Deronda as Alternate History." *Extrapolation*, vol. 27, no. 3, 1986, pp. 185–96.

McGee, Glenn. *The Perfect Baby: Parenthood in the New World of Cloning and Genetics*. Rowman & Littlefield, 2000.

McGuire, Seanan. *Every Heart a Doorway*. Kindle ed. Tor.com, 2016.

———. "Fifty Thoughts on Writing." *SeananMcGuire.com*, https://seananmcguire.com/50thoughts.php. Accessed 20 Sept. 2022.

Mcleod, Deborah Susan. *The 'Defective' Generation: Disability in Modernist Literature*. Dissertation, U of South Florida, 2014. Scholar Commons 5272.

McRuer, Robert. "The Then and There of Crip Futurity." Review of *Feminist, Queer, Crip* by Alison Kafer. *GLQ: A Journal of Lesbian and Gay Studies*, vol. 20, no. 4, 2013, 532–534.

Miceli, Michael George, and Jason Kenneth Steele. "Masking Eugenics as Science: A Critical Disability Studies Perspective of New Reproductive Technologies: Commentary on Stowe Et Al." *Journal on Developmental Disabilities*, vol. 13, no. 2, 2007, pp. 85–88.

Michals, Teresa, and Claire McTiernan. "'Oh, Why Can't You Remain Like This Forever!': Children's Literature, Growth, and Disability." *Disability Studies Quarterly*, vol. 38, no. 2, 2018, https://dsq-sds.org/article/view/6107/4914. 28 Dec. 2020.

Miller, Laura, ed. *Literary Wonderlands: A Journey Through the Greatest Fictional Worlds Ever Created*. Kindle ed., Black Dog & Leventhal, 2016.

Minich, Julie Avril. "Disability, Losers, and Narrative Remediation." *Comparative Literature* 66.1, 2014, 35–42, https://www.jstor.org/stable/24694534/.

Miserandino, Christine. "Spoon Theory." *But You Don't Look Sick?: The Stories Behind the Smiles*, 2003, https://butyoudontlooksick.com/articles/written-by-christine/the-spoon-theory/. Accessed 14 June 2014.

Mitchell, David T., and Sharon L. Snyder. "Compulsory Feralization: Institutionalizing Disability Studies." *PMLA* 120, 2005, 627–634.

———. *Narrative Prosthesis: Disability and Dependencies of Discourse*. University of Michigan Press 2001.

Moglen, Seth. *Mourning Modernity: Literary Modernism and the Injuries of American Capitalism*. 1st ed. Stanford University Press, 2007.

Moore, Raylyn. *Wonderful Wizard Marvelous Land*. Popular Press, 1974.

More, Thomas. 1516. *Utopia*. Project Gutenberg, 2005, https://www.gutenberg.org/files/2130/2130-h/2130-h.htm. Accessed 15 July 2018.

Morris, William. *News from Nowhere; Or, an Epoch of Rest*. 1890. Project Gutenberg, 2007, http://www.gutenberg.org/files/3261/3261-h/3261-h.htm. Accessed 17 Feb. 2017.

Morrison, Grant, and Dave McKean. *Batman: Arkham Asylum*. 1989. New ed., DC, 2020.

Moyes, Jojo. *Me Before You*. Kindle ed., Penguin, 2012.

Muñoz, José Esteban. *Cruising Utopia: The Then and There of Queer Futurity*. New York University Press, 2009.

Murdock, Maureen. *The Heroine's Journey*. Shambhala, 1990.

Works Cited

Murkoff, Heidi. "The Benefits of Prenatal Testing." *What to Expect*, 23 March 2017, https://www.whattoexpect.com/pregnancy/pregnancy-health/benefits-of-prenatal-testing/. Accessed 8 Feb. 2018.

National Institutes of Health [NIH]. "Cleidocranial Dysplasia." *GARD*, 19 Aug. 2020, https://rarediseases.info.nih.gov/diseases/6118/cleidocranial-dysplasia. 28 Dec. 2020.

Nelson, Alondra, and Nalo Hopkinson. "'Making the Impossible Possible': An Interview with Nalo Hopkinson." *Social Text*, vol. 20, no. 2, 2002, pp. 97–113.

Nepveu, Kate. "Diana Gabaldon & Fanfic Followup." *LiveJournal*, 10 May 2010, https://kate-nepveu.livejournal.com/483239.html. Accessed 30 Sept. 2022.

The NeverEnding Story. Directed by Wolfgang Petersen, Warner Bros., 1984.

The NeverEnding Story II: The Next Chapter. Directed by George T. Miller, Warner Bros., 1990.

Nielsen, Kim E. *A Disability History of the United States*. Kindle ed. Beacon, 2012.

O'Kane, Claire. "Reflections on the Benefits of Participatory Techniques." *Research with Children: Perspectives and Practices*, ed. Pia Christensen and Allison James, Routledge, 2000, pp. 136–159.

Ouellette, Alicia. "Selection Against Disability: Abortion, ART, and Access." *Journal of Law, Medicine, & Ethics*, Summer 2015.

Owens, Robert. "How Much Does a Boat Cost in 2022? (With Ownership Costs)." *Quicknav*, 17 Jan. 2017, https://quicknav.com/how-much-does-a-boat-cost/. Accessed 20 Sept. 2022.

Pan's Labyrinth. Directed by Guillermo del Toro, Warner Bros., 2006.

Parker, David B. "The Rise and Fall of the Wonderful Wizard of Oz as a 'Parable on Populism.'" *Journal of the Georgia Association of Historians*, vol. 15, 1994, pp. 49–63.

Parrinder, Patrick. "Entering Dystopia, Entering 'Erewhon.'" *Critical Survey*, vol. 17, no. 1, 2005, pp. 6–21.

Paterson, Katherine. *Bridge to Terabithia*. 1977. Special 40th Anniversary Ed. Kindle ed. Harper, 2017.

Patterson, Annette, and Martha Satz. "Genetic Counseling and the Disabled: Feminism Examines the Stance of Those Who Stand at the Gate." *Hypatia*, vol. 17, no. 3, Summer 2002, pp. 118–142.

Perkins Gilman, Charlotte. *Herland*. 1915. *Project Gutenberg*, 2008, http://www.gutenberg.org/files/32/32-h/32-h.htm. Accessed 22 Feb. 2017.

Petersen, Anne Helen. *Too Fat, Too Slutty, Too Loud: The Rise and Reign of the Unruly Woman*. Kindle ed., Plume, 2017.

Pindar, Peter. *The Works of Peter Pindar*. 1787. *Archive.org*, https://archive.org/details/worksofpeterpind00pind. Accessed 15 July 2018.

Pinkola Estés, Clarissa. *Women Who Run with the Wolves: Myths and Stories of the Wild Woman Archetype*. 1992. Kindle ed., Wolf River Press, 2017.

Plumly Thompson, Ruth. *The Giant Horse of Oz*. Kindle ed., Del Rey, 1956.

"Pope Calls Abortion 'White Glove' Equivalent of Nazi Crimes" ["Pope"]. *The New York Times*, 16 June 2018, https://www.nytimes.com/2018/06/16/world/europe/pope-abortion-nazi-crimes.html. Accessed 30 June 2018.

Prop Anon. "Grant Morrison Surveys the Situation in 'The Age of Horus.'" *Mondo 2000*, 26 Oct 2020, https://www.mondo2000.com/2020/10/26/grant-morrison-surveys-the-situation-in-the-age-of-horus/. Accessed 20 Sept. 2022.

Pugh, Tison. "'There Lived in the Land of Oz Two Queerly Made Men': Queer Utopianism and Antisocial Eroticism in L. Frank Baum's Oz Series." *Marvels & Tales*, vol. 22, no. 2, 2008, pp. 217–239.

Quayson, Ato. *Aesthetic Nervousness: Disability and the Crisis of Representation*. Kindle ed., Columbia University Press, 2007.

Works Cited

Randall, Alice. "Bio." *AliceRandall.com*, 2015, http://www.alicerandall.com/bio. Accessed 25 June 2018.

———. *The Wind Done Gone*. 2001. Reprint ed., Mariner, 2002.

Rawles, Nancy. *My Jim*. 2005. Second ed., Broadway, 2006.

Reindal, Solveig Magnus. "Disability, Gene Therapy and Genetics: A Challenge to John Harris." *Journal of Medical Ethics*, no. 26, 2000, pp. 89–94.

Remake The Last Jedi. *Remake the Last Jedi*, https://www.remakethelastjedi.com/. Accessed 30 June 2018.

Return to Oz. Directed by Walter Murch, Disney, 1985.

Rhys, Jean. *Wide Sargasso Sea*. 1966. Reissue ed., Norton, 2016.

Roberts, Amy. "As Long as They Are Healthy?" *Raising Arrows*, 29 Nov. 2016, https://www.raisingarrows.net/2016/11/as-long-as-they-are-healthy/. Accessed 16 June 2017.

Rocca, Francis X. "Pope Francis Likens Abortion to Nazi Eugenics." *The Wall Street Journal*, 16 June 2018, https://www.wsj.com/articles/pope-francis-likens-abortion-to-nazi-eugenics-1529178587. Accessed 30 June 2018.

Rogers, Katherine M. *L. Frank Baum: Creator of Oz*. St. Martin's Press, 2002.

Roper, Kem. "From the 'War on Poverty' to Reagan's 'New Right,' What's in a Name?: The Symbolic Significance of the 'Welfare Queen' in Politics and Public Discourse. 2012. University of Louisville, PhD dissertation. *Electronic Theses and Dissertations*, https://ir.library.louisville.edu/cgi/viewcontent.cgi?article=2231&context=etd. Accessed 20 Sept. 2022.

Ross, Josephine. "From Slavery to Prison in Rinkitink in Oz." *Southern California Interdisciplinary Law Journal*, vol. 20, no. 107, 2010–2011, pp. 107–120.

Roychoudhuri, Onnesha. *The Marginalized Majority: Claiming Our Power in a Post-Truth America*. Kindle ed., Melville House, 2018.

Rukstad, Michael G., and David Collis. "The Walt Disney Company: The Entertainment King (Abridged)." *Harvard Business School* Case 713-475, April 2013.

Rutledge, Gregory E., and Nalo Hopkinson. "Speaking in Tongues: An Interview with Science Fiction Writer Nalo Hopkinson." *African American Review*, vol. 33, no. 4, Winter 1999, pp. 589–601.

Sarkeesian, Anita. "JoCo Cruise Interview #1: Talking Writing, Worldbuilding and Games with Sci-fi Author N.K. Jemisin." Interview with N.K. Jemisin, *Fem Freq Radio*. 12 March 2018.

Scanlan, Sean. "Introduction: Nostalgia." *Iowa Journal of Cultural Studies*, vol. 5, issue 1, Fall 2004, pp. 3–9.

Schwartz, Evan I. *Finding Oz: How L. Frank Baum Discovered the Great American Story*. Houghton Mifflin, 2009.

Serviss, Garrett P. *Edison's Conquest of Mars*. 1898. *Project Gutenberg*, 2006, https://www.gutenberg.org/files/19141/19141-h/19141-h.htm. Accessed 22 Feb. 2017.

Shakespeare, Tom. "Social Model of Disability." *Disability Studies Reader*, 5th Kindle ed., ed. Lennard J. Davis, Routledge, 2017.

Sharda, Megha, et al. "Music Improves Social Communication and Auditory-motor Connectivity in Children with Autism." *Translational Psychiatry*, vol. 8, art. 1.231. 23 Oct. 2018, https://www.ncbi.nlm.nih.gov/pmc/articles/PMC6199253/. Accessed 28 Dec. 2020.

Sharf, Zack. "Disability Groups Speak Out Against 'Us' Over Lupita Nyong'o Doppelgänger Voice." *IndieWire*, 27 March 2019, https://www.indiewire.com/2019/03/disability-groups-speak-out-us-lupita-nyongo-red-voice-1202053942/. Accessed 28 Dec. 2020.

Shaw, Harry E. *The Forms of Historical Fiction: Sir Walter Scott and His Successors*. Cornell University Press, 1983.

Shea, Sarah E., et al. "Pathology in the Hundred Acre Wood: A Neurodevelopmental Perspective on A.A. Milne." *Canadian Medical Association Journal*, vol. 163, no. 12, Dec. 2000, pp. 1557–1559.

Works Cited

Sicher, Efraim, and Natalia Skradol. "A World Neither Brave Nor New: Reading Dystopian Fiction After 9/11." *Partial Answers: Journal of Literature and the History of Ideas*, vol. 4 no. 1, 2006, pp. 151–179.

Siebers, Tobin. "Disability Trouble." *Civil Disabilities: Citizenship, Membership, and Belonging*, ed. Nancy J. Hirschmann and Beth Linker, University of Pennsylvania Press, 2015, pp. 223–236.

Siskel, Gene. "'Return to Oz' Is Missing a Welcome Mat." *Chicago Tribune*, 21 June 1985, https://www.chicagotribune.com/news/ct-xpm-1985-06-21-8502090797-story.html. Accessed 28 Dec. 2020.

Smiley, Tavis. "Could America Enslave Black People Again? The Question Is Haunting Me." Public Radio International, 28 July 2016, https://www.pri.org/stories/2016-10-21/could-america-enslave-black-people-again-question-haunting-me. Accessed 28 Dec. 2020.

Snyder, Sharon L., and David T. Mitchell. "Re-engaging the Body." *Public Culture* 13, 2001, 367–390.

Stam, Robert. "Beyond Fidelity: The Dialogics of Adaptation." Self-published, 2000.

Stein, Perry. "Disability Advocates Arrested During Health Care Protest at McConnell's Office." *Washington Post*, 22 June 2017, https://www.washingtonpost.com/local/public-safety/disability-advocates-arrested-during-health-care-protest-at-mcconnells-office/2017/06/22/f5dd9992-576f-11e7-ba90-f5875b7d1876_story.html. Accessed 7 Jan. 2021.

Stim, Rich. "Copyright Basics FAQ." *Stanford University Libraries*, 2010, https://fairuse.stanford.edu/overview/faqs/copyright-basics/. Accessed 25 June 2018.

Stoppard, Tom. *Rosencrantz and Guildenstern Are Dead*. Samuel French, 1966.

Stubby the Rocket. "Mapping Fantasies Into a Single Multiverse Through Seanan McGuire's 'Wayward Children' Series." Tor.com, 12 June 2017, https://www.tor.com/2017/06/12/mapping-fantasies-into-a-single-multiverse-through-seanan-mcguires-wayward-children-series/. Accessed 28 Dec. 2020.

Sturrock, Donald. *Love from Boy: Roald Dahl's Letters to His Mother*. Kindle Ed., Blue Rider Press 2016.

———. *Storyteller: The Life of Roald Dahl*. Kindle ed., HarperCollins, 2011.

Suntrust Bank v. Houghton Mifflin Co. Nos. 268 F.3d 1257. US Court of Appeals, Eleventh Circuit. 2001. *Copyright.gov*, https://www.copyright.gov/fair-use/summaries/suntrust-houghton-11thcir2001.pdf. 25 June 2018.

Swartz, Mark Evan. *Oz Before the Rainbow: L. Frank Baum's The Wonderful Wizard of Oz on Stage and Screen to 1939*. Johns Hopkins Univ. Press, 2000.

Taylor, Amber. "Ripples in the Water." *Today Parenting*, 25 May 2016, http://community.today.com/parentingteam/post/a-ripple-in-the-water. Accessed 16 June 2017.

Tennant, Michael. "Disabled U.K. Lawmaker: End Abortion Discrimination Against Disabled." *The New American*, 25 Oct. 2016, https://www.thenewamerican.com/world-news/europe/item/24470-disabled-uk-lawmaker-end-abortion-discrimination-against-disabled. Accessed 8 Feb. 2018.

Thomas, Donald. *Lewis Carroll: A Portrait with Background*. Murray, 1997.

Thomas, Ebony Elizabeth. *The Dark Fantastic: Race and the Imagination from Harry Potter to the Hunger Games*. Kindle ed., NYU Press 2019.

Thomas, Sheree R. *Dark Matter: A Century of Speculative Fiction from the African Diaspora*. Kindle ed., Grand Central, 2014.

Thorpe, Vanessa. "The Prime of Miss Jean Rhys." *The Guardian*, 30 Sept. 2006, https://www.theguardian.com/media/2006/oct/01/tvnews.books. Accessed 25 June 2018.

Tolkien, J.R.R. *The Fellowship of the Ring*. 1954. Ballantine, 1973.

———. *The Hobbit*. 1937. Ballantine, 1973.

Works Cited

———. *The Return of the King*. 1955. Ballantine, 1973.

———. *The Two Towers*. 1954. Ballantine, 1973.

Understanding Media and Culture: An Introduction to Mass Communication. University of Minnesota Libraries Publishing, 2010. https://open.lib.umn.edu/mediaandculture/front-matter/publisher-information/. Accessed 20 Sept. 2022.

United Kingdom Ministry of Food. Records of the Ministry of Food. 1873–1985, https://discovery.national archives.gov.uk/details/r/C786. Accessed 20, Sept. 2022.

U.S. Centers for Disease Control and Prevention (CDC). *CDC*, "Current Trends Mortality Attributable to HIV Infection/AIDS—United States, 1981–1990." *MMWR*, 25 Jan. 1991, https://www.cdc.gov/mmwr/preview/mmwrhtml/00001880.htm. Accessed 20 Sept. 2022.

———. "Facts About Cleft Lip and Cleft Palate." *CDC*, https://www.cdc.gov/ncbddd/birthdefects/cleftlip.html. Accessed 13 June 2018.

———. "Who Should NOT Get Vaccinated with These Vaccines?" *CDC*, https://www.cdc.gov/vaccines/vpd/should-not-vacc.html. Accessed 16 June 2017.

U.S. Social Security Administration. "Disability Evaluation Under Social Security: 12.00 Mental Disorders—Adult." *SSA.gov*, n.d., https://www.ssa.gov/disability/professionals/bluebook/12.00-MentalDisorders-Adult.htm#12_00E3. Accessed 28 Dec. 2020.

Us. Directed by Jordan Peele, Universal, 2019.

"Utopia, N." *OED Online*, Oxford University Press, June 2018, www.oed.com/view/Entry/220784. Accessed 13 June 2018.

Variety. "Lupita Nyong'o's Voice in 'Us' & Cast Reactions to Hearing It." 25 March 2019, https://www.youtube.com/watch?v=vI4JB05PTM0.

Vidal, Fernando. "Brainhood, Anthropological Figure of Modernity." *History of the Human Sciences*, vol. 22, no. 1, 2009, pp. 5–36.

Walt Disney Productions v. Air Pirates. Nos. 75–3116, 75–3243. United States Court of Appeals, Ninth Circuit. 1978. *OpenJurist*, https://openjurist.org/581/f2d/751/walt-disney-productions-v-air-pirates. Accessed 25 June 2018.

Wagenknecht, Edward Charles. *Utopia Americana*. University of Washington Press, 1929.

Waters, Darren. "Rowling Backs Potter Fan Fiction." *BBC*, 27 May 2004, http://news.bbc.co.uk/2/hi/entertainment/3753001.stm. Accessed 14 June 2018.

Webster, Richard. *Why Freud Was Wrong: Sin, Science, and Psychoanalysis*. Kindle ed., Basic, 1996.

Weinraub, Bernard. "Famine in Africa Is Called Worst in a Decade." *New York Times*, 7 June 1983, Sect. A, pp.1, https://www.nytimes.com/1983/06/07/world/famine-in-africa-is-called-worst-in-a-decade.html. Accessed 20 Sept. 2022.

Wells, H.G. *The Time Machine and the Invisible Man*. 1895. Kindle ed., Signet, 1984.

Wherry, Timothy Lee. *Trademarks in the Digital Age*. Scarecrow, 2004.

Whitford, Emma. "Lev Grossman, S.E. Hinton, and Other Authors on the Freedom of Writing Fanfiction." *Vulture*, 13 March 2015, https://www.vulture.com/2015/03/6-famous-authors-whove-written-fanfiction.html. Accessed 20 Sept. 2022.

Williams, Kam. "Misty Copeland: The 'Life in Motion' Interview." *AALBC*, https://aalbc.com/interviews/interview.php?id=131. Accessed 20 Sept. 2022.

Williams, Raymond. *Keywords: A Vocabulary of Culture and Society*. 1976. Revised ed., Oxford University Press, 1983.

Willmott, Glenn. "Wonder Vs. Science in Speculative Fiction: Stupid or Profound?" *MSA*, 2016. Unpublished.

The Wizard of Oz. Directed by Victor Fleming, MGM, 1939.

"Wonderland, N." *OED Online*, Oxford University Press, June 2018, www.oed.

Works Cited

com/view/Entry/229951. Accessed 15 July 2018.

The World Health Organization [WHO]. "Violence Against Adults and Children with Disabilities." *World Health Organization*, 2021, https://www.who.int/disabilities/violence/en/#:~:text=The%20review%20indicated%20that%20children,be%20victims%20of%20sexual%20violence. Accessed 7 Jan. 2021.

Wray-Lake, Laura, et al. "Developmental Patterns in Decision-Making Autonomy Across Middle Childhood and Adolescence: European American Parents' Perspectives." *Child Development*, vol. 81, no. 2, March/Apr. 2010, pp. 636–651.

Yeats, William Butler. *Fairy and Folk Tales of the Irish Peasantry*. 1888. Project Gutenberg, 2010, http://www.gutenberg.org/files/33887/33887-h/33887-h.htm. Accessed 28 Dec. 2020.

Young, Stella. "I'm Not Your Inspiration, Thank You Very Much." *TEDxSydney*, April 2014, https://www.ted.com/talks/stella_young_i_m_not_your_inspiration_thank_you_very_much/transcript?language=en.

———. "We're Not Here for Your Inspiration." *ABC Australia*, http://www.abc.net.au/rampup/articles/2012/07/02/3537035.htm. Accessed 14 June 2018.

Index

Numbers in **_bold italics_** indicate pages with illustrations

Across the Zodiac 1, 46, 49
adaptation 5–7, 11, 15–16, 93, **_105_**, **_108_**, 110, **_117_**
affect theory 51–52
aging 26–27, 46, 55, 74, 78
Ahmed, Sara 35–38, 44, 51–52
Alice (film) 8, **_167–168_**
Alice in Wonderland (book) 5, 12, 13, 21, 55–56, 60–61, 64, 105, 108, 167
Alice: Madness Returns 147
American McGee's Alice **_146_**, 154
And Then Emily Was Gone 6, 97, **_150–152_**, 156
Arkham Asylum 8–9, 157, 168, 169

Batman 8–9, 157, 159, 169
Baum, L. Frank 2, 3, 12, 66, 72–73, 79, 87–88, 94–95, 169
Bridge to Terabithia (book) 100–101, 102, 115, 116

care 12, 42, 51, 74, **_85–88_**, 90–91
Carroll, Lewis *see* Dodgson, Charles
Charlie and the Chocolate Factory (book) 4–5, 27–28, 99, 102–103, 105, **_110–115_**, 116
Christianity 27, 44, 45, 59, 72, 162
cinema studies *see* film studies
Cold War 94, 101
copyright **_118–125_**, 126, 128, 134–135, 136
CRISPR 39, 172
cure 2, 4, 9, 31, 68, 144, 153

Dahl, Roald 5, 110, **_111–113_**, 115, 116
death 3, 4–5, 19, 22, **_24–31_**, 44, 48, 55, 73, 78, 80, 89, 95–96, 97, 98, 100–101, 102, 112, **_113–116_**, 138–139, 153, 155, 157, 167
disability history 14, 17, 21, 22, 33, 34–35, 45, 139, 144–145, 173
Disney 117, 120–122, 124
Dodgson, Charles 107, 108, 168

ethnicity *see* race
Erewhon 46, 47–48
eugenics 2, 21, 39, **_41–43_**, 47, 50, 139, 172
euthanasia 19, 50, 74, 81

fairies 54, 55, 132–133, 151–152; Tinkerbell 114
fairy tales 52, 59, 107, 142
feminism 18, 35–36, 44, 52, 69, 82, 128, 134–135
Feminist Frequency 127–128, 170
film studies 11, 16, 19, 28–31, 83, 108–109, 128, 137–138, 141, 163
futurity **_18–20;_** 34–35, 42–43, 172–173

Gabaldon, Diana 118, 119, 124, 125, 127
A Game of Thrones (book) *see* A Song of Fire and Ice
Game of Thrones (TV series) *see* A Song of Fire and Ice
Glinda of Oz 94–95
great compass *see* multiverse compass

happiness **_35–38_**, 44, 48, 85
health 34–35, 38–41, 42, 46, 48, 87, 94, 113, 114, 146, 172, 173
Herland 50, 74
heroine's journey 31, **_52–60_**, 64, 67, 68, 69, **_71–76_**, 140–142, 166–167

Index

hero's journey **53–54**, 55, 56, 58, 72, 171
Hopkinson, Nalo 20, 132–133
horror 6, 20, 26–27, 59, 94, 97, 140, 146, 159, 167

Jones, Diana Wynne 63, 66–67

Kafer, Alison 18, 34, 43, 74

The Last Battle 26–27
The Lathe of Heaven 2, **36**, 50, 171, 174
L'Engle, Madeleine 100, 115–116
Lewis, C.S. 23–24, 101–102
LGBTQ studies *see* queer studies
The Lion, the Witch, and the Wardrobe (book) 23–24, 55, 56, 59–60, 64, 96–97, 101–102
The Little Prince 99, 100, 102, 108
Looking Backward 45–46, 74, 89, 109
The Lord of the Rings 54, 66, 121, 122, 170
Lovecraft, H.P. 108, 123

magic 13, 21, 24, 26, 54–55, 56, 57–60, 62–63, 75, 76, 84, 86, 99–100, 103, 114, 140, 142, 152–153, 166
Martin, George R.R. 66, 119, 120–121, 122–123, 125
medium 5, 16, 106–110
modernism 11–12, 13, 14
monomyth *see* hero's journey
monsters 54, 60, 97, 108, 142, 147, 150–152, 155
Morrison, Grant 157–158
multiverse compass **96–98**, 135

Narnia 24, 26–27, 55, 57–60, 64–64, 67, 96–97, 101–103, 113–114
The Neverending Story (book) 28–31, 97, 98, 103, 115
The NeverEnding Story (film) 28–31
The NeverEnding Story: The Next Chapter 30–31
Neverland 24, 55, 57, 58, 59, 60, 65, 67, 114, 140
Nielsen, Kim E. 14, 21, 45, 46, 139
nonsense 12, 96–98

Outlander series 118, 127
Oz 2–3, 11, 24, 26, 55–59, 62–63, 65, 66, 68, 69, **71–93**, 95–96, 109, 110, 114–115, 137–140, 146, 150

Pan's Labyrinth 152–153, 156
Paterson, Katherine 100–101, 115–116
Peter Pan (book) 5, 12–13, 24–25, **55–59**, 167, 169
Peter Pan (play) 5, 108, 109–110, 117
Pinkola Estés, Clarissa 52, 59

queer studies 18–19, 35, 40, 71, 74, 93, 126, 136, 157–158, 162, 173

race 36, 70, 71, 92, 128, 133, 139, 163–165
RaceFail 171, 174
Return to Oz 137–139, 146, 149–150

sorcery *see* magic
Star Wars 54, 170–171; *The Last Jedi* 170, 174
Stranger Things **148–150**, 154–155

theater 5, 108
Thomas, Ebony Elizabeth 70, 169
Through the Looking-Glass 12, 59, 98
Tik-Tok 80, **87–88**, 90, 92
The Time Machine 50, 166
Tin Man 25, 63, 68, 69, 76, 77, **80–86**, 87–88, 90, 114–115, 137, 138
Tolkien, J.R.R. 66, 121, 170
Toto 25, 57, 59, 75–77, 81–83, 88, 91–92
trauma 3, 8–9, 29, 31, 99, 102–104, 116, 144, 153–156

Us 6–7, **140–146**, 158–168
Utopia (book) 44–45

Wicked 93, 124
Willy Wonka & the Chocolate Factory 5, 27–28
The Wizard of Oz (film) 11, 16, 69–85, 92, 117
The Wonderful Wizard of Oz (book) 11, 12, 25–26, 56, 57, 69–85, 88, 89, 110, 114, 117, 167
Wonderland 13, 23, 55, 58, 64, 146, 147, 154
world compass *see* multiverse compass
World War I 4, 15, 21–22, 94–95, 116
World War II 4, 21, 24, 58, 103, 111–112, 115, 139
A Wrinkle in Time 99, 100, 103

www.ingramcontent.com/pod-product-compliance
Lightning Source LLC
Chambersburg PA
CBHW032046300426
44117CB00009B/1204